AF342142

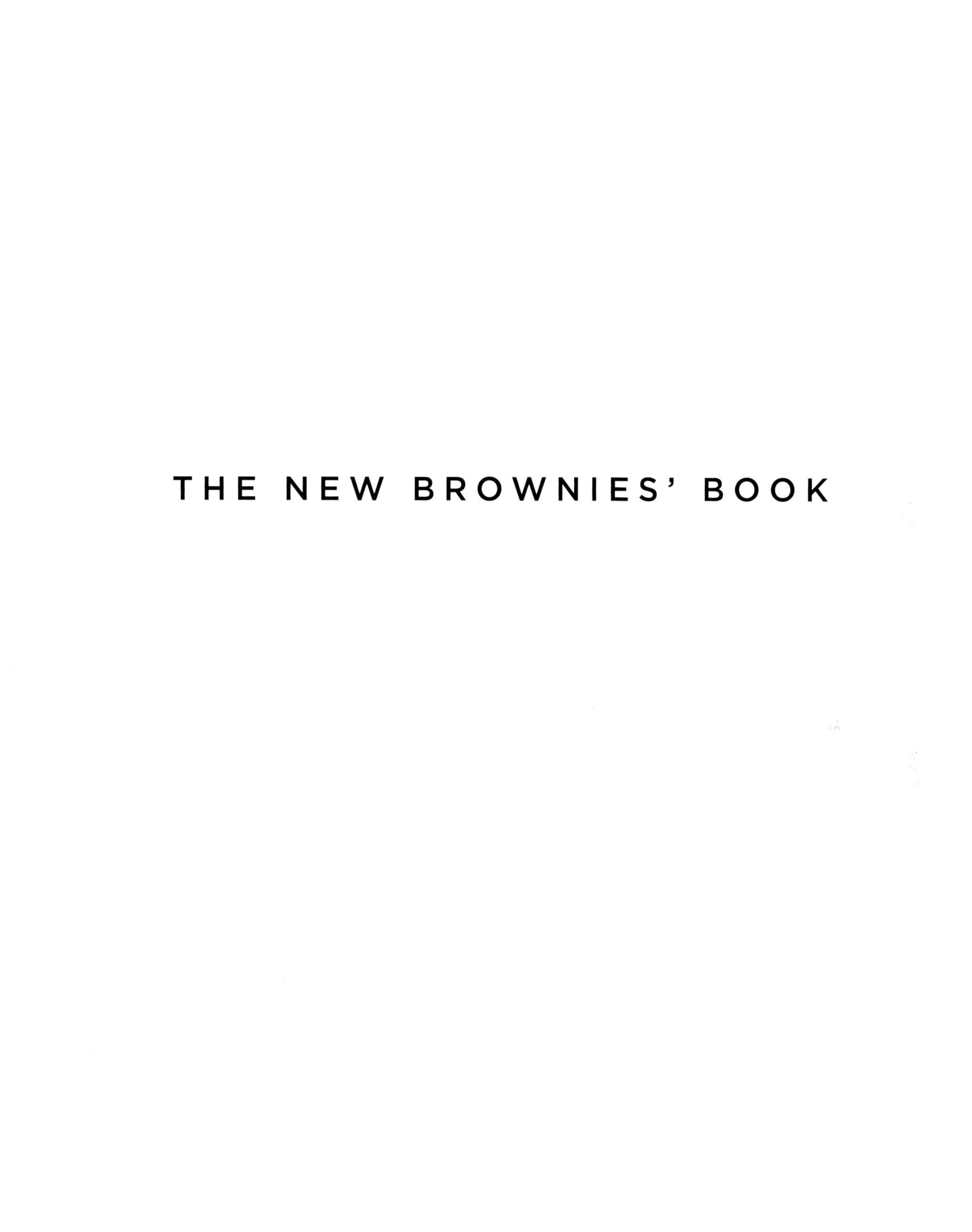

THE NEW BROWNIES' BOOK

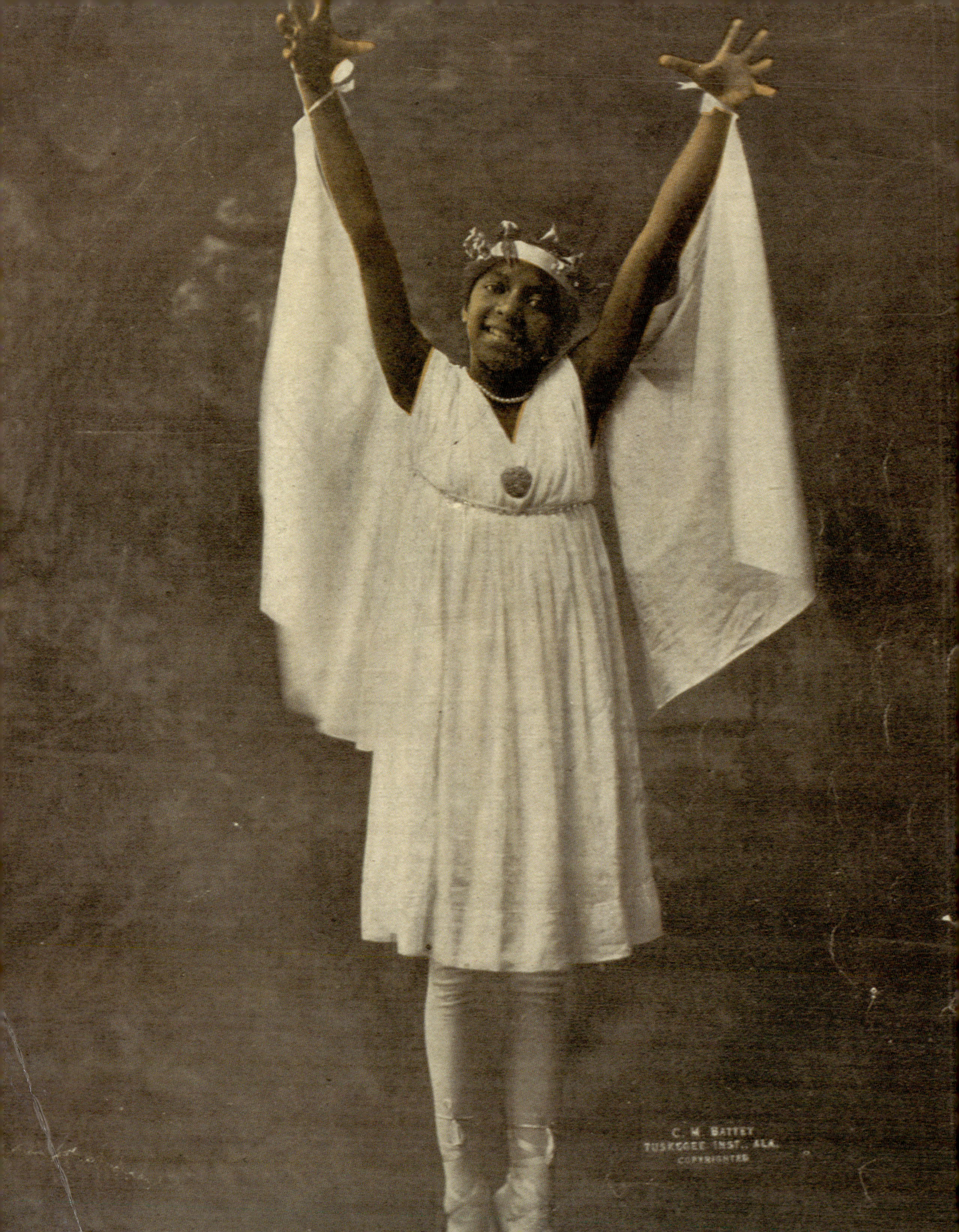
C. M. BATTEY
TUSKEGEE INST., ALA.
COPYRIGHTED

THE NEW BROWNIES' BOOK
A LOVE LETTER TO BLACK FAMILIES

By Karida L. Brown and Charly Palmer

CHRONICLE BOOKS

SAN FRANCISCO

First and foremost, we thank W. E. B. Du Bois for creating the original *Brownies' Book*
more than one hundred years ago for Black and brown youth: the Children of the Sun.

Thank you to all the writers and artists who responded with an enthusiastic
"Yes!" when asked to contribute to this project.

We dedicate this book to Mary, Larry, Mark, Thornton, and Katina, our most recent family to have joined the Ancestors.

Lastly, we dedicate this book to Black Love. Where would the world be without it?

We love YOU,
Karida and Charly

Library of Congress Cataloging-in-Publication Data:
Names: Brown, Karida, 1982- editor. | Palmer, Charly, editor.
Title: The new Brownies' book : a love letter to black families / by Karida L. Brown and Charly Palmer.
Other titles: Brownies' book.
Description: San Francisco: Chronicle Books, [2023] | Includes bibliographical references.
Identifiers: LCCN 2023012517 | ISBN 9781797216829 (hardcover)
Subjects: LCSH: African Americans. | African American arts.
Classification: LCC E185.86 .N485 2023 | DDC 305.896/073—dc23/eng/20230331
LC record available at https://lccn.loc.gov/2023012517

Manufactured in China.

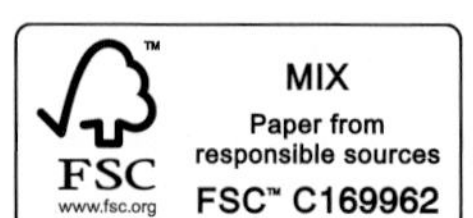

Design by Kieron Lewis.

Cover art: *Child of God*, Tokie Rome-Taylor.

10 9 8 7 6 5 4 3 2 1

Chronicle books and gifts are available at special quantity discounts to corporations, professional associations,
literacy programs, and other organizations. For details and discount information, please contact our premiums department at
corporatesales@chroniclebooks.com or at 1-800-759-0190.

Chronicle Books LLC
680 Second Street
San Francisco, California 94107
www.chroniclebooks.com

CONTENTS

THE ORIGINAL BROWNIES' BOOK

By Karida L. Brown

In 1920, W. E. B. Du Bois, Augustus Granville Dill, and Jessie Redmon Fauset founded a periodical called *The Brownies' Book: A Monthly Magazine for Children of the Sun.* Issued as an offshoot of the infamous *The Crisis* magazine and sold for $1.50 for a six-month subscription or fifteen cents a copy, *The Brownies' Book* remained in circulation for nearly two years. The inside cover of each issue contained the same declaration:

"DESIGNED FOR ALL CHILDREN BUT ESPECIALLY FOR OURS. It aims to be a thing of Joy and Beauty, dealing in Happiness, Laughter and Emulation, and designed especially for Kiddies from Six to Sixteen. It will seek to teach Universal Love and Brotherhood for all little folk—black and brown and yellow and white. Of course, pictures, stories, letters from little ones, games and oh—everything!"

Du Bois and his co-editors intended that this children's magazine serve as a much-needed medium for Black and brown children and families to learn about the many contributions made by people of color around the world, as a public forum to discuss current issues they faced, and most of all, as a space of literary and artistic joy!

In a call to generate a sense of pride and awareness among the "Children of the Sun" worldwide, Du Bois announced the aims of the newly created *Brownies' Book* in a 1919 issue of the *Crisis*:

1. To make colored children realize that being "colored" is a normal beautiful thing.
2. To make them familiar with the history and achievements of the Negro race.
3. To make them know that other colored children have grown into beautiful, useful and famous persons.
4. To teach them a delicate code of honor and action in their relations with white children.
5. To turn their little hurts and resentments into emulation, ambition and love of their homes and companions.
6. To point out the best amusements and joys and worthwhile things of life.
7. To inspire them to prepare for definite occupations and duties with a broad spirit of sacrifice.

In his role as editor-in-chief of *The Brownies' Book*, Du Bois would reach out to Black creatives of his time and ask them to contribute a piece of their "best work" to the periodical so that Black children would know that they are thought about, and LOVED. He also solicited submissions from unknown creatives to give them an opportunity to publish their work. For example, it was in *The Brownies' Book* where the young Langston Hughes would first publish his works. In time, Du Bois, Dill, and Fauset brought on the prolific artist and teacher Hilda Rue Wilkerson as the magazine's art director and illustrator. The issues of the original *Brownies' Book* are dripping with contributions from

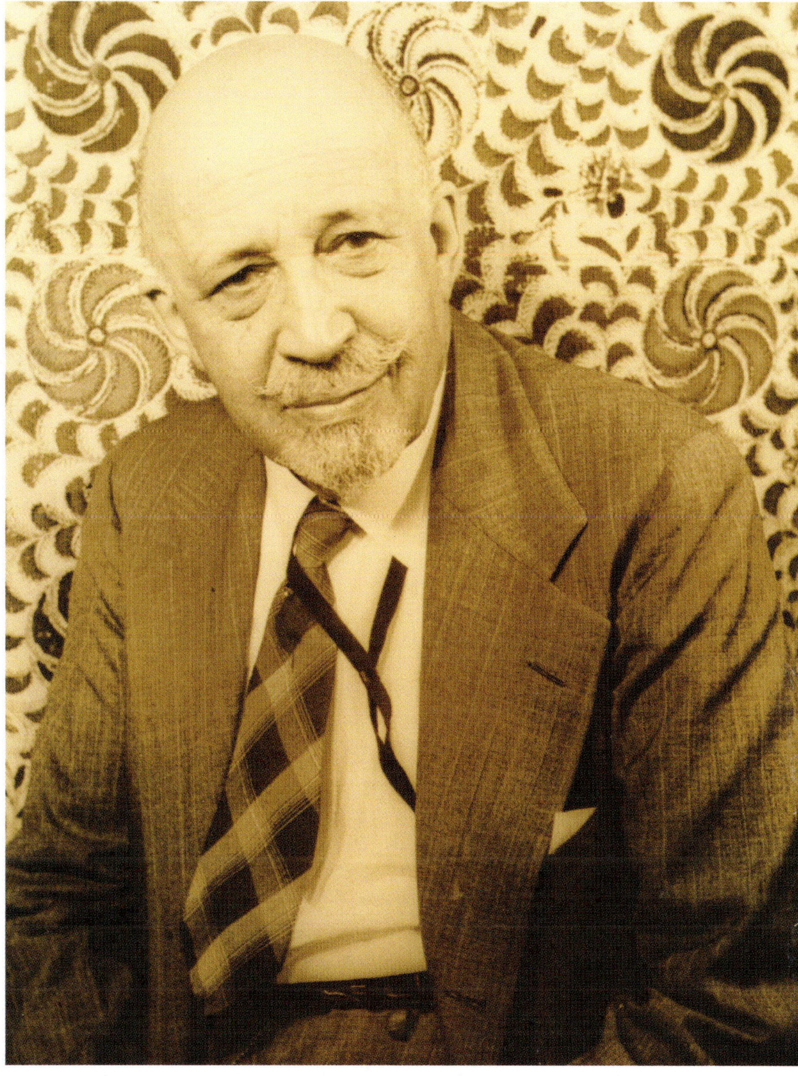

W. E. B. Du Bois, July 18, 1946. Photograph by Carl Van Vechten, from the W. E. B. Du Bois Papers, Special Collections and the University Archives, University of Massachusetts Amherst Libraries.

a multitude of Black creatives, known and not-so-known, from the Harlem Renaissance era. In this way, it is a crown jewel of African American children's literature.

LOVE LETTER

By Karida L. Brown and Charly Palmer

Dear Reader,

Within these pages we have set out to evoke the spirit of W. E. B. Du Bois's original *Brownies' Book* magazine. Like Du Bois, we invited some of the most talented Black artists and writers of our time to contribute original works—from short stories, artwork, and poetry to plays—as a personal expression of their resounding Love for you: the Children of the Sun.

Together, we believed that we could create something bigger than the two of us could ever have come up with alone. An artist and a sociologist, husband and wife, both creatives in our own right—we produced *The New Brownies' Book* as a labor of love.

Karida: As a sociologist, my love for W. E. B. Du Bois has been life-giving. It was his genius and unwavering commitment to Black people that inspired me to become a scholar. It was his luxurious prose, however, that let me know that I could be a beautiful writer too. Throughout this process, I cast my net wide to friends and colleagues in the writing community asking them to imprint a stroke of their genius on this book.

Charly: For me, it was also very important that I get a chance to work with this great brain next to me, Dr. Karida Brown. I believed that we could assemble an A-team of creative people that shared the same passion and commitment to Black Love. It was important to pull from some of the most creative visual artists that I know so that this book would have a strong representation of Black Art. I hope that this book becomes a fixture in the homes of every Black family—on your coffee tables, and on your bookshelves.

What follows is a collection of works that serve as a strong expression of inspiration, recognition, love, laughter, reflection, and celebration of what we mean to one another. From your nuclear, extended, and chosen family to your play cousins and your motley crew of friends—*The New Brownies' Book* is a collective love letter to YOU.

Love,
Karida and Charly

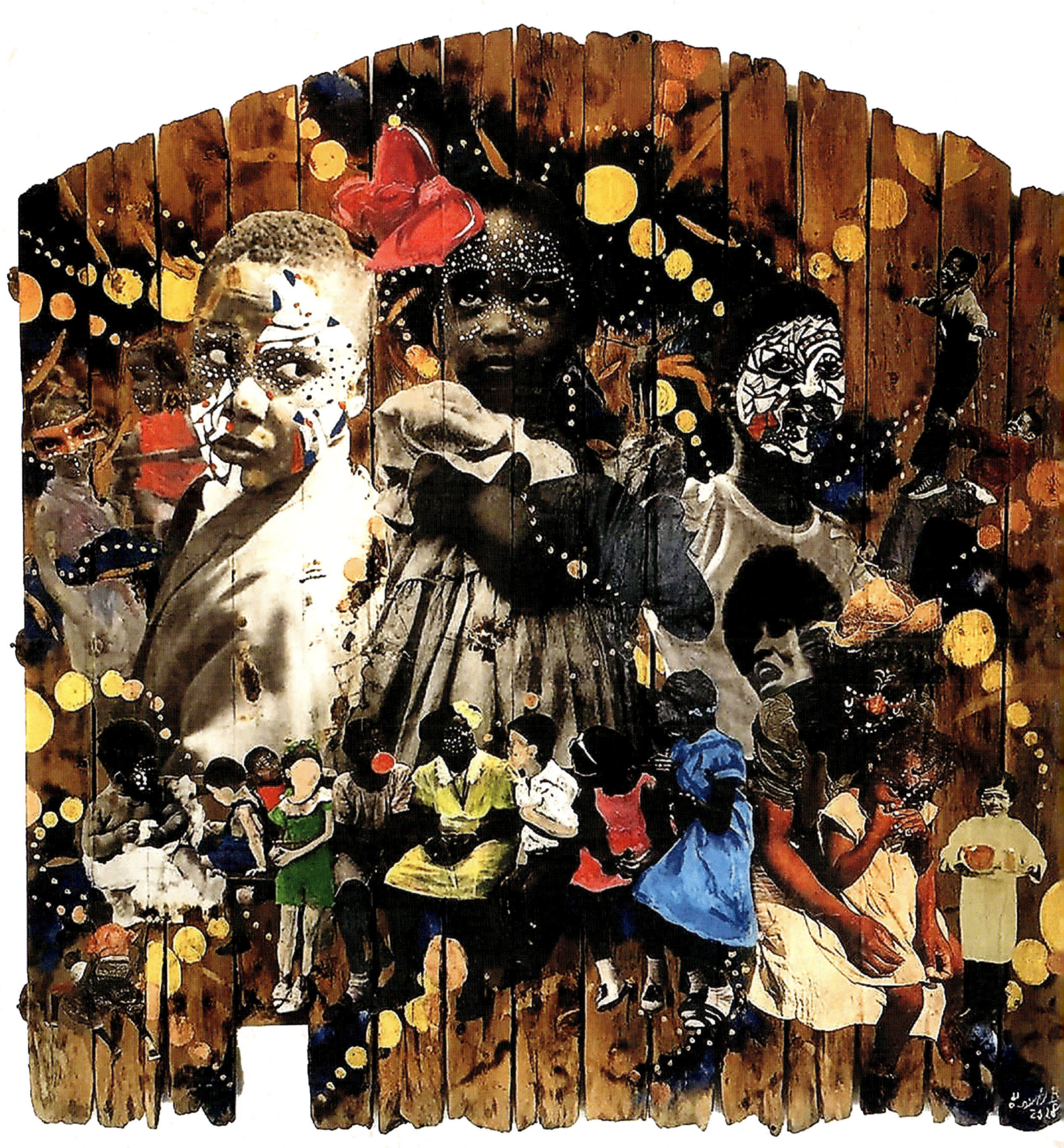

Lavett Ballard, *Hey Black Child*
(Mixed media collage on reclaimed wood fencing)

THIS IS

The Brownies' Book

A Monthly Magazine
For the Children of the Sun

DESIGNED FOR ALL CHILDREN,
BUT ESPECIALLY FOR *OURS*.

It aims to be a thing of Joy and Beauty, dealing in Happiness, Laughter and Emulation, and designed especially for Kiddies from Six to Sixteen.

It will seek to teach Universal Love and Brotherhood for all little folk--black and brown and yellow and white.

Of course, pictures, stories, letters from little ones, games and oh--everything!

One Dollar and a Half a Year
Fifteen Cents a Copy

W. E. B. DU BOIS, ... Editor
A. G. DILL. . . . . . Business Manager

Address: THE BROWNIES' BOOK
2 West 13th Street   New York, N. Y.

THE
CHILDREN OF THE SUN

By Marcus Anthony Hunter

Riding on water from Venus
      thcir appearance
           forged the Nile
gold, brown, blue, & black shining
         smiles casting light everywhere

amazed at their wonder
        they were encountered
          they were accompanied
               peacocks
                 hummingbirds
                    eagles
                     & doves
above their heads, following their lead

awesome though they were
        a fear trap came upon them
for something as brightly lit has never before been seen
        captured & surprised they cried

'We are the children of the Sun.
We traveled here on our mother's rays.'

Their cries went unheard for days
        praise became prayers
                days became years
                        trapped on planes, ships, & oceans of fears
                    Years became centuries
        soon enough the children were unable
                                    to remember
                                            or recall
        their glorious arrival
                their divine call

then came the ultimate cost
                    to be lost
                            scattered east & west
                                    north & south
before long the days before the pyramids a distant memory
afraid the children would remember
                    to cast light
in their mouths a bit was placed
                preventing the sunshine in their hearts becoming again bright
                        in their smiles
                                underneath
                                    they still cried & believed
'We are the children of the Sun.
We traveled here on our mother's rays.'

& still they would be betrayed
            some even strayed
                    finding refuge in the darkness
        others pleaded with the moon
                hoping soon their mother would swoon
                        swoop down to their rescue

after a while, she returned in dreams of a chosen few

Malcolm, Nelson, Winnie, Coretta & Martin
        Stokely, Chiekh, Mariame, Ella & Aretha
Maya, James, Langston, Toni & Whitney
Fela, Zora, Steve, Marley & Ali too
words became songs
        songs became poems
                poems became light
        sunlight & future sunshine
                where their story returned to them to be told

Behold!
        You are the children of the Sun.
        You traveled here on her rays.
                Arrived & targeted as other
                        you sought cover
                                were nearly covered up.
        only to learn you cannot hide shine
                        or sheen
                                for you were sent here to be seen
                                        to show
                        below & above
                        that love is God & God is love
                                residing everywhere
                                        especially in you,
the children of the Sun.

Chapter 1

FAMILY TIES

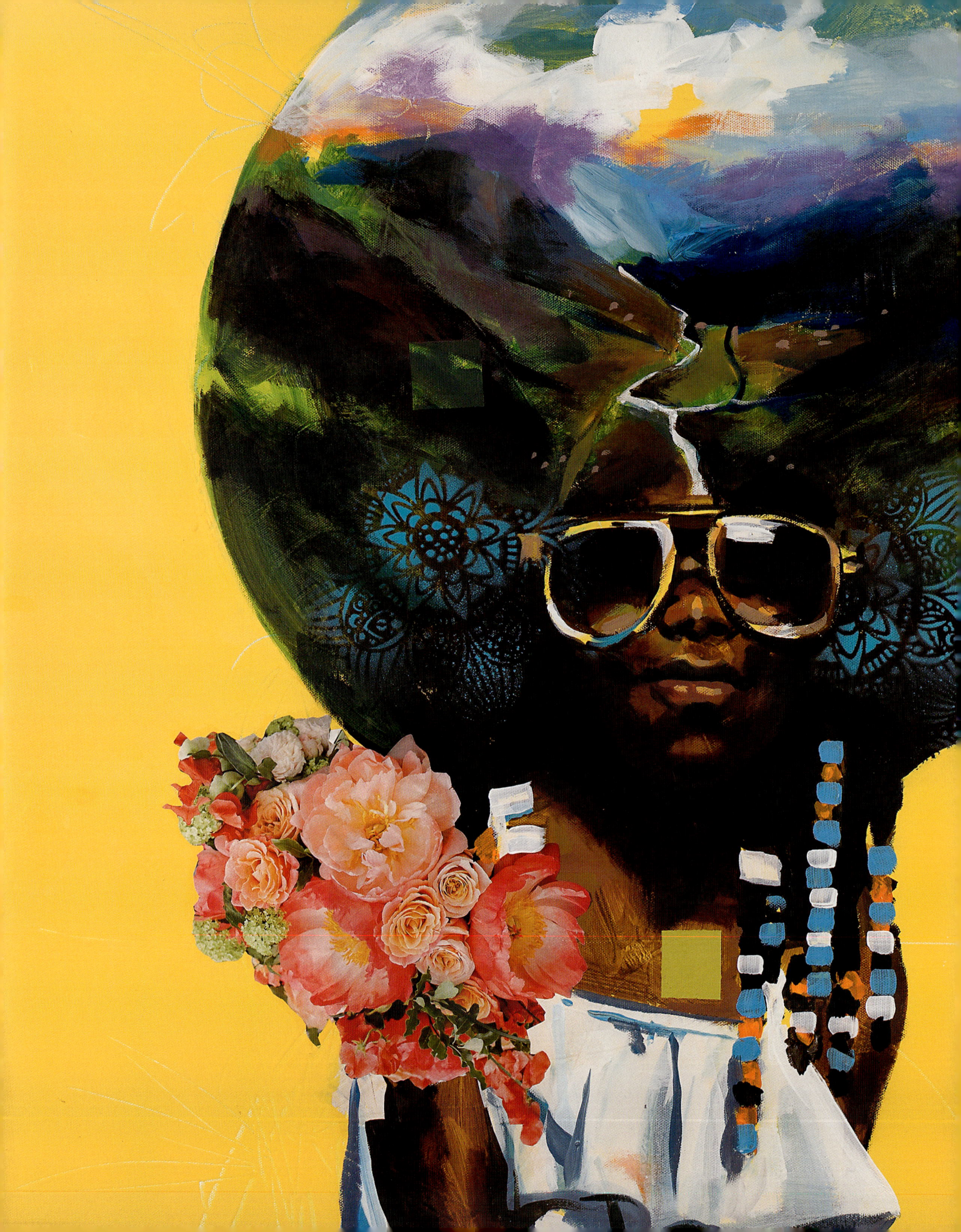

◀ Charly Palmer, *Her World*
(Acrylic on canvas)

KISSES MAKE THINGS BETTER (BUT SOMETIMES THEY DON'T)

By Zoe Jones | Age 5

Kisses make bad dreams better,
  but they don't make hard things feel soft
They make ouchies feel better,
  but kisses don't make cuts stop hurting
They don't make water safer,
  but they do make swimming fun
Kisses make things better that are sad,
  but not everything that is bad
Because sometimes kisses make things better
  but sometimes they don't.

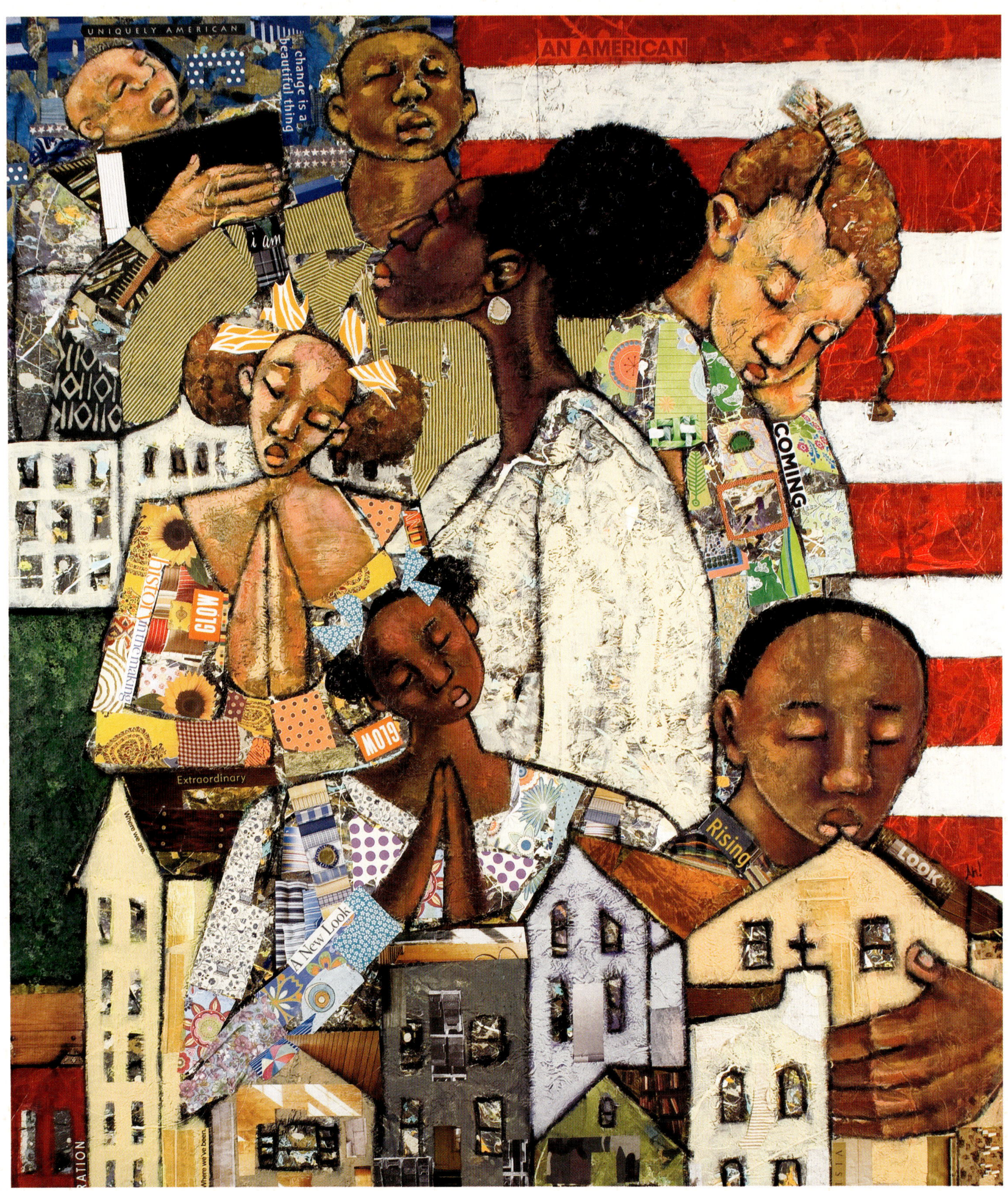

April Harrison, *Community Prayer*
(Acrylic and collage on canvas)

TIME CAPSULES

By Laurence Ralph

To my daughter Amina,

Did your mother ever tell you that a full day after you were born we still hadn't settled on a name? We wanted to get to know you first. So we devised a plan. If you had a calm, easygoing personality, we would name you Amina Lynette, after my mother. But if you had a more aggressive nature, we would call you Justice, simply because we were fond of the name. After our first day together, your mother and I looked at each other and then at you—a precious and tranquil baby girl. Amina.

That was the first trick you ever played on us. Your real personality came out on the second day! But by that time, we had already signed the birth certificate. It was too late.

Let me tell you something, Amina: It is terrifying, raising a strong-willed Black child in the United States today. It might seem silly to worry. People say I should be more afraid for your little brother, that he'll have it worse than you. But I'm not so sure. Black girls are over five times more likely to be suspended from school, and seven times more likely to receive multiple suspensions than white girls—a rate even higher than the gap between Black boys and white boys. When Black girls are "pushed out" of school, as the educator and activist Monique Morris has noted, they are set on paths to abuse, economic insecurity, and incarceration. This is why I'm giving you this book—so you may know the dangers that may lie ahead. And so you can also know hope.

When I was thirteen years old, my eighth-grade class created a time capsule. We gathered a copy of the local newspaper (the *Columbia Flyer*) and national publications like *USA Today* and *Time* magazine. We listed our favorite movies, *Batman Forever* and *Clueless*. We posed for a class picture and put it in the box. And each of us wrote a letter about what we loved about our class. We buried it next to the bench that our class dedicated to the school. Our idea was that, in fifty years, students our age would dig up the box and come to learn about history in a way that related to them.

You might think of this book (and this very letter) as my time capsule for you, Amina. ▶

When I was growing up in Baltimore and then Columbia, Maryland, my parents sat me down and told me, "You could be walking down the street, and a police officer could stop you, and question you, and they won't know that you're an honor roll student, and it won't matter to them, and it wouldn't be your fault if they harassed you, it is just so dangerous outside for Black kids like you."

I'm referring to a coming-of-age conversation about racial awakening that Black families know so well, commonly referred to as "the talk."

I imagine that parents across the United States—all over the world, in fact—have had similar conversations with their children about what it feels like to be underprotected in the age of Breonna Taylor, George Floyd, and COVID-19. They probably sound a lot like my folks did back then. I can still hear them now: "Honey, you must stay calm, but also vigilant. I'm telling you this because I love you."

When you're my age, your children will ask you what it was like growing up. And you might recall that year that you couldn't go to school—the year that you asked your parents why the people on TV were marching down the street and holding signs.

You can tell your kids that their granddad had some ideas about why this happened.

I think that being isolated in quarantine made Americans pay closer attention to the brutal effects of police violence. Sitting in their homes, with nowhere to go, people were shaken, in a visceral way, by the injustices they witnessed. In the process, something remarkable happened, Amina. As tens of thousands of people fell ill and died from COVID-19—and millions lost their livelihoods—we could not escape our own vulnerability.

This shared sense of vulnerability reminds me of "the talk" about the law and the police that my parents had with me, and that I am having with you now—the talk that Black parents have been having with their children for generations.

I think about vulnerability a lot these days.

Your great-grandmother passed away in a nursing home in New York City at the height of COVID-19. She lived a full life, though. In fact, she was considered a "miracle baby." She was born during the Spanish flu, one of the deadliest pandemics in human history. Your brother, Langston, was born two months after your great-grandmother died. I dread the day that I'll have to have "the talk" with him.

When I think about these intimate transitions, it's clear to me what our country needs, now more than ever: a larger alliance committed to uniting people around human dignity. "Hope is a discipline," the prison abolitionist Mariame Kaba once said. I realize now that my loved ones have been teaching me, for as long as I can remember, to maintain optimism and resolve in the face of injustice. And I want to pass on that hope to you, Amina.

That hope has been our family's secret weapon. It will be your key to success.

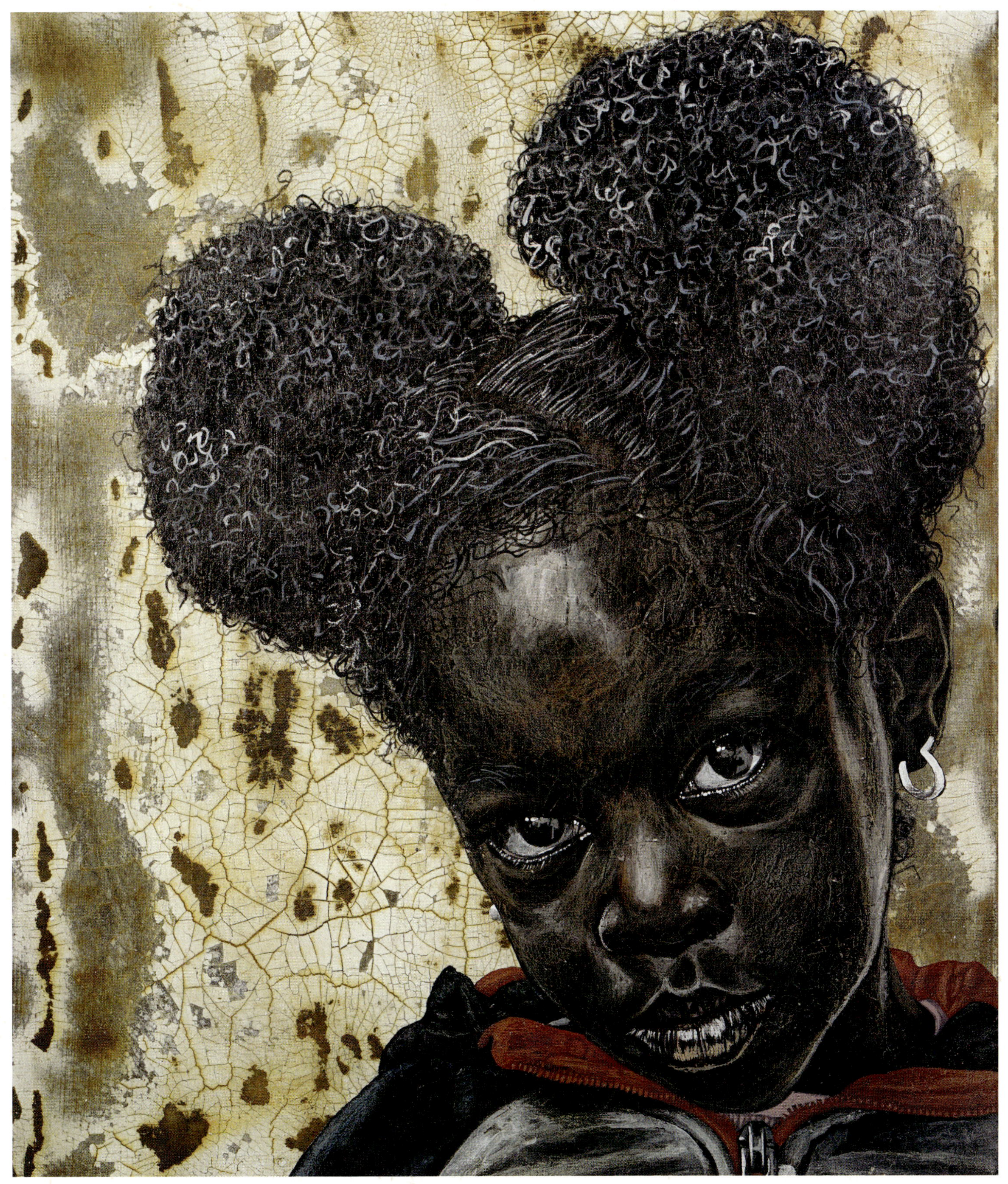

Alfred Conteh, *Neveah*
(Acrylic, urethane plastic, and atomized steel dust on paper)

NOBODY LOVES THE DEBBIL

By Charly Palmer

On this particular Halloween day, I was going to be taking out my goddaughter, Winter, who was four-and-a-half years old, and my two-and-a-half-year-old godson, Kalief. Winter said, "I'm the devil." "Oh, that's wonderful," I replied. Kalief was dressed as Winnie-the-Pooh.

We were going to walk our neighborhood. Now keep in mind our neighborhood is the neighborhood that everybody came to for Halloween because all the houses participated in trick-or-treating. Everybody gave lots of candy. Near the start of our little journey, we were heading toward house number two. I'm holding the hand of the two-year-old, as the four-year-old leads on, because this is not her first trip in the neighborhood for trick-or-treating. We go to the door and the person opens the door and the kids say, "Trick or treat!" And my little Winnie-the-Pooh wants to step into the house because this whole thing is new to him, so, of course, when someone opens the door, you enter.

But I said, "No, no, no. Say 'Trick or treat' and get your candy." And so the people said, "Oh, that's cute. That's Winnie-the-Pooh."

Then we go onto the next house and the next house. Someone says, "Oh, Winnie-the-Pooh. I love Winnie-the-Pooh!" And the kids say, "Trick or treat." They receive their candy. We go to the next house, and this continues throughout the whole trip. Everybody is excited about Winnie-the-Pooh. However, they don't know what to say to a child dressed in full garb as the devil. We go to about ten houses. We're not even halfway through the houses with candy in the neighborhood.

My goddaughter turns to me, forlorn, and says, "Charly, I'm ready to go home."

"Why?" I asked.

My little goddaughter responded, "I just don't want to do it anymore."

I said, "There's a lot of candy to get here. We can't go home yet." And so we continued.

Then we walked to the next house, and when they opened the door, before we could say "Trick or treat!" this woman says, "Oh my God, Winnie-the-Pooh! I love Winnie-the-Pooh!!!" She calls her husband, "Honey, you have to come see Winnie-the-Pooh!"

And so the husband comes down and says, "Look, Winnie-the-Pooh." They give us lots of candy.

At this point, my goddaughter is fed up. Winter says, "Charly, I want to go home."

And I'm like, "What's wrong, sweetie?" She says, "I just don't want to do this anymore."

"Come on, we got to try a little bit more." Then we go up this long driveway and then these long stairways. We have to climb up to a second level. We go up and we ring the doorbell.

They open the door and it's a little girl this time, and the little girl says, "Winnie-the-Pooh!"

The people in the house say, "Trick or treat." My goddaughter says nothing. They give us candy, and as we're going down the stairs, she's mumbling to herself.

"Sweetie, what is wrong?"

She said, "I want to go home."

"Why?"

She says, "Everybody loves Winnie-the-Pooh. Don't nobody love the debbil."

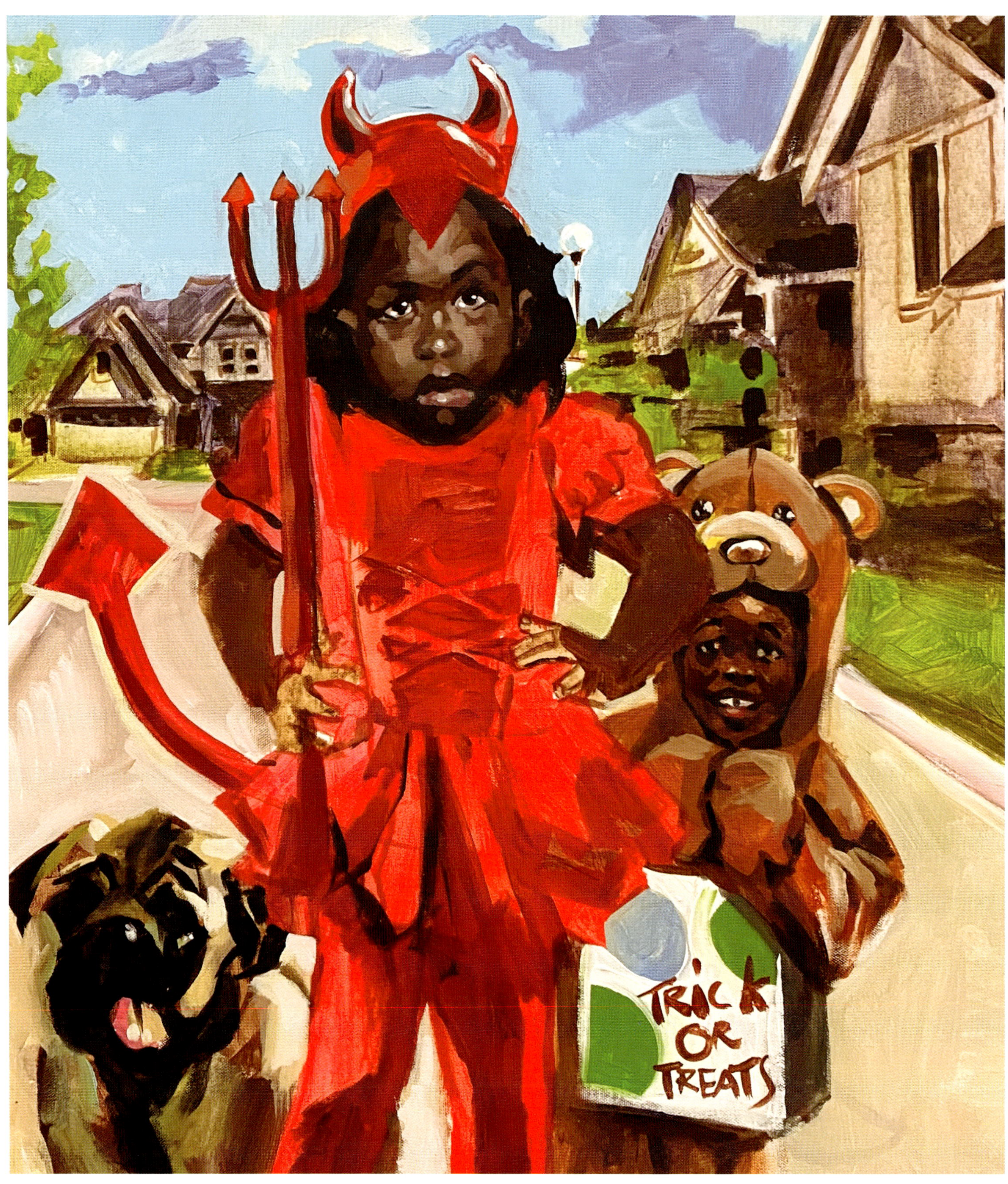

Charly Palmer, *Nobody Loves the Debbil*
(Acrylic on canvas)

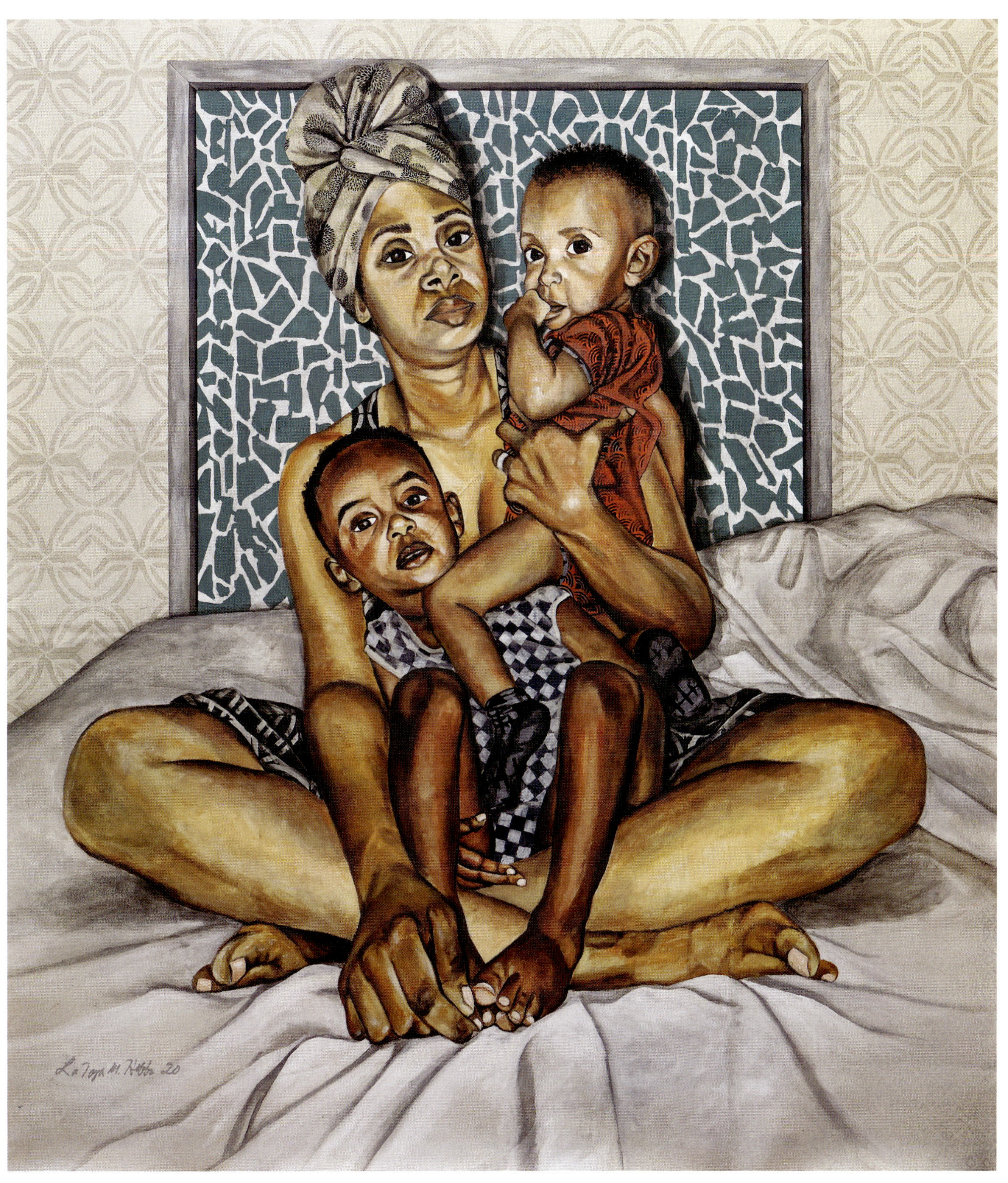

Latoya Hobbs, *The Everyday*
(Acrylic and collage on canvas)

PLAYTIME: SIX GAMES

Arranged by Mekhi Yant | Fisk University, Class of 2023

MUSICAL CHAIRS

This is a popular game for children. It's a game of elimination involving, of course, music and chairs. A group of chairs are placed in a circle; as the music plays, participants walk around the chairs; and when the music stops, the participants race for a chair to sit in. At the end of each round, the number of chairs decreases. The person sitting in the final chair is declared the winner. As simple as it seems, this game can be a real challenge. This game is especially good for children because it keeps them engaged with one another, it gets them active, and it allows them to listen to a nice tune. While the game is meant for children, it still often appeals to adults and teenagers.

CAPTURE THE FLAG

This game is also good for children to participate in. It's most often played outdoors, in big fields. Players are placed on teams of two or more. Each team has a flag. The flags will likely be placed (or sometimes hidden) on opposite sides of the fields, one on each team's base. One team must retrieve the other team's flag and bring it to their own base. This game is good for children because it keeps them active, it teaches them teamwork, and it enables them to hone their strategic skills.

SIMON SAYS

This is a great game that many people will remember from their childhoods. There is a designated leader who gives out the directions. All the other participants in the game must follow the exact instructions the leader gives *if* the leader includes the phrase "Simon says" in front of it. For instance, if the leader says, "Simon says touch your head," you must touch your head, but if the leader says, "Touch your head," following the instructions would result in a penalty followed by elimination from the game on the second infraction. This game is good for children because it shows them how to use their listening and comprehension skills in an amusing way.

HOPSCOTCH

This is another quite popular game that you can play just about anywhere, like playgrounds, neighborhood sidewalks, driveways, or any other concrete surface. Numbered rectangular boxes are drawn on the ground to give participants an outline of where to hop. The participants of the game must toss a small object (preferably a small rock or marble) into the rectangles. Following this, the participants must hop through the rectangular boxes to retrieve the small object they tossed. This game can be played with one participant or multiple participants. This game is good for children because it's always convenient to play, it builds physical coordination, and it displays numbers and shapes for children to see.

FOUR SQUARE

This great game for children requires four players. This game can be played outside on a playground or in a gym. The playing field is divided into four squares, as the name suggests, and each player has their own individual square. Using a ball that is capable of bouncing, each player must tap the ball into the next player's square. The ball can only bounce one time before a player must tap it; if a player misses a ball or lets the ball bounce twice in a square, they are eliminated. This game is good for children because it forces them to think fast and strategically. It is also another way to keep them active and healthy. Most importantly, it puts them in a competitive yet friendly environment.

HEADS UP, SEVEN UP

This is a game that is very popular with grade-schoolers and is often played in a classroom setting. Seven students are selected, and the other students sit with their heads down on their desks and their thumbs up. The selected students must move around the classroom silently and touch the thumbs of the students with their heads down. Once a student's thumb is touched, they must put it down. The students must guess which of the seven selected touched their thumbs. This game is good for students because it shows them how to use other senses to find clues. It's often a silent game, so it is not disturbing to other classes when being played. Most importantly, it gives students a chance to relax and just have fun at school.

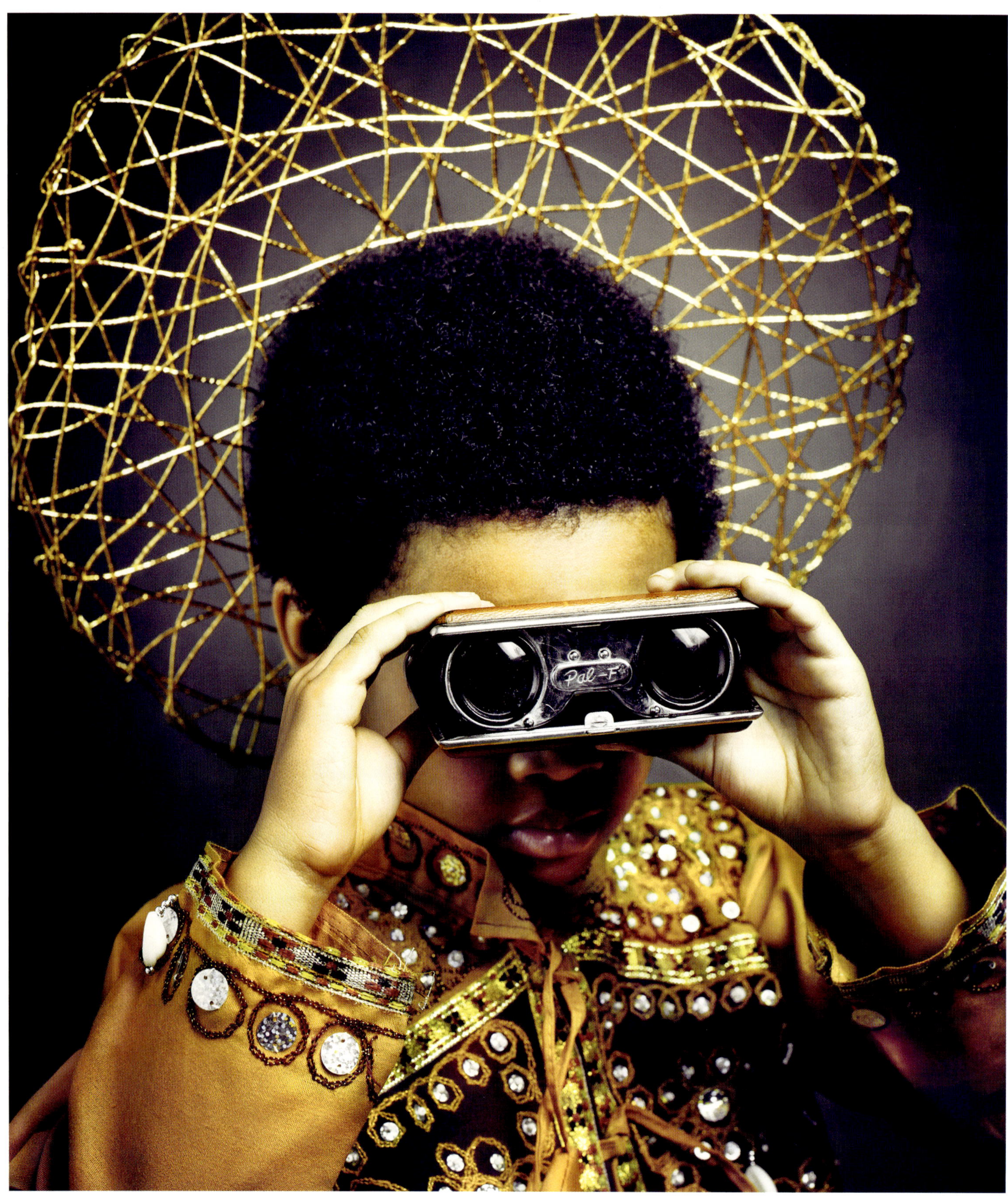

Tokie Rome-Taylor, *Scout*
(Archival pigment photograph)

THE ISLAND OF LOST FATHERS

By Bertice Berry

Once upon a time, in a far, faraway place, lived a little boy named Jabril. Jabril had a brother named William, a sister named Fatima, and a sister named Mariah. Now, he had a wonderful mother, but she was a chosen mother, a mother who came to care for them because their mother was sick.

Well, Jabril wished more than anything for a father. One day he said to his friends, "I know where all the fathers are."

His friends said, "No one knows where our daddies are! They are lost. My mommy said so."

Jabril said, "I do know where they are! I was dreaming one day in class. The teacher said, 'Stop that daydreaming!' But I wasn't daydreaming. I was just dreaming. They say I have ADHD, which means I can't focus, but I focus on everything, and that day I focused so hard that I saw where our fathers are!"

So Jabril grabbed up all his friends and his sisters and his brother and they went in search of the island of lost fathers. The island wasn't that far. It was just a few leaps away, but you had to use your imagination to get there. They leapt, and they leapt, and they leapt but they couldn't find it.

Just as they were about to lose hope, Jabril heard a voice.

"We're here! We're here and we love you! We're here and we love you!"

Jabril closed his eyes and followed the voice. But his friends couldn't follow because they couldn't hear! So Jabril went ahead alone, and finally he landed on the Island of Lost Fathers. There he saw fathers toiling, physically in their bodies, walking to and fro, lost to those who could not see them, but there to Jabril, who could imagine. He saw that the fathers were weak, and their consciousness had been stolen away. There on that island of lost fathers was the consciousness of each of those fathers who walked away from their families, the consciousness they had lost to all the hardships of life. Some hardships were caused by others, and some the fathers had chosen. There on that island of lost fathers, the consciousness of each man was alive and well and seeking a way to get back to the children. Jabril knew the way. Only he could show those fathers the way back.

The end. Until tomorrow!

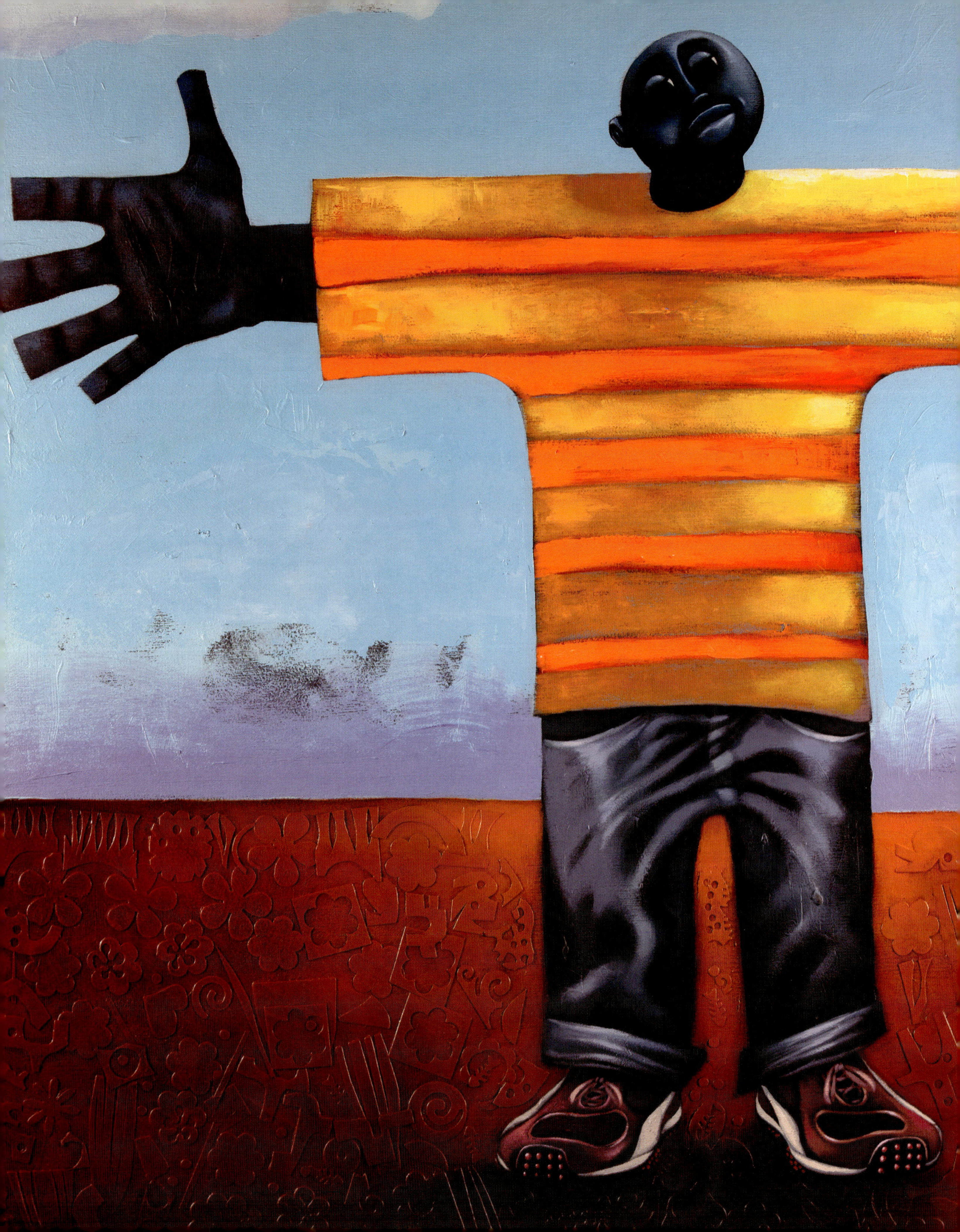

THE LACTOSE INTOLERANT CLUB FOR PICKY EATERS

By Waverly Duck

It was a cold winter day in February. The cold didn't bother me, though, because it was my birthday. It was also a Saturday—the best day for a party! It was sunny outside, and the clouds overhead were strung together like polka dots in the sky.

I had been planning my birthday for weeks and invited my entire third-grade class. The invitation read:

**JOIN US FOR A PIZZA PARTY TO CELEBRATE
WAVERLY'S 8TH BIRTHDAY
SATURDAY, FEBRUARY 21ST
NOON TO 3 PM
ALL ARE WELCOME!**

I had a detailed plan. It was going to be the best party ever. I made a list of my favorite foods, including chocolate cake, chocolate ice cream, cupcakes, and lots of pizza—some with just cheese, some with pepperoni, some stacked with veggies, and even one with pineapple. That's right, pineapple! I'd never tried that before, but I liked pineapple, and I liked pizza, so putting the two together seemed like a perfect combo.

I'd even gotten food for my best friend, Kamal. Kamal doesn't like pizza or ice cream, so my dad made him grilled hamburgers and homemade French fries. I even helped my mom and dad make party favors for my friends and classmates—noisemakers, paper hats, puzzles, and small bags of chocolates to take home from the best party ever.

On the day of the party, I was so excited I could hardly breathe. My oldest brother, Keith, who was in high school, helped me decorate. My sister, Sharon, who was three years older, helped me set the table. My mom made me a music playlist of my favorite songs by Stevie Wonder.

Everyone showed up, and we played games until the party ended. I had my fill of chocolate cake and gobbled down so many bowls of ice cream I lost count of them. Then I heard my mom say, "Waverly, stop eating all that ice cream. You'll get a stomachache and spoil your dinner!" "Ha," I thought. "Who can think about dinner when there's all this ice cream to be eaten?"

Well, it turned out my mom was right. By dinnertime, I had the worst stomachache of my life. I could hear my stomach grumbling and bubbling. My mom put a plate of fish and spaghetti in front of me, but I couldn't eat it.

"Waverly, you've had your fill of sweets for the day, now finish your dinner," my mom said. My family called me a picky eater because I didn't like any of the food my parents made. If they gave me a piece of bread, I just ate the crust. If they offered me milk, I declined. Even though I loved ice cream, milk always made me feel sick.

My sister chimed in. "See, Mom? Even on his birthday he's a picky eater!"

"No, it's not that, Mom. My stomach hurts!" I protested.

But my sister kept going. "He eats all the time and never gains weight. Maybe he has a tapeworm."

That sounded bad. "A TAPEWORM! What!?" I exclaimed.

"Yeah," said my sister. "It's when a worm lives in your belly and eats all your food."

My dad looked up. "Stop teasing your brother; he doesn't have a tapeworm."

But my sister was persistent. "You should let me hold a cookie up to your mouth to see if the worm will come out of your belly to eat it!" she said.

Dad was getting annoyed. "Stop trying to scare your brother! He doesn't have a tapeworm. But we will go to the doctor tomorrow to get it checked out."

While I lay in bed that night, I was kept awake by the sound of my stomach rumbling and gas pains. I also kept thinking about that tapeworm. If he was in there, could I talk him into coming out? Couldn't he go find his own food instead of eating mine?!

The next morning my parents took me to urgent care to see the doctor.

The doctor came in and asked me if I could think of any other times my stomach felt this bad. I thought for a moment, then answered, "Well, mostly it happens when I drink milk, and sometimes during pizza day at school."

The doctor nodded, and I asked about the tapeworm.

"My sister said that my stomach hurts because a worm in my belly eats all my food. Is that true?"

The doctor laughed. "No, there isn't a tapeworm in your stomach."

Phew, that was a close one, I thought.

"But you are lactose intolerant."

"Lactose what?" I replied. "What's that?"

The doctor explained, "Lactose intolerance is when your body can't process the lactose in dairy products like milk and ice cream. It's pretty common for a boy your age, and it usually develops as we get older."

A sense of dread came over me. This didn't sound good.

"Does this mean I can't have ice cream anymore?" I asked.

"Well, it depends," answered the doctor. "You can have lactose-free food, including ice cream, but you should be careful about eating any dairy from now on."

I was devastated.

On Monday I returned to school knowing that there would be no more cheeseburgers, ice cream

cups, chocolate milk, or pineapple pizza in my future. I loved all those foods, but I hated the stomachaches.

I told my best friend, Kamal, that I was lactose intolerant. I thought he'd be confused. Instead, he laughed and said, "Me too. So are Keisha, Rosabelle, Tyler, Jamal, Shannon, and Jackson—you're not alone."

"Wow, so I'm not the only one?" I asked, suddenly feeling much better. "Nah," replied Kamal. "Lots of people have it. It's no big deal."

That gave me an idea. We could form a lactose intolerance club for picky eaters!

During lunch, all my lactose-intolerant friends helped put together a lactose-free lunch for me.

Jackson gave me an apple.

Keisha gave me fruit juice.

And Kamal gave me one of his chicken tacos.

I realized that while I'd lost a few foods, I had gained a whole club! The Lactose Intolerant Club for Picky Eaters!

It was a good day!

FLIGHT LESSONS
FOR KUMASI

By Frank X Walker

You stare back at me
with my own eyes
and command that I *"fix it,"*
endowing me with magic powers
to uncrash or unbreak the results
of the Faith you place
in the pretend wings attached
to anything that fits in your hands.

The too-full toy box won't even close,
yet the veggies on your plate
are your new favorite playthings.

Our Benin brass bell is missing
its clapper. Every single piece of furniture
we own is chipped, scratched or dented.

There isn't a single wall in our house
you haven't kissed with a crayon.

When you were too quiet
you had flooded the bathroom.

Yesterday, I considered trading you
for a puppy, but your mother said, "No."

Today, you attach magnetic triangles
to a square and proudly show us
your *"picture of blue mountains."*

I let my smile out of its cave,
swell with pride and float
out of the room on new wings.

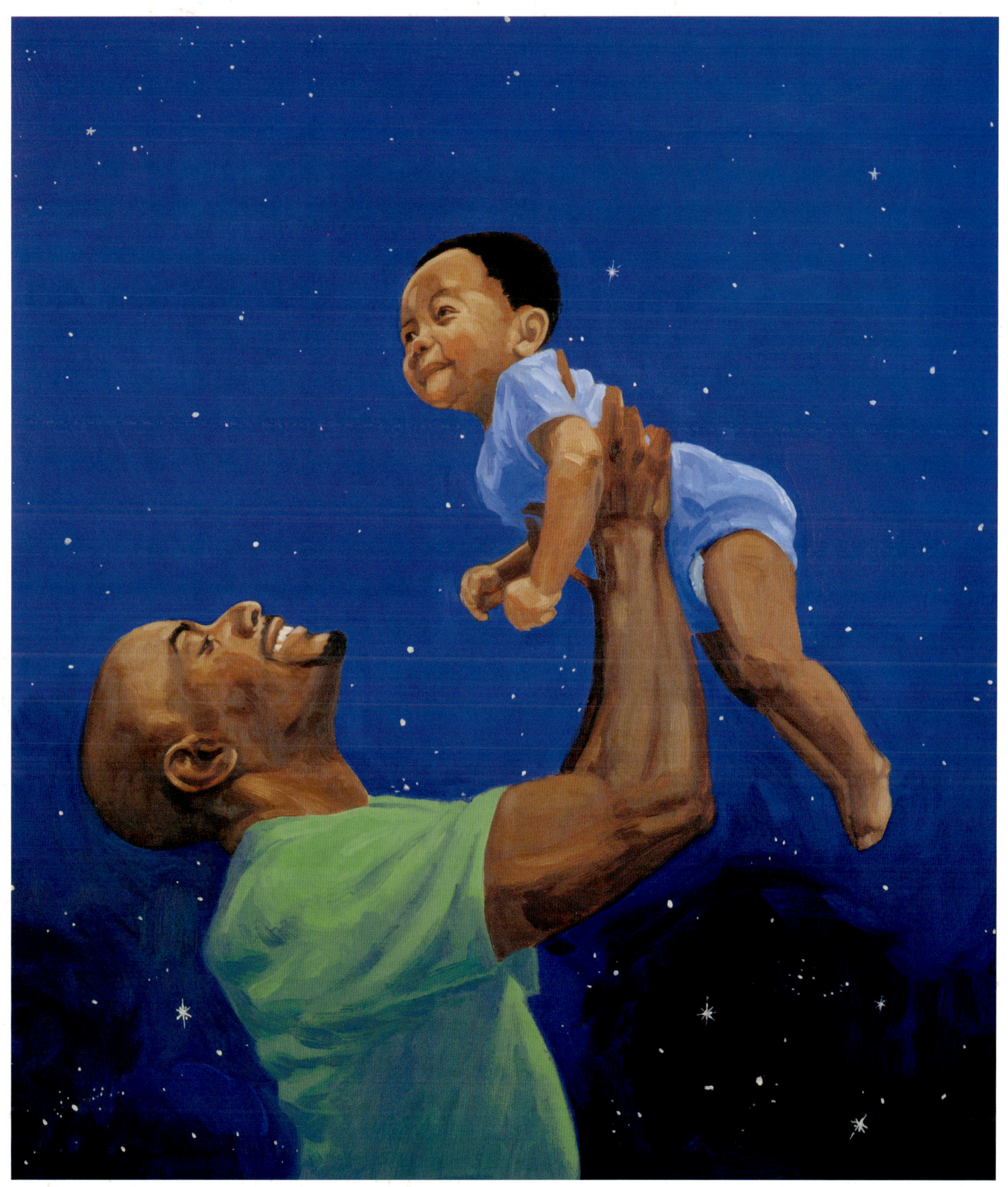

James Ransome, *Baby Blessing*
(Oil on paper)

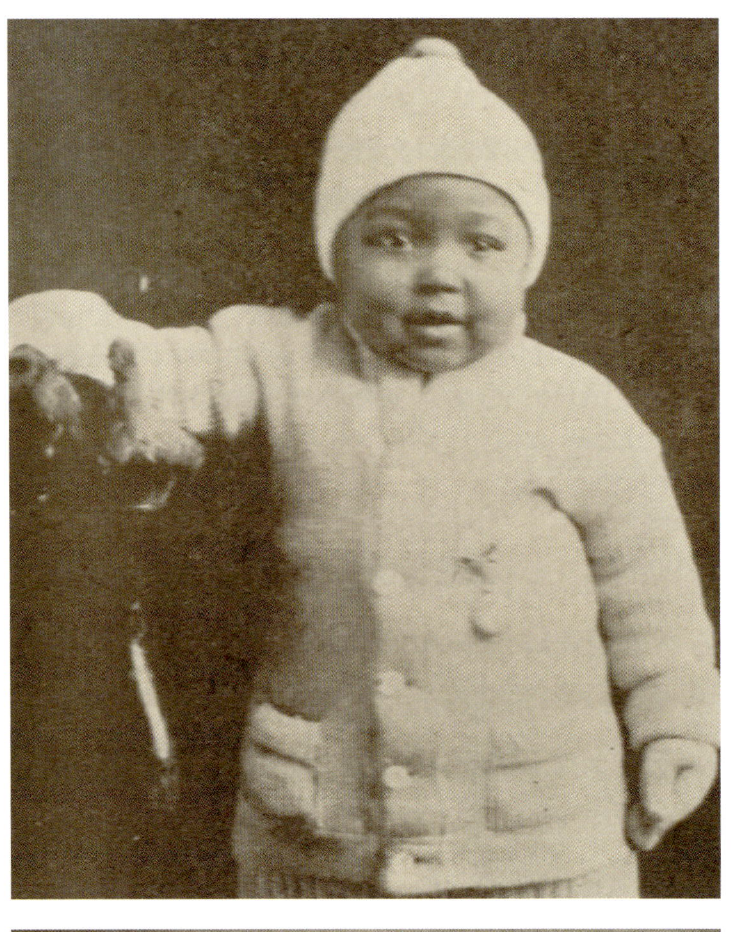 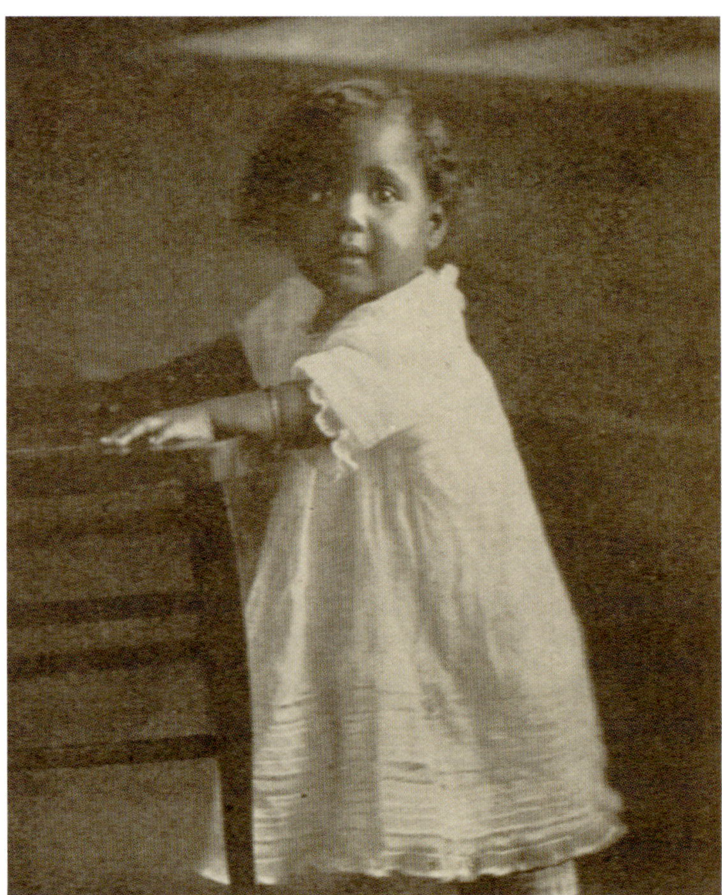

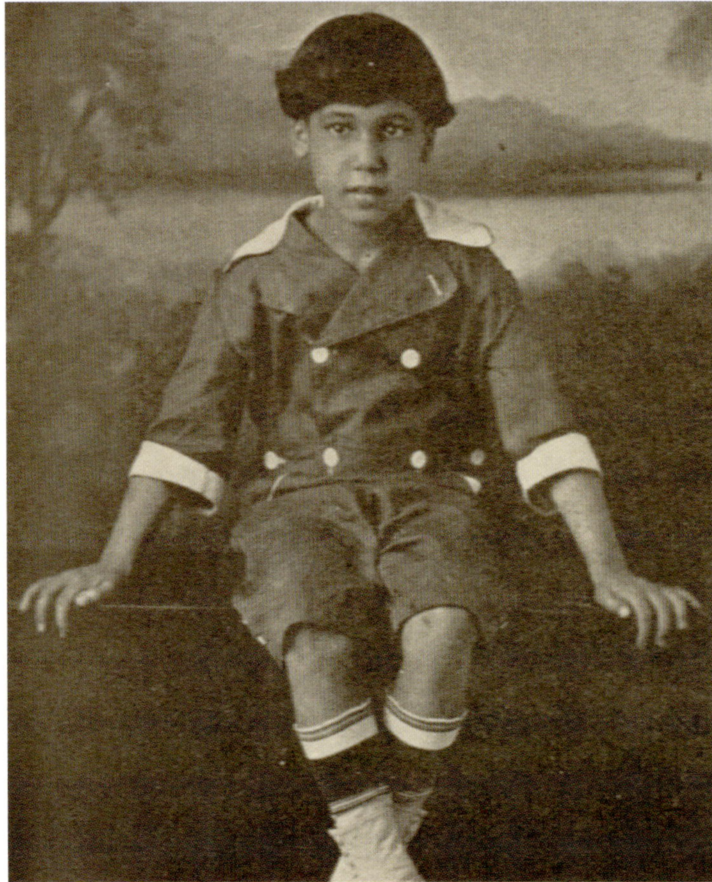 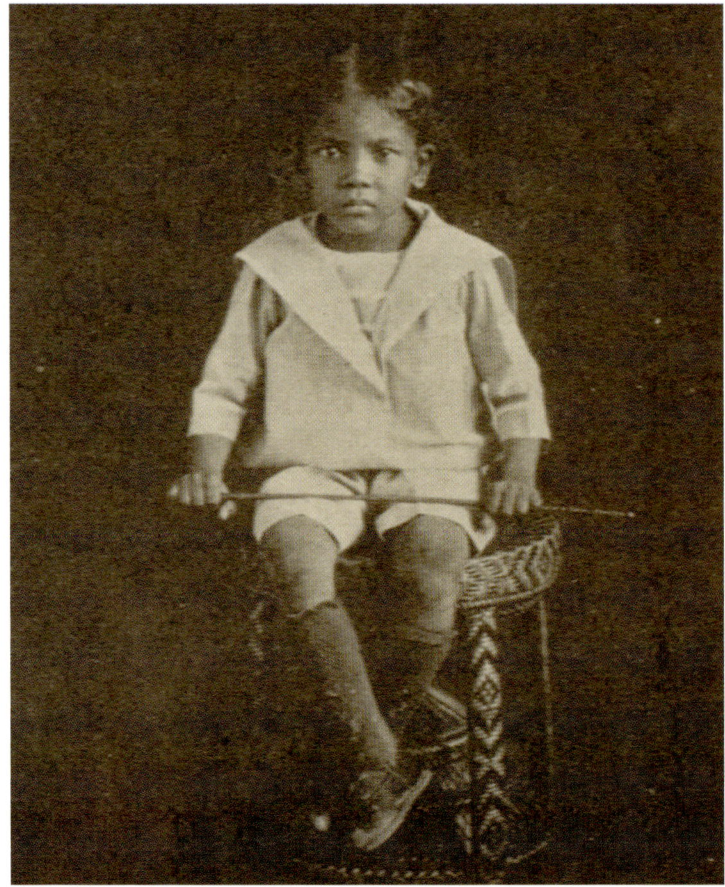

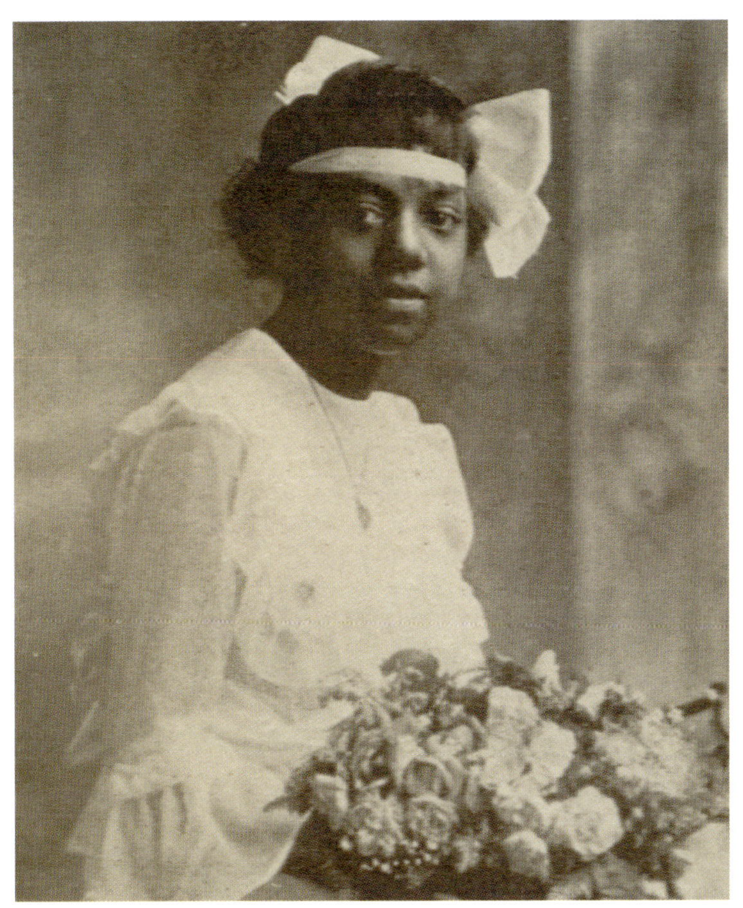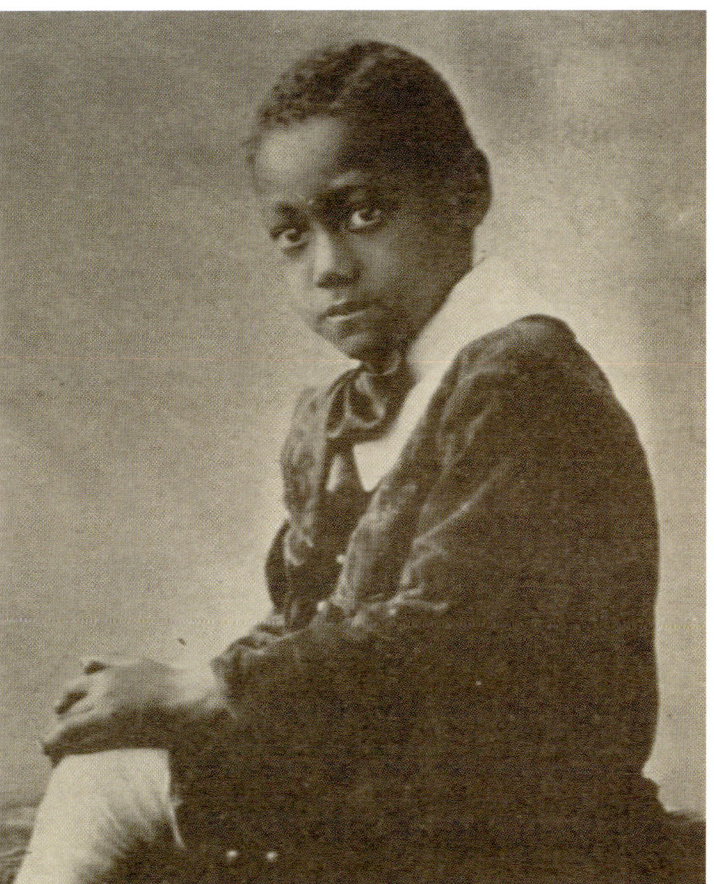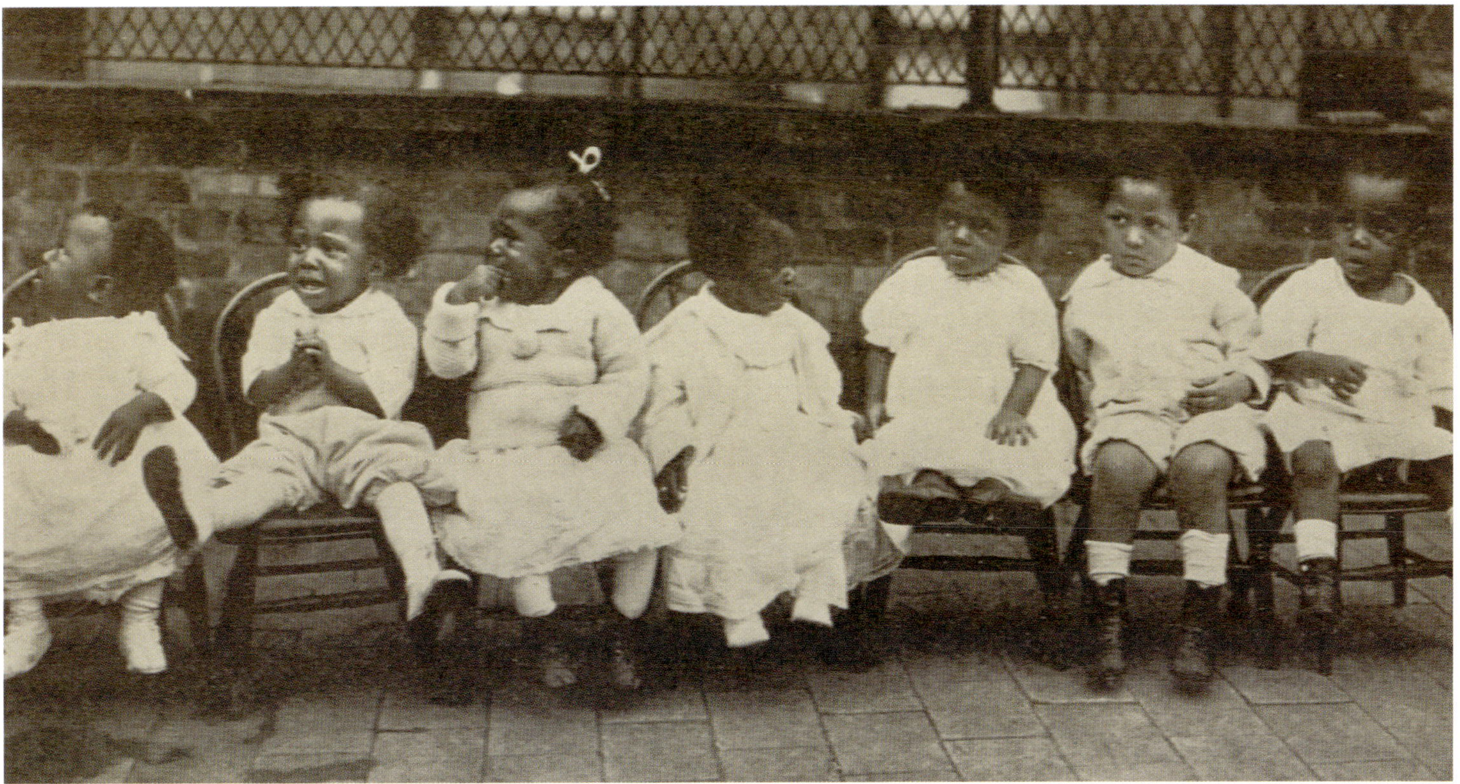

Images from *The Brownies' Book*, Volume 2, Issue 3, March 1921.
This page, top: Louise Ruth Morgan and John Lucas, from "Little People of the Month"; bottom: Underwood & Underwood, "Seven Prize Winners of New York City"; opposite page: from "Our Little Friends."

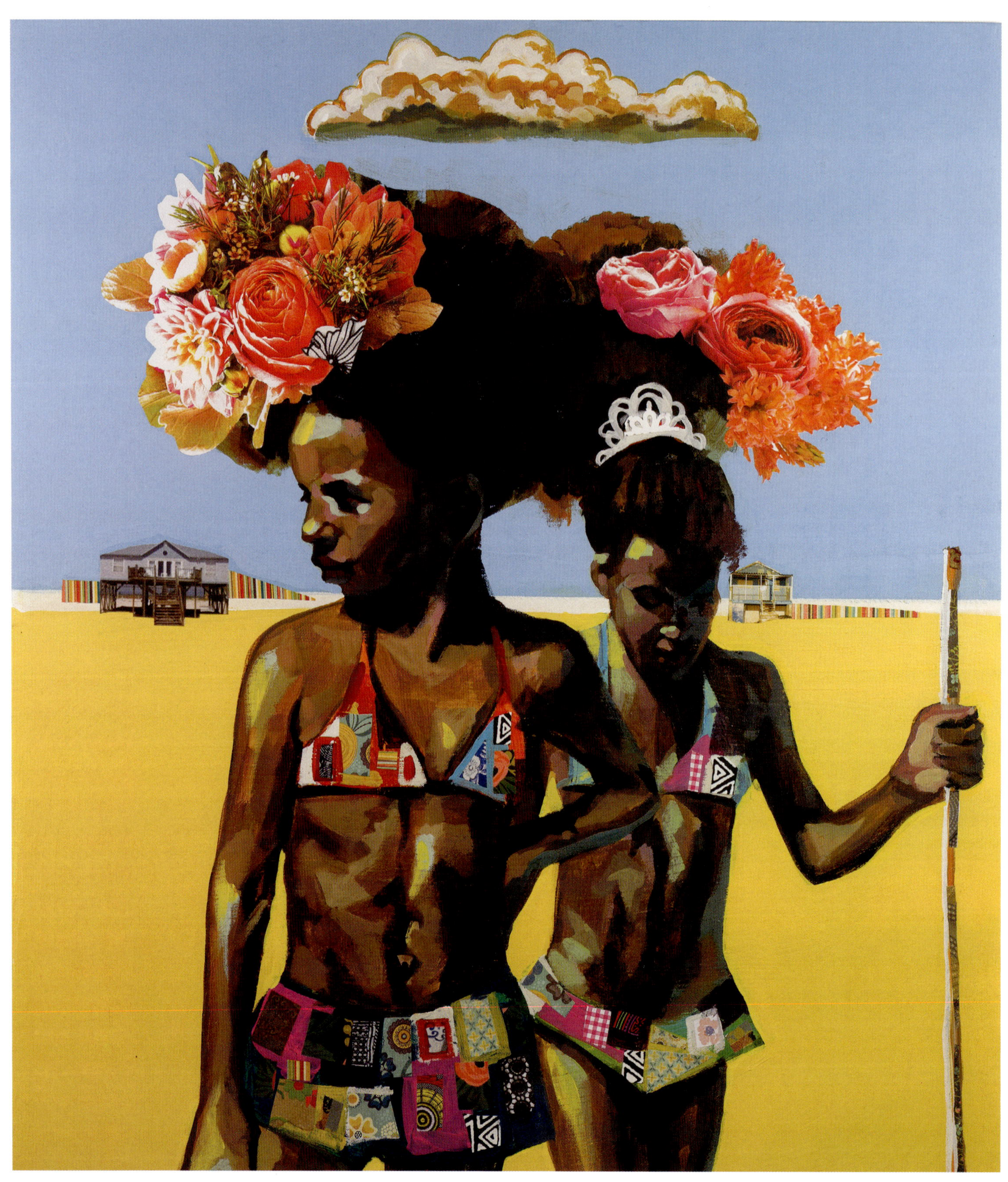

Charly Palmer, *Sister Warriors*
(Acrylic on canvas)

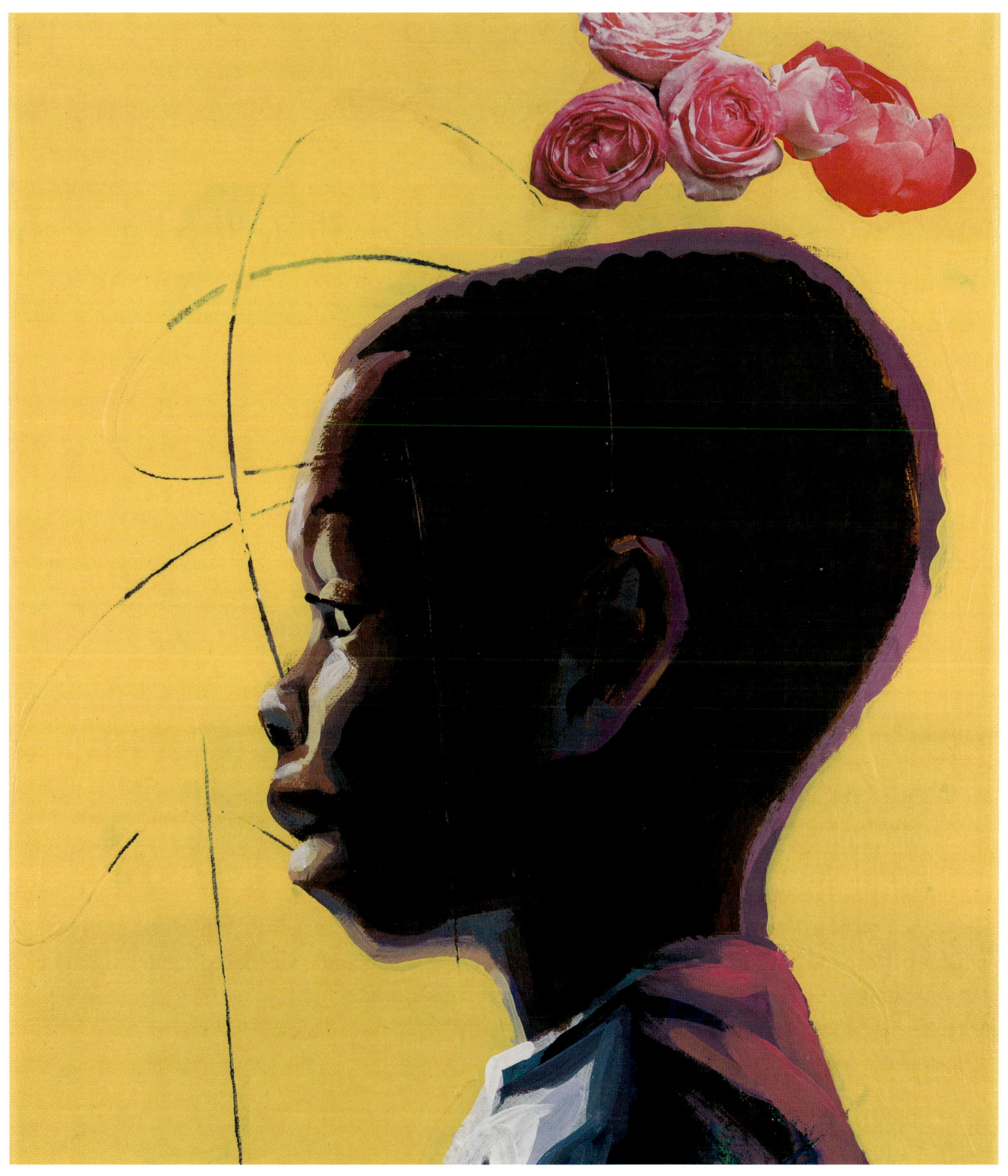

Charly Palmer, *Hudson*
(Acrylic on canvas)

FOR BREANNA AND OTHER CHILDREN WHO LOVE TO LAUGH WITH THE ADULTS IN THEIR LIVES

By Courtney J. Patterson-Faye

Do you remember the way you overflowed with giggles when you mocked Stevie J rubbing his hands together, showing me how I would "make dat bread" when I started my new job? If you do, good, you should! If you don't, then I will remember and hold all that laughter between us for us. You were sharp with your mimicry. Keen in your hand gestures and more than accurate with that Grinch-like smile curled up on both sides of your face, you were beaming. We are more than twenty years apart in age, but that day reminded me that what binds our family is the type of love that knows no type of boundary and we wrap that love in humor and adoration.

There are countless instances of our love for gut-busting laughs. It's almost as if our laughter is as unconditional as the love between us. When you were six you perfected Wendy Williams's "How you doin?" (and her hand gestures, too) and I videotaped you—in your princess heels—just in case you needed a "remember when" video when you became a superstar. I showed the video to my friends and their guffaws were all the validation I needed. You are hilarious! When you set up a Facebook account for our Aunt Ann and the next day she complained that her Facebook "calls" went "ding all night!" you and I cackled over FaceTime. My mother, your Aunt

Gwen, informed her, "They ain't calling you, Ann—they friend requests!" and your mother, my Aunt Angie (to her sister, our Aunt Jan, on the phone), said, "They were just notations, you know?" You and I both screamed "NOTIFICATIONS" before we fell out and into raucous laughter. I may have been home in Connecticut while all of you were at my mother's house in South Carolina, but I felt like I was there. That particular moment brought all four sisters, their sense of humor, you, and me together and fortified us in a legacy of our grand-mother's humor.

Mama Sis, as she was affectionately called, was one of the funniest people in the entire world. She was a woman who did not mince words. She bit her tongue for no one and only her intelligence was sharper than her wit (although I believe they were never mutually exclusive). While raising us both at two different times, she cooked us our favorite foods, passed the most horrible-smelling gas, and when she threw her head back and laughed we could hear her in every room. Your comedic timing reminds me of her. Your responses to your mother nagging you or my mother chastising you made me spit out my water/ginger ale/wine cooler many a time. Even when you argued with me or said something slick about my appearance I would have to turn away so that you wouldn't see the laughter bubbling in my face. But it's the way we say the wrong words about the right things that get me every time. Mama Sis's anger once made her cuss when she recalled seeing an "efficiency note" on her brother's door when his hospital bills overwhelmed his pockets. Your mother complained about how her birthday dinner turned sour when she realized her friends went overboard with the tip because the restaurant did not tell the group that the "gratility" was already included. That still sends me over the edge every time I pay the bill at a restaurant. Let us never forget when you, Breanna, boasted to me about you making salmon "crocakes" for breakfast. You blame your mother for saying salmon "croquettes" this way, but I'm blaming you too! And I'm still laughing about it. I love how we keep Mama Sis alive through our humor and I am forever grateful.

I laughed with her and her sisters much like how you laugh with me and your aunts now. We fill generational gaps with jokes and sidesplitting giggles about our day-to-day happenings. Whether it be a misspoken word, off-key singing, or something we watched on the newest episode of one of the Real Housewives franchises, we find humor—our brand of love—anywhere. We find it in sadness, anger, disappointment, and betrayal and eventually transform them all into some form of joy. Our discoveries really tap into what it means to be beautiful Black people making our way in the world. We don't often get the positive, redemptive stories about us, especially us Black women, but you and I know that we've always already had a multitude of emotions, feelings, beliefs, and values. We are allowed to change as time demands, but we know who we are. We are our grandmother's daughters, and she gave us the sights and sounds of Blackness. We have them in abundance. I say don't hold back when basking in how we love on each other. Be boastful, loud, and attentive while laughing with the adults in your life. Our relationships with each other truly ground us and reflect the magnitude of who we are.

This is not a call for you and all the Black children that I hold dear to cuss (more), watch more reality television, or grow up too fast, but rather a hope that you will find common ground with the adults around you using all the tools that you can find. Stay close to the ones that you feel safe around, those who love and protect you, and especially those, like me, who get on your nerves when they try to share their life experiences. They (we) are your wells of knowledge and wisdom. We are your people. I also fully understand that our exchanges go both ways; we must pay attention when you speak. If we become hardheaded, just remind us that we were once children, too. Remind us that you are the future and show just how impeccable and hilarious you are. All of you teach us so much and we don't know where we would be without you. We—and our laughter—are each other's blessings.

Chapter 2

LET ME COUNT THE WAYS

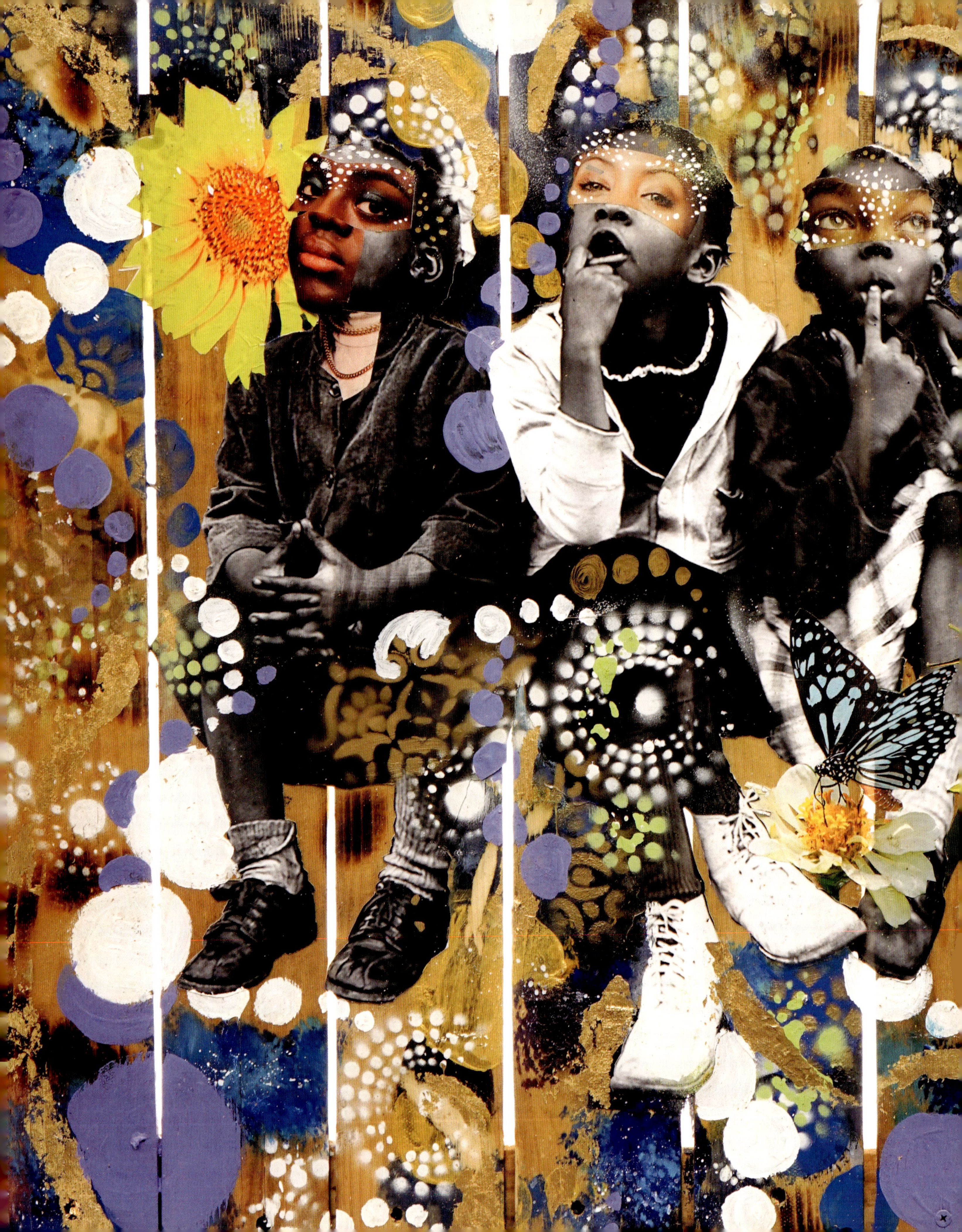

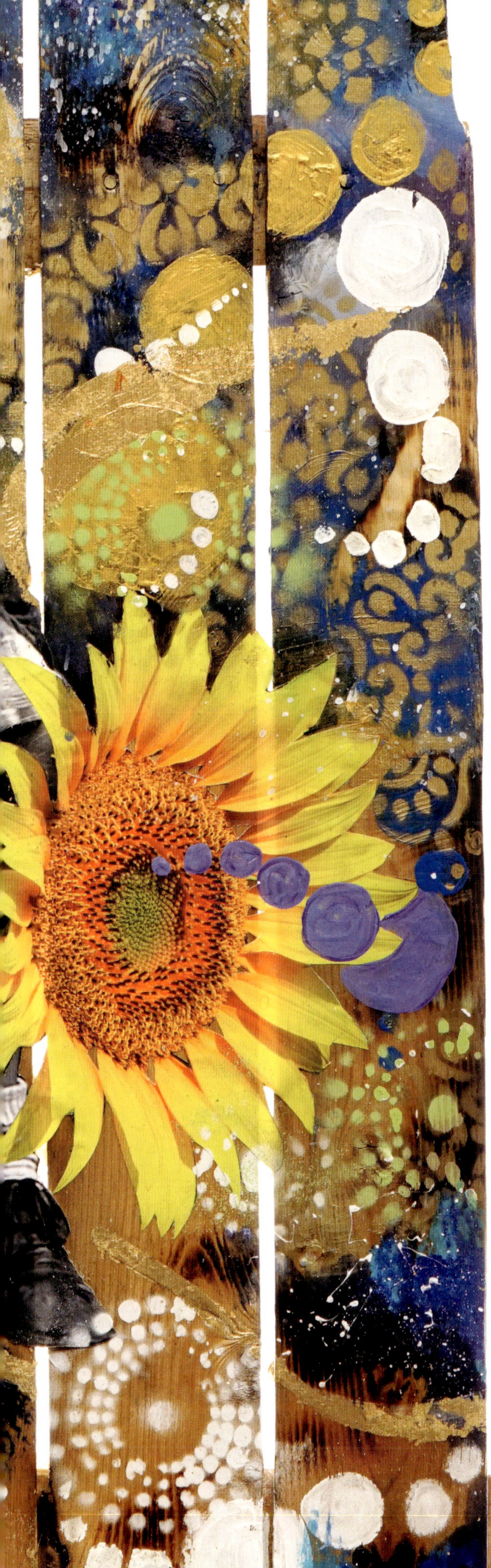

SWEET BEE

By Kai Adia

A fat bundle of nerves,
she looks exactly like her father.
Filled with the brilliance of her mother.
A sweet bee, she is
Striped with the colors of eternal knowing
A kind intelligence that tells her to unfurl
her wings and flutter until she flies . . .

She's in training now,
learning to own her smile.
Despite the bumps on the wind
that threatened to shake her off the board
on her first flight in,
She's here to stay
In her black and gold skin.

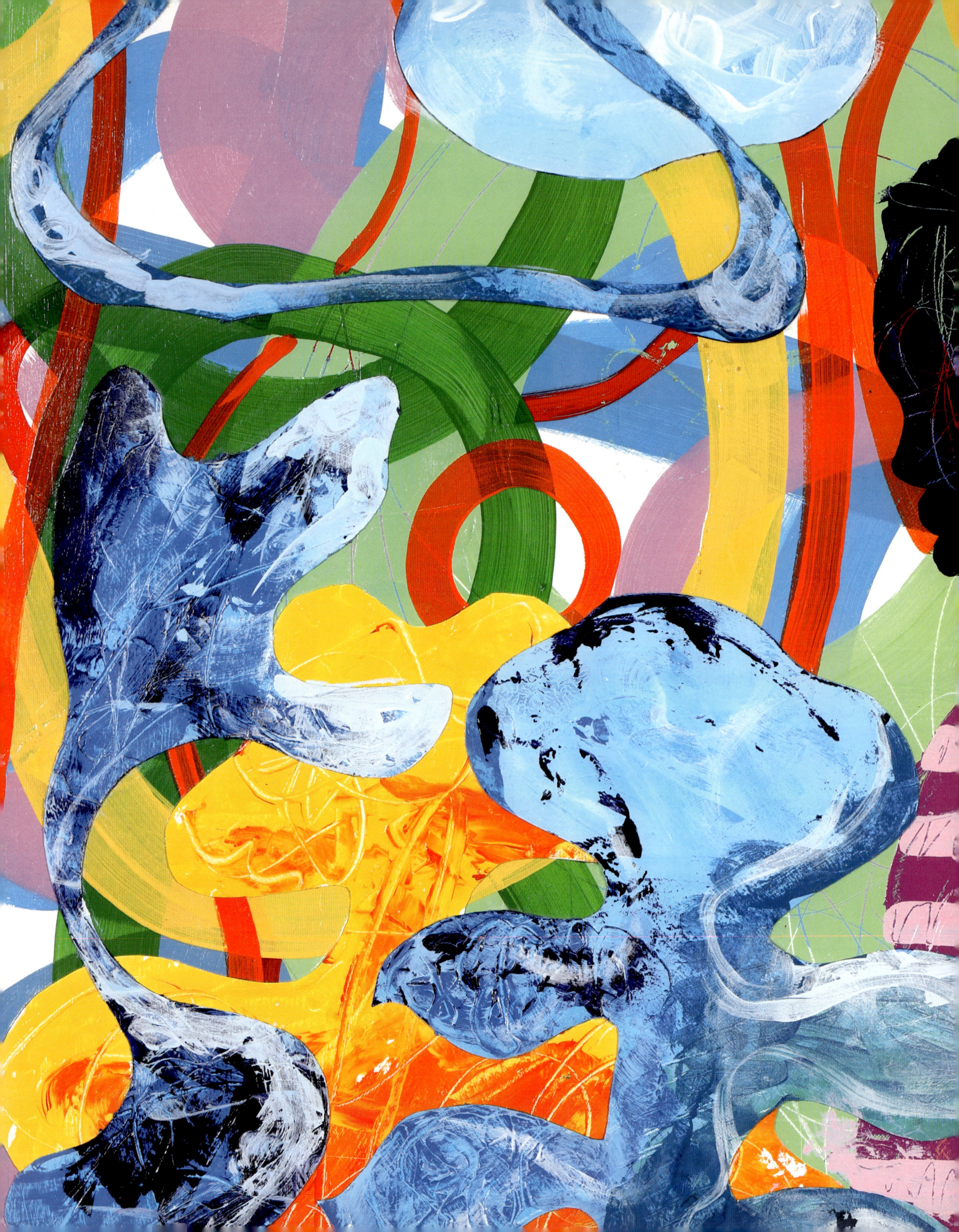

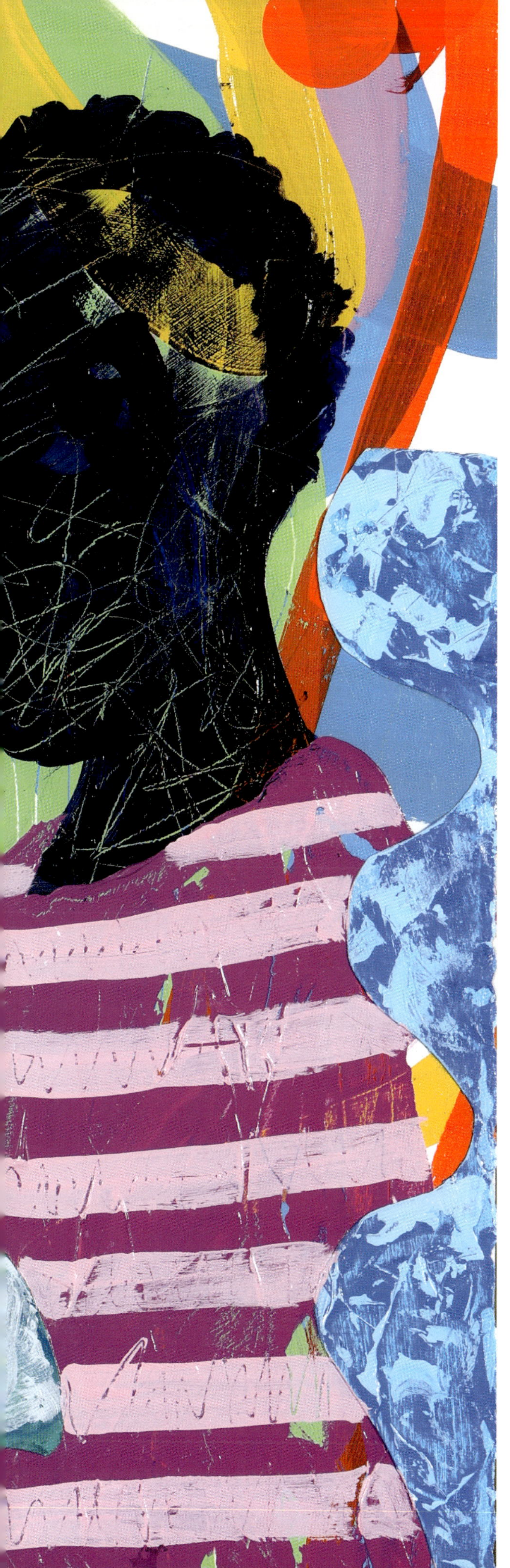

LITTLE BROWN BOY

By Annette Christine Browne |
From *The Brownies' Book*, January 1921

God loved you an awful lot, I know.
  Why do I think so?
Why he tinted your body that beautiful brown,
So the angels might guard you from Heaven
  on down;
While trailing clouds of glory you came down
  here to stay,
They watched that little soul in brown all the long
  way.
They loved you dearly there, I know.
Don't you feel it so?
They might have made hair plain and straight on
  your head,
But they fashioned those crisp little curls
  there instead;
They gave them with their love for you and
  put them on to stay
And wanted them always to grow just that way.
I wonder that they ever let you go;
They loved you so.
They gave you a heart full of laughter and song,
And lips that go merrily all the day long.
I guess they let you come to us so we might
  see what joy
And loveliness can dwell within a little boy.

LITTLE BLACK BOY

By Lucian B. Watkins |
From *The Brownies' Book*, January 1921

Little Black boy with your little black feet,
Fanned and tanned by the wild-winds fleet;
Caught and kissed by the morning's cool,
Christened with dew from the lily-cup pool:
Sable Youth! Crown Prince of Night!
Royal in the reign of Right!
Heaven-born Heart! naught can destroy
Your faith-bright visions, little Black boy.
Little Black boy with your little black hands,
Seared by desert suns and sands;
In the crucible of time,
Seasoned for your task sublime:
From the depth unto the height,

These shall bear your Lamp of Light;
These shall build your Rome and Troy,
Beyond life's mountains, little Black boy.
Little Black boy with your little black head,
Crinkled hair of midnight shred;
Mystic moons have wrought a grace
Into the molding of your face:
Lo, the splendor in your eyes,
Like a wonder in dark skies,
Seems a sign from worlds unknown,
Glory-gleams from a distant throne;—
Ah, it is your soul, O joy!—
God's gift of Love to the little Black boy!

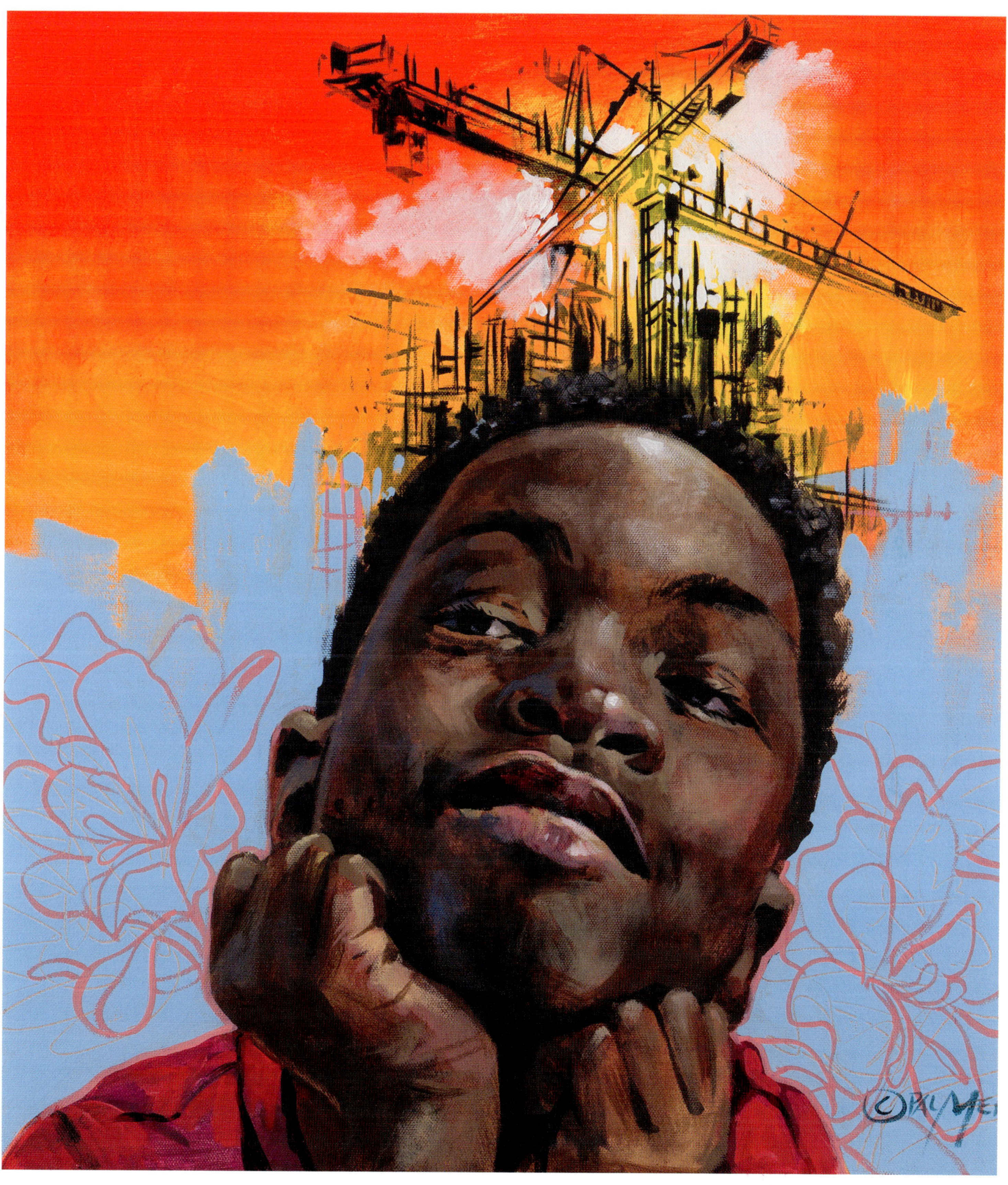

Charly Palmer, *Our Future*
(Acrylic on canvas)

½ cup Flour
¾ cup sugar
3T cup Butter
1 teaspoon cinnamon
½ tea sp nutmeg
1 cup prum
1 cup Butter
1¼ tea sp soda
2 egg
1 teas Flour
Bock 1 hour — 325

Gloze 1 stick Butter
1 cup Butter milk
1 cup sugar

Lena

mayonnaise

A LOVE LETTER FOR YOU

By Halima Taha

Beloved,

Yes, YOU! I have been thinking about you ever since you were born. And now that you are older and know the difference between right and wrong, I have a secret that I want to share with you always to remember.

This secret is like a raincoat for every season to protect you from ideas, energy, and projections about you that are not true today or ever. This raincoat will help you to stay the course to accomplish your goals and make your dreams for yourself come true.

The secret is called TRUTH, which is in accordance with fact and reality. The easiest way to see TRUTH is to look in the mirror. Give yourself a joyful smile as you look at your beautiful skin. Hug yourself. You are as unique as your fingerprints. This is TRUTH.

Beloved, you are the reflection of resplendent beauty, ancient history, substantive quality, discerning intelligence, capable talent, and irreplaceable value. Your eyes are the portal to see many extraordinary and spellbinding places, captivating people, and inspiring ideas in art, architecture, and design.

Your ears are a highway of wave patterns that hear sounds in syllables, music, and knowledge. Your nostrils will be filled with perfumed bouquets of fragrant oils, cooking herbs, and flavors that excite the palate. Your mouth will create words of joy, wonder, protest, and adoration and enjoy delicious foods from Africa, Europe, Asia, the Caribbean, North, South, and Central American kitchens in the homes of your family and friends.

> **THIS TRUTH IS THE FOUNDATION FOR YOUR SPIRITUAL, INTELLECTUAL, AND PHYSICAL FREEDOM TO BE THE UNIQUE PERSON YOU ARE.**

Beloved, you were created from DIVINE Love through an essence of pure love that brought your parents together, or other special circumstances. Some people call this pure Love the Creator, God, Allah, Lord, Netcher, Ptah, Yahweh, Jehovah, Adonai, or Jesus. The most important thing to know is that you are lovable as an attribute of DIVINE Love.

This TRUTH is the foundation for your spiritual, intellectual, and physical freedom to be the unique person you are. You were born free to be whole without limitations. You are free to become the best human being you can be. As you learn more about the world around you, you will also discover what is important and makes ▶

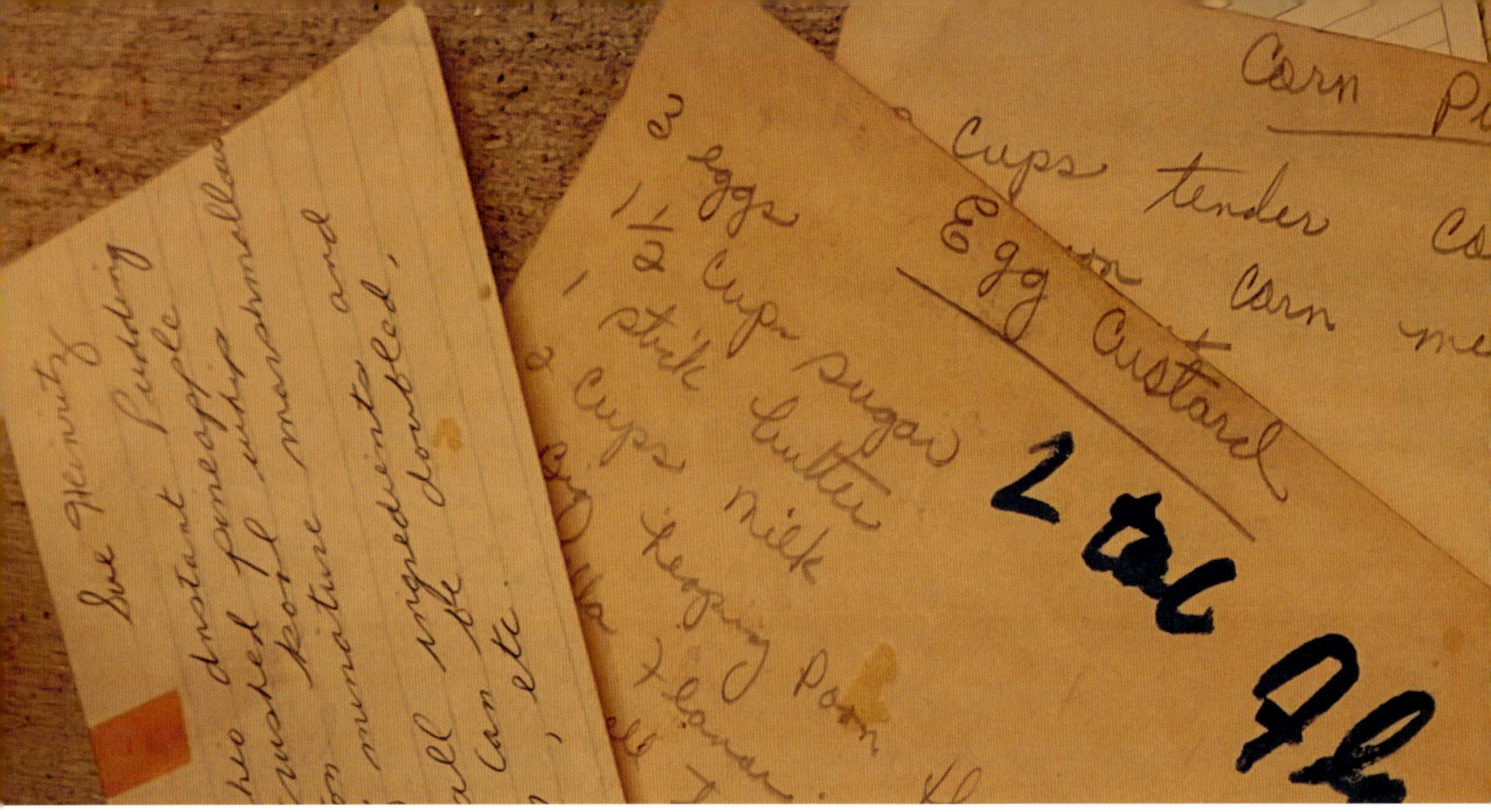

your life meaningful. This could be playing sports, painting, taking photographs, drawing, jewelry making, carpentry, dance, theater, writing, reading, fishing, hunting, skating, snowboarding, skiing, singing, traveling, or helping people in need.

Beloved, whatever gives you joy and purpose, your beautiful face will always radiate the TRUTH about you. It will also inspire encouragement, support, hugs, and kisses from family and friends who see the value of who you are. Sometimes, the best intentions of those who love you can be overwhelming, and the best thing to do is to silently listen and think about how the experiences of others can help you have success with your goals. Often being still like a mountain—looking, listening, and thinking about the world around you—is the best way to develop your ideas so your TRUTH can shine through.

Beloved, as you mature, there will always be people who value you, but there will also be people who try to make you feel less than who you are. They will attempt to take away your freedom to do or become your best self. This comes in the form of telling you that you cannot do something that you are capable of, telling you that you are not good enough because of the way you look, speak, and dress, or simply tearing you down because you can do many things better than they can. This can make you feel sad and angry or disinterested in the things that once gave you joy because you decided to allow another person to distract you from the TRUTH about yourself.

In this instance, you chose not to wear your raincoat in a storm of deceitful lies that emerge from other people's shortcomings, not yours. Jealousy, dishonesty, poor character, greed, and selfishness are shortcomings. Often when people have these qualities, they have forgotten the TRUTH about themselves because other people have said and done the same things to destroy their TRUTH.

Beloved, the greatness of your TRUTH is that when you fully accept, nurture, and embrace it,

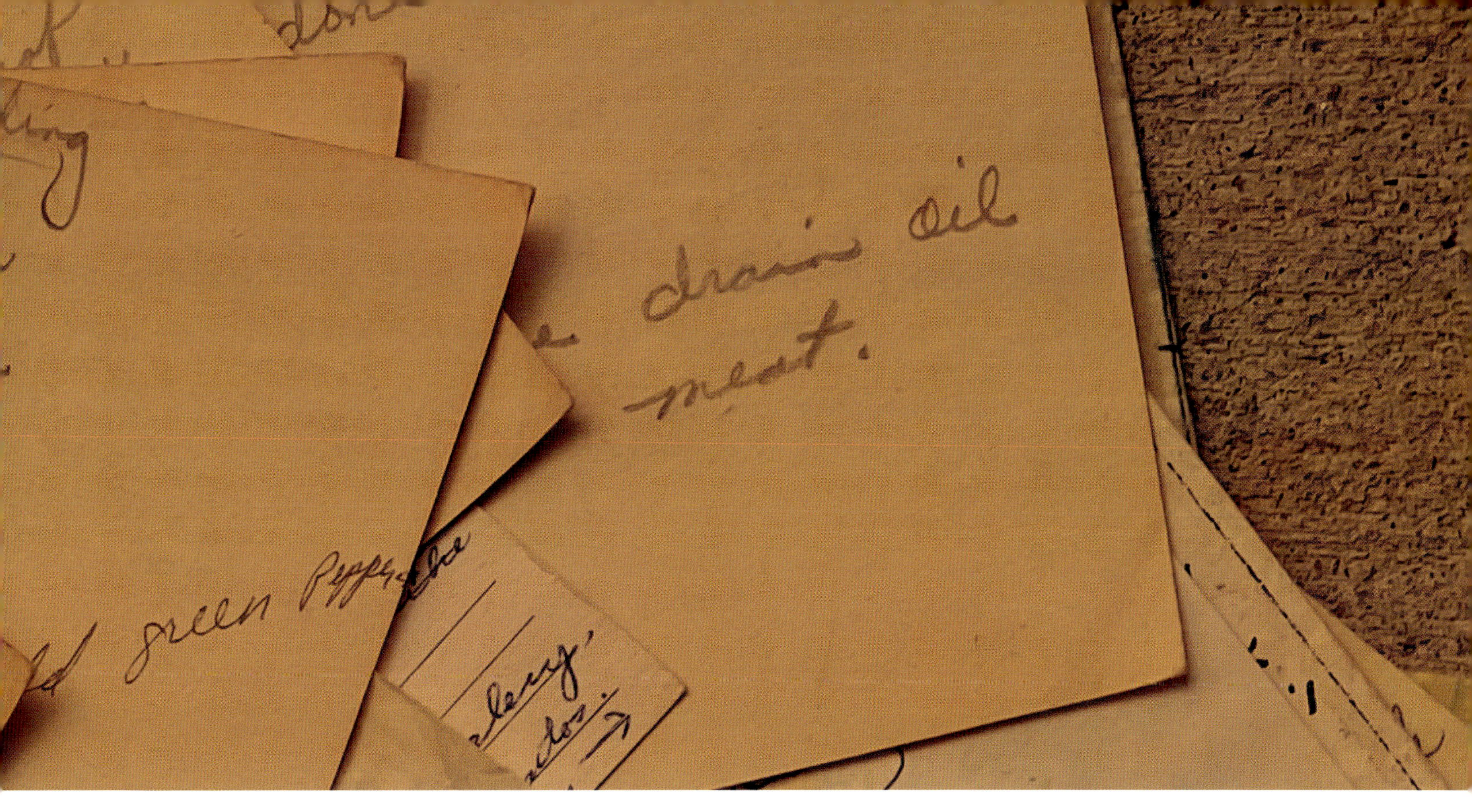

your humanity expands and enables you to become a valuable, mature, contributing member of society. You can be generous, kind, honest, sincere, trustworthy, accountable, responsible, admired, loved, and cherished within all the communities you are a member of. Your TRUTH is the most important reality to protect, defend, and honor.

As a child of African descent, your **TRUTH** is built on a solid foundation of DIVINE Love. Many of your relatives live and come from every country, territory, commonwealth, and island. You come from ancient people whose art and technology have taught us who they were and what their hopes, dreams, challenges, and successes were. Through art—pottery, paintings, sculptures, architecture, and design—you can discover innovative ideas about the world and yourself within it. The differences and similarities in language, culture, and values reiterate that art and civilization coexist. Combined, they are a gateway for you to discover your place and purpose in the world.

To that end, one of the oldest forms of art making is pottery. Pottery began in Africa 11,400 years ago. Pottery—modeled, dried, and fired clay—has many practical uses. YOU, like pottery, are modeled by your TRUTH, dried as you hold onto your TRUTH, and fired so that your TRUTH gives you the strength to overcome adversity. Once you are modeled, dried, and fired like a clay vessel, YOU are protected by your TRUTH.

Beloved, hold fast to TRUTH. Carry your TRUTH and wear it as a protective and eloquent raincoat. Remember that you are—always—the DIVINE reflection of resplendent beauty, ancient history, substantive quality, discerning intelligence, capable talent, and irreplaceable value, always. Lovingly,

YOUR TRUTH

EMPATHY

By Joy Angela DeGruy

"The art of stepping imaginatively into the shoes of another person, understanding their feelings and perspectives, and using that understanding to guide you."
—**Roman Krznaric**

There was a documentary years about ago about a famine in eastern Africa impacting an estimated thirteen million people across Somalia, Kenya, and Ethiopia. People were left without basic life-sustaining resources. The documentary followed individuals and families walking across miles of scorched cracked earth in search of food. Among them were two young children. The oldest child looked to be about seven or eight and the younger child about four. It was hard to determine because their tiny bodies were frail and compromised. They were among thousands of people seeking food, water, and shelter during the brutal famine that swept over their homelands.

The cameras followed these two children as they walked for miles in grueling heat. The older child was carrying the younger one, who had become too weak to walk. After an extraordinary journey they came to a refugee camp where health workers were walking through the crowds of people sitting on the parched ground awaiting assistance, the adults holding up their infant children with hopes they would be fed and saved. The doctors and health care workers would examine each child quickly to determine which infants had a hope of survival. If the child seemed too small or sick they would simply hand them back to their parents.

The two children now stood in line for their first meal in days, or perhaps even weeks, the older child still carrying the smaller one on their back. Eventually the children were brought into a huge tent and seated on benches at long tables. The older child sat their young sibling next to them. A small bowl of food was then placed in front of the older child, who without hesitation pushed the bowl in front of the younger child.

Starving and weary, the older sibling, knowing that the next bowl was less than a few seconds away, still thought first of the younger sibling before taking as much as one spoonful for themselves. Surely the cognitive capacity of this youngster was diminished from malnutrition and exhaustion —clearly this child was in undeniable crisis! Yet notwithstanding these harsh conditions,

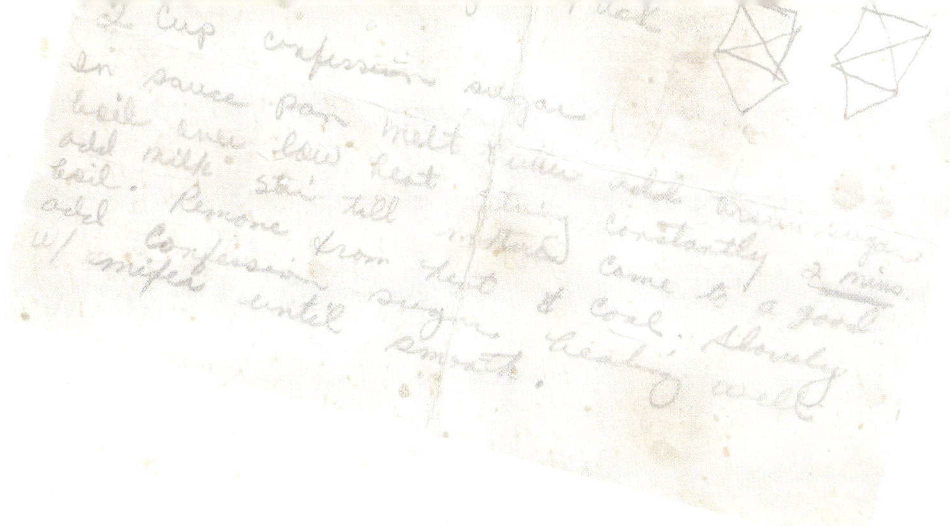

empathy and selflessness reigned supreme!

Years ago I had a personal experience with my granddaughter Zufan and my grandson Avi. Zufan was two years old and her brother Avi was one. Both children were playing on the floor in the living room. Zufan was making Avi laugh as she often did by making faces and twirling around in front of him. I stood watching them as I washed the dishes when things went terribly awry really fast!

Zufan had leaned forward momentarily, giving Avi just enough time to reach over and grab her hair. Within seconds Avi had her by the hair and had pulled her head to the floor. Zufan was wailing in pain as I struggled to disentangle Avi's tiny fingers from her hair. I picked Avi up and sat him a few feet away so I could attend to Zufan, who had tears rolling down her cheeks. I reached out my arms to her to comfort her, but much to my astonishment, Zufan immediately ran over to her baby brother, who sat looking perplexed. Zufan, while still crying, hugged and kissed him before running over to me and sobbing in my arms. As I held my sweet Zufan I thought to myself, How wonderful!

Thinking back today I realize that it is no coincidence that my granddaughter would manifest such empathy. She shares the qualities of her Ethiopian mother, Eden, her grandparents, and her great-grandparents, going all the way back to our ancient ancestor Dinknesh, the oldest human from which all of humanity descended. The Europeans called her Lucy but she was African, from Ethiopia, and the Ethiopian people called her "Dinknesh," which means "thou art wonderful."

> **THE TWO CHILDREN NOW STOOD IN LINE FOR THEIR FIRST MEAL IN DAYS, OR PERHAPS EVEN WEEKS, THE OLDER CHILD STILL CARRYING THE SMALLER ONE ON THEIR BACK.**

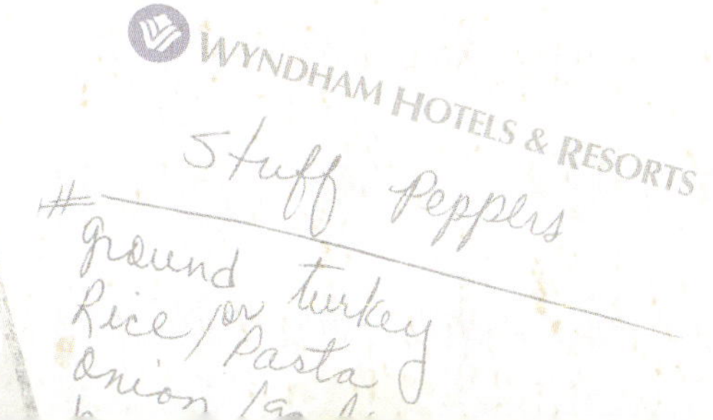

I DON'T WANNA BE BLACK

Story and art by KEEF Cross | Written by Shannon Byrd

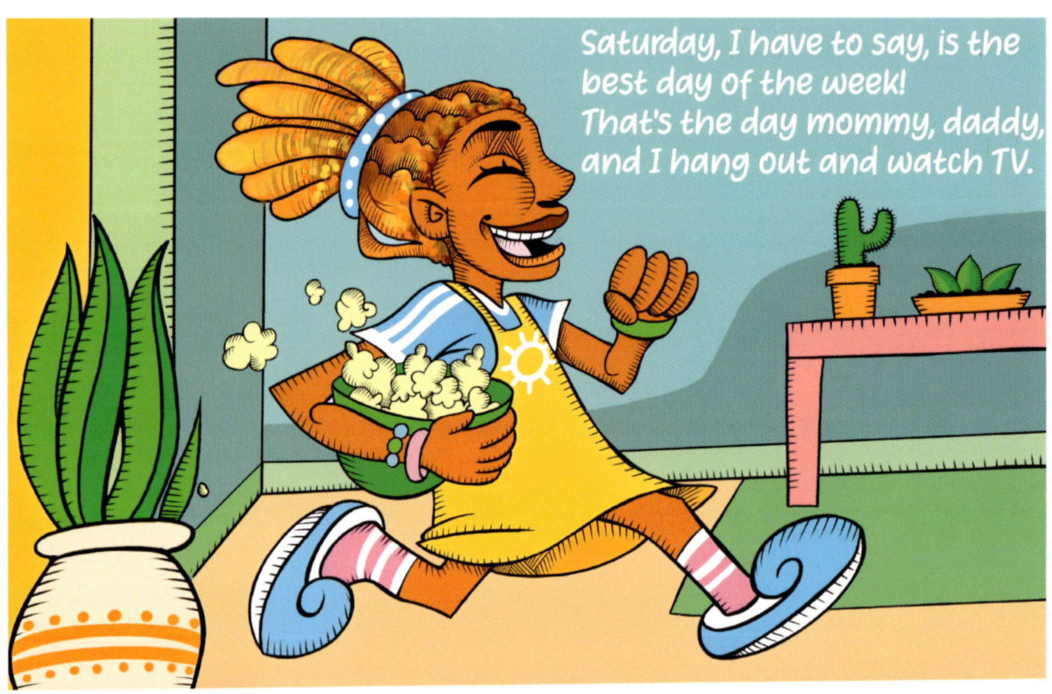

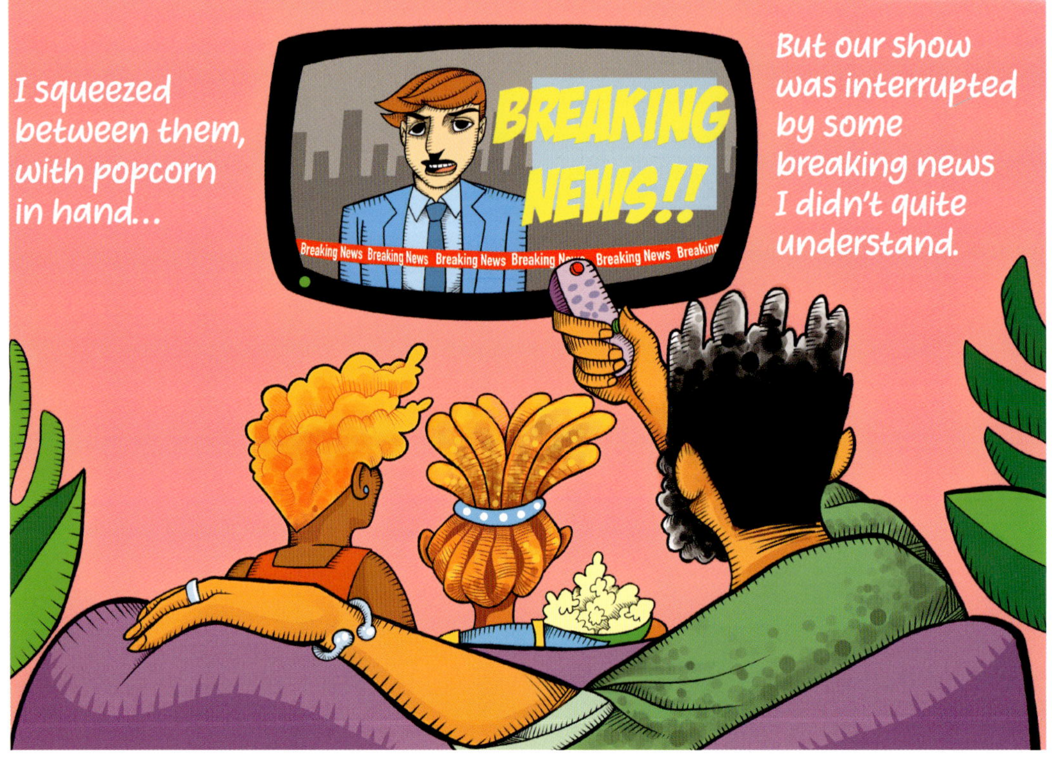

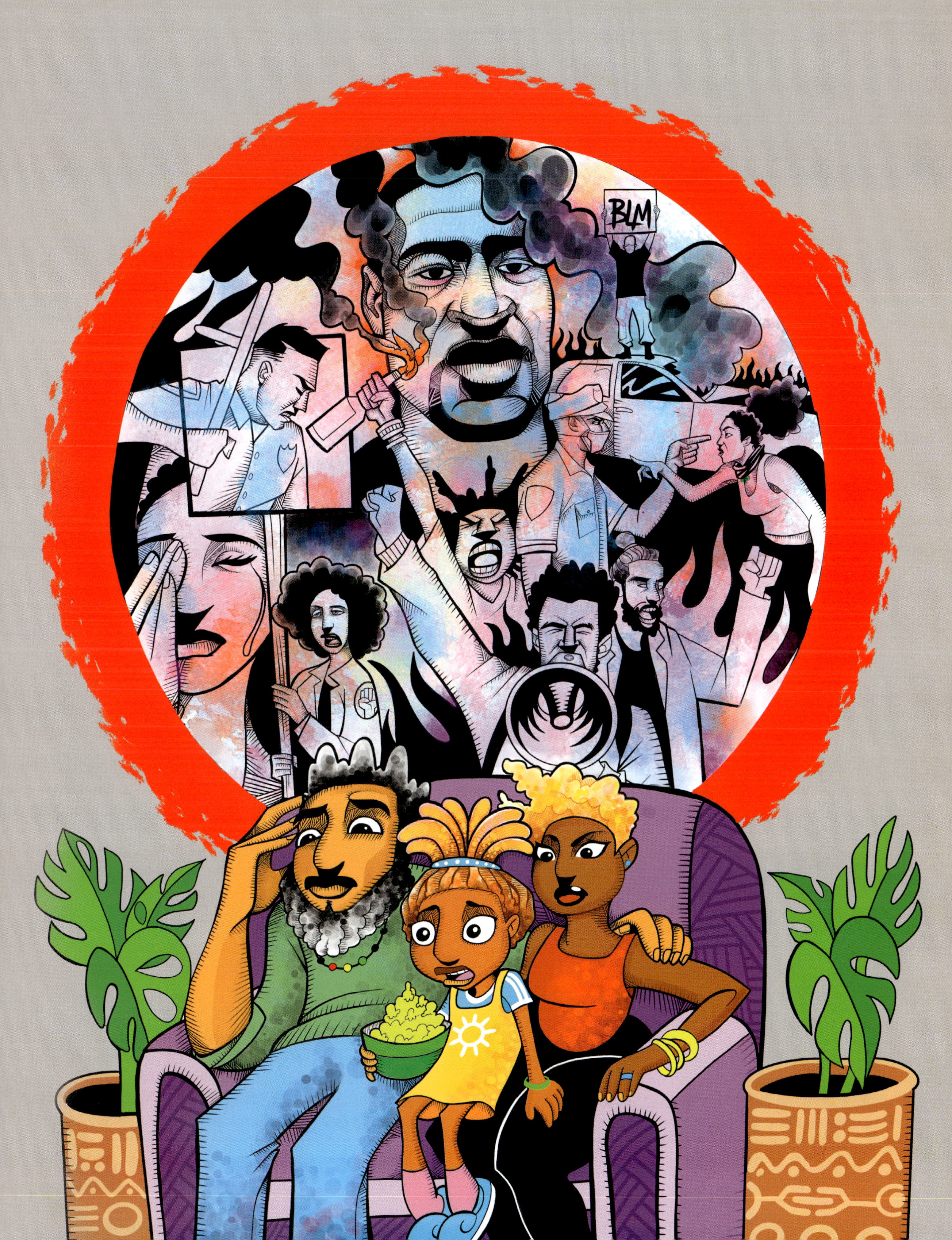
BLM

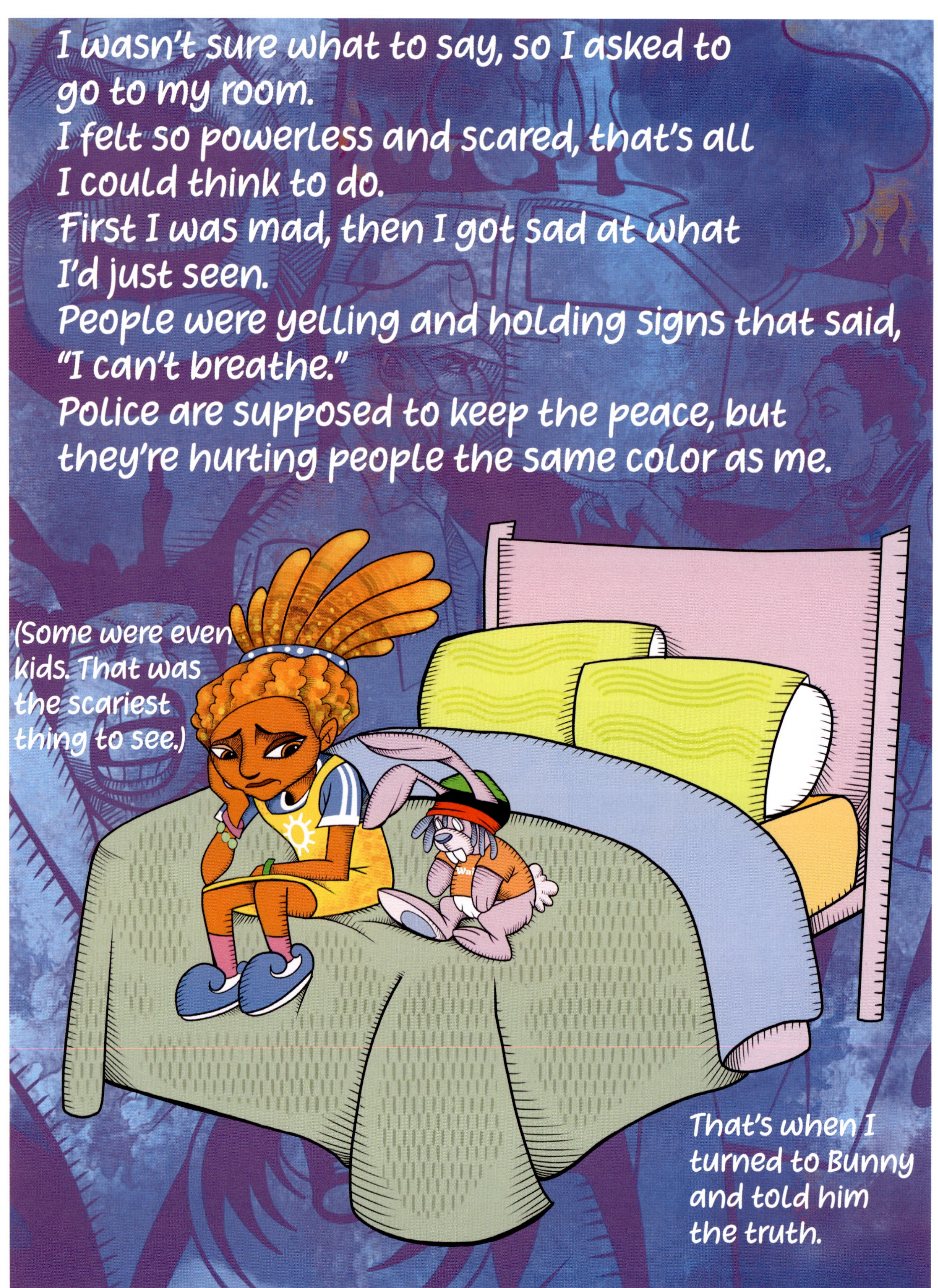

I wasn't sure what to say, so I asked to
go to my room.
I felt so powerless and scared, that's all
I could think to do.
First I was mad, then I got sad at what
I'd just seen.
People were yelling and holding signs that said,
"I can't breathe."
Police are supposed to keep the peace, but
they're hurting people the same color as me.

(Some were even
kids. That was
the scariest
thing to see.)

That's when I
turned to Bunny
and told him
the truth.

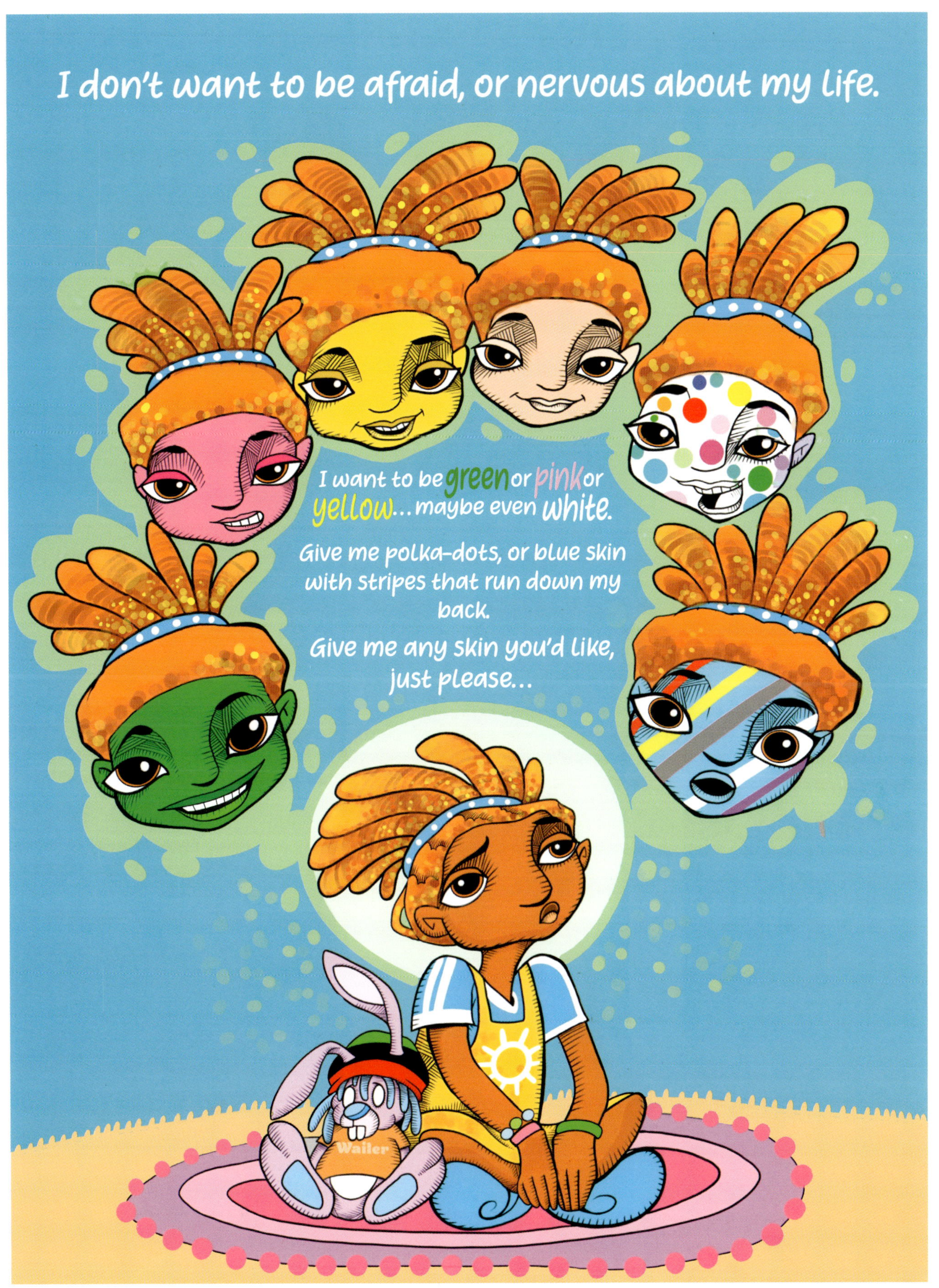

I don't want to be afraid, or nervous about my life.

I want to be green or pink or yellow… maybe even white.

Give me polka-dots, or blue skin with stripes that run down my back.

Give me any skin you'd like, just please…

Wailer

I don't wanna be Black.

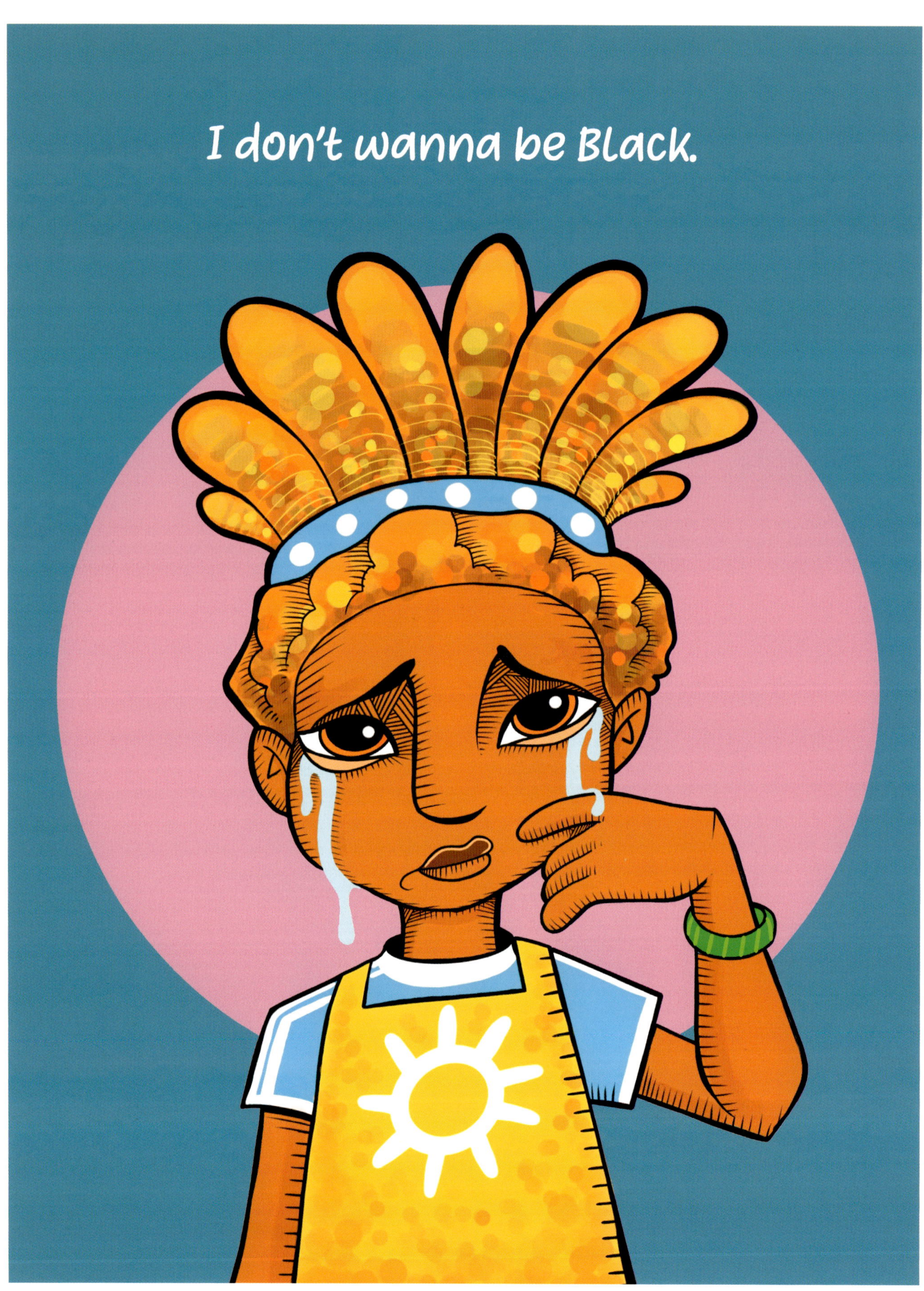

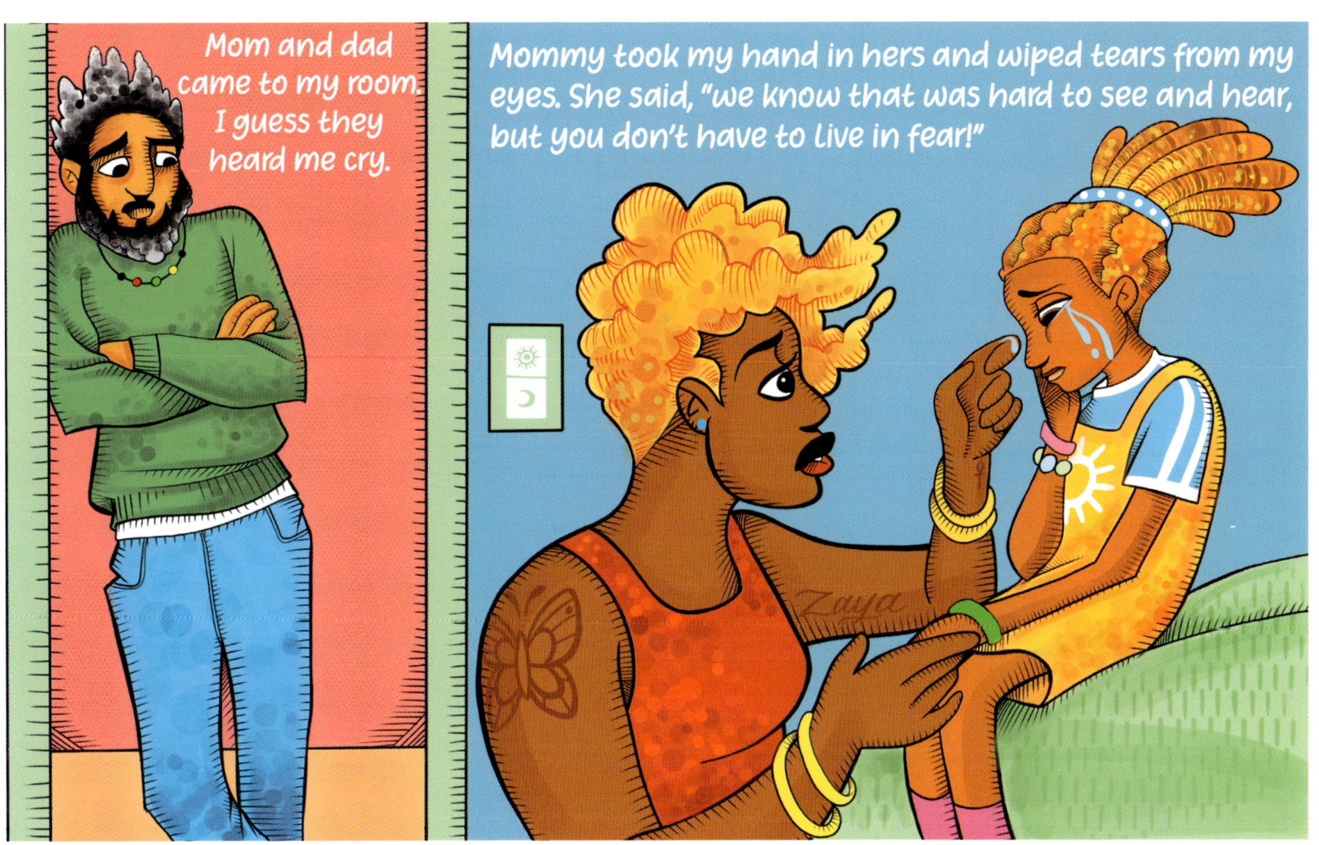

Mom and dad came to my room. I guess they heard me cry.
Mommy took my hand in hers and wiped tears from my eyes. She said, "we know that was hard to see and hear, but you don't have to live in fear!"

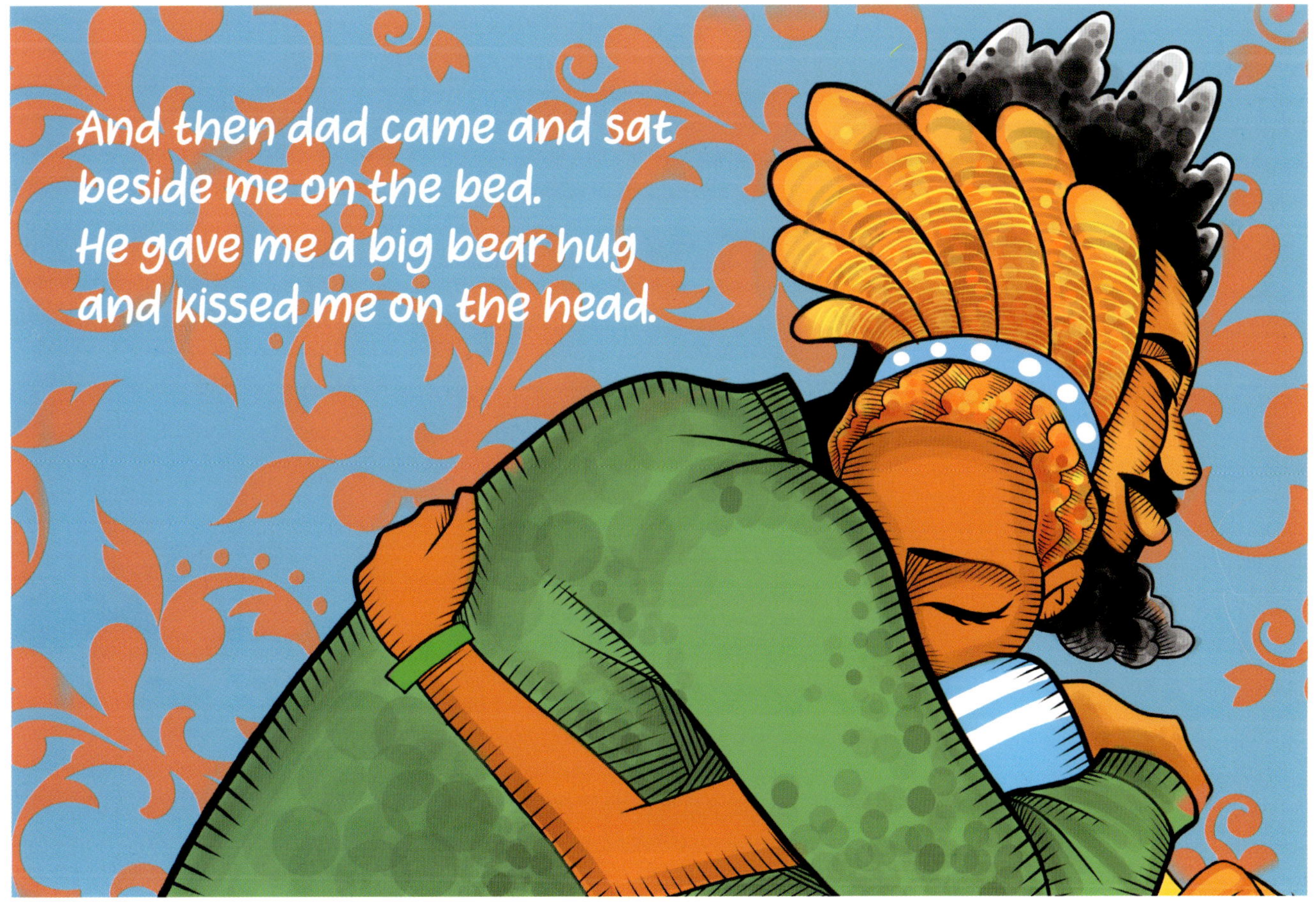

And then dad came and sat beside me on the bed. He gave me a big bear hug and kissed me on the head.

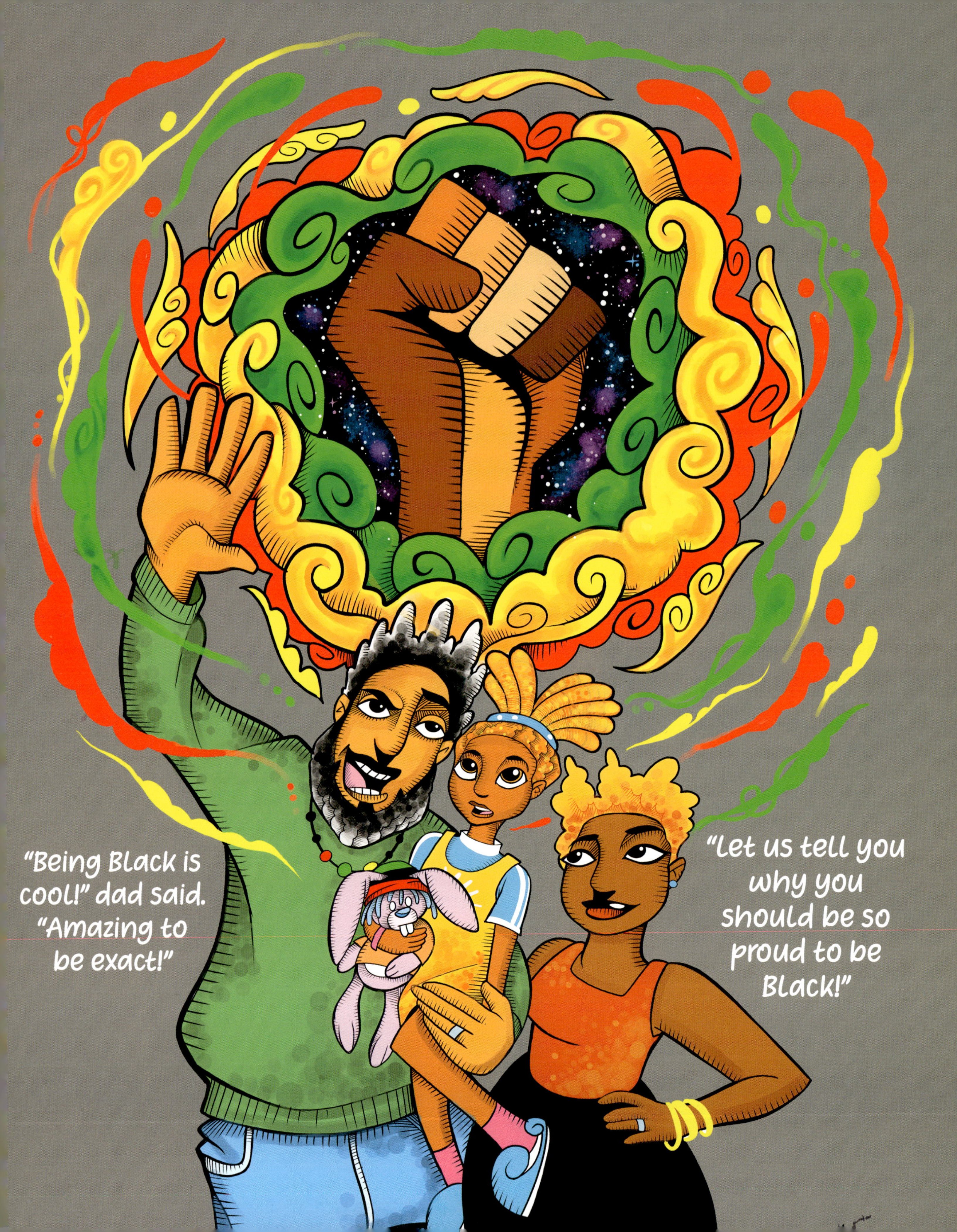

"Being Black is cool!" dad said. "Amazing to be exact!"
"Let us tell you why you should be so proud to be Black!"

"

YOU DON'T HAVE TO LIVE IN FEAR!

"

Chapter 3

YOUNG LANGSTON

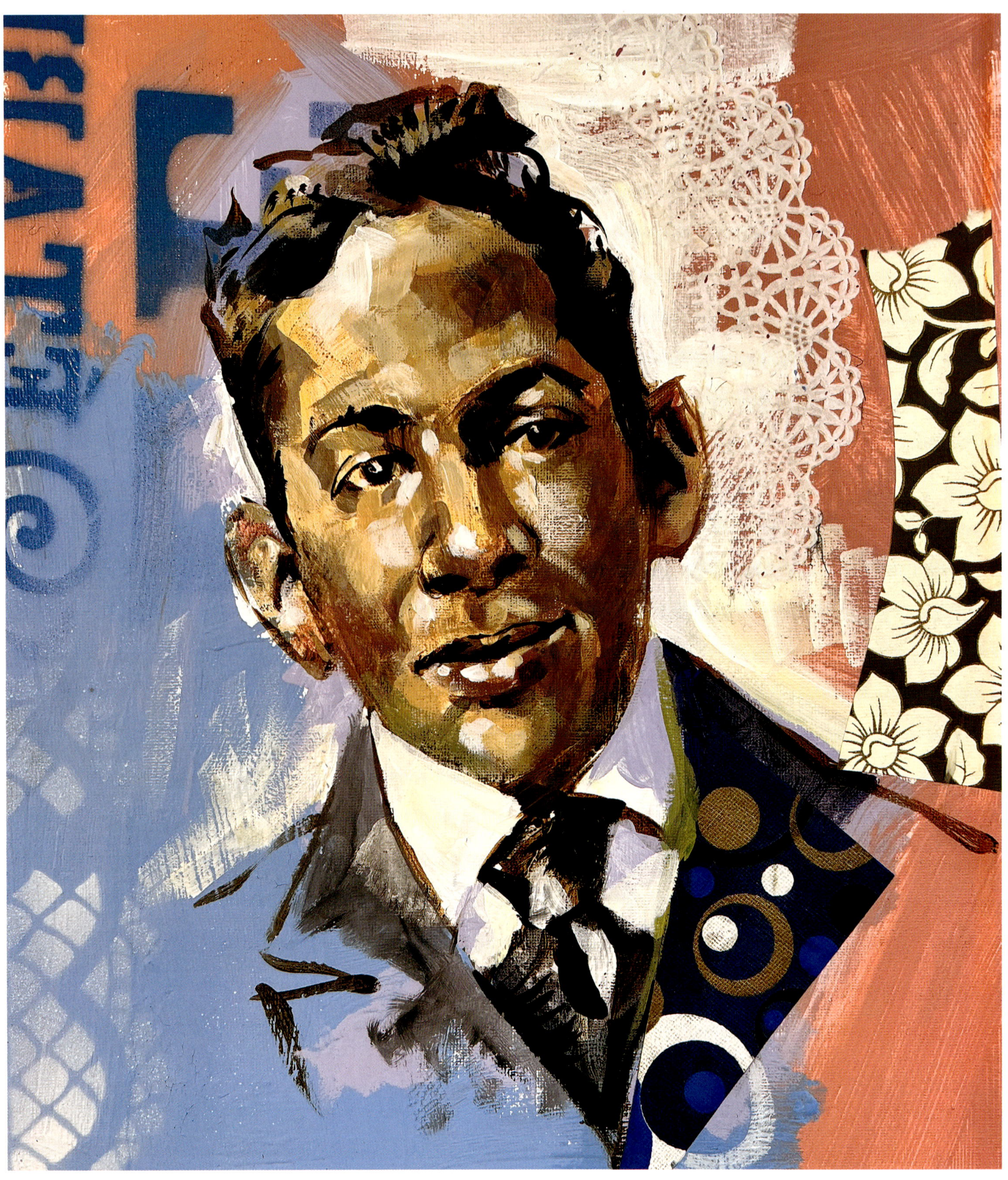

Charly Palmer, *Young Langston*
(Acrylic on canvas)

INTRODUCTION

By Karida L. Brown

Langston Hughes is one of the most prolific writers in the history of American letters. He was born in 1901, coming into his literary genius just at the start of the Harlem Renaissance, in the early 1920s. In his lifetime he penned nearly a thousand poems, more than forty plays, ten nonfiction novels, eight children's books, two autobiographies, dozens of short stories . . . and even a few operettas!

What a lot of people don't know is that, as a young man, Langston Hughes published his very first works in *The Brownies' Book!* W. E. B. Du Bois served as the editor-in-chief of *The Crisis* magazine for almost twenty-five years, from 1910 to 1934. During that time, he and his friends Augustus Granville Dill and Jessie Redmon Fauset also founded *The Brownies' Book.* As editor, W. E. B. Du Bois recognized Langston's talent and was the first to publish the young writer's works—in none other than *The Brownies' Book*! These writings include Hughes's first published play, *The Gold Piece,* several poems, and two short stories—all published when Hughes was just twenty years old.

We have reprinted all of Langston Hughes's original pieces in this *New Brownies' Book* for you to enjoy. As you read through his works we want you to notice this: Although Hughes became renowned for his insightful social criticism, commentary, and fictional stories related to Black life, he started off by writing about topics like nature and his surroundings.

From these early works by young Langston we can learn that we all start somewhere. It is never too early for you to try your hand at your craft.

So we ask you, dear reader, what is *your* genius?

AUTUMN THOUGHT

By Langston Hughes | From *The Brownies' Book*, November 1921

Flowers are happy in summer;
In autumn they die and are blown away.
Dry and withered,
Their petals dance on the wind,
Like little brown butterflies.

SIGNS OF SPRING

By Langston Hughes | From *The Brownies' Book*, March 1921

Bright, jolly sunshine and clear blue skies,
Green trees and gardens and gay butterflies,
Soft little winds that balmy blow,
A golden moon with a love light glow,
And the music of bird songs, blithe and clear,
Are the things which tell us that Spring is here.

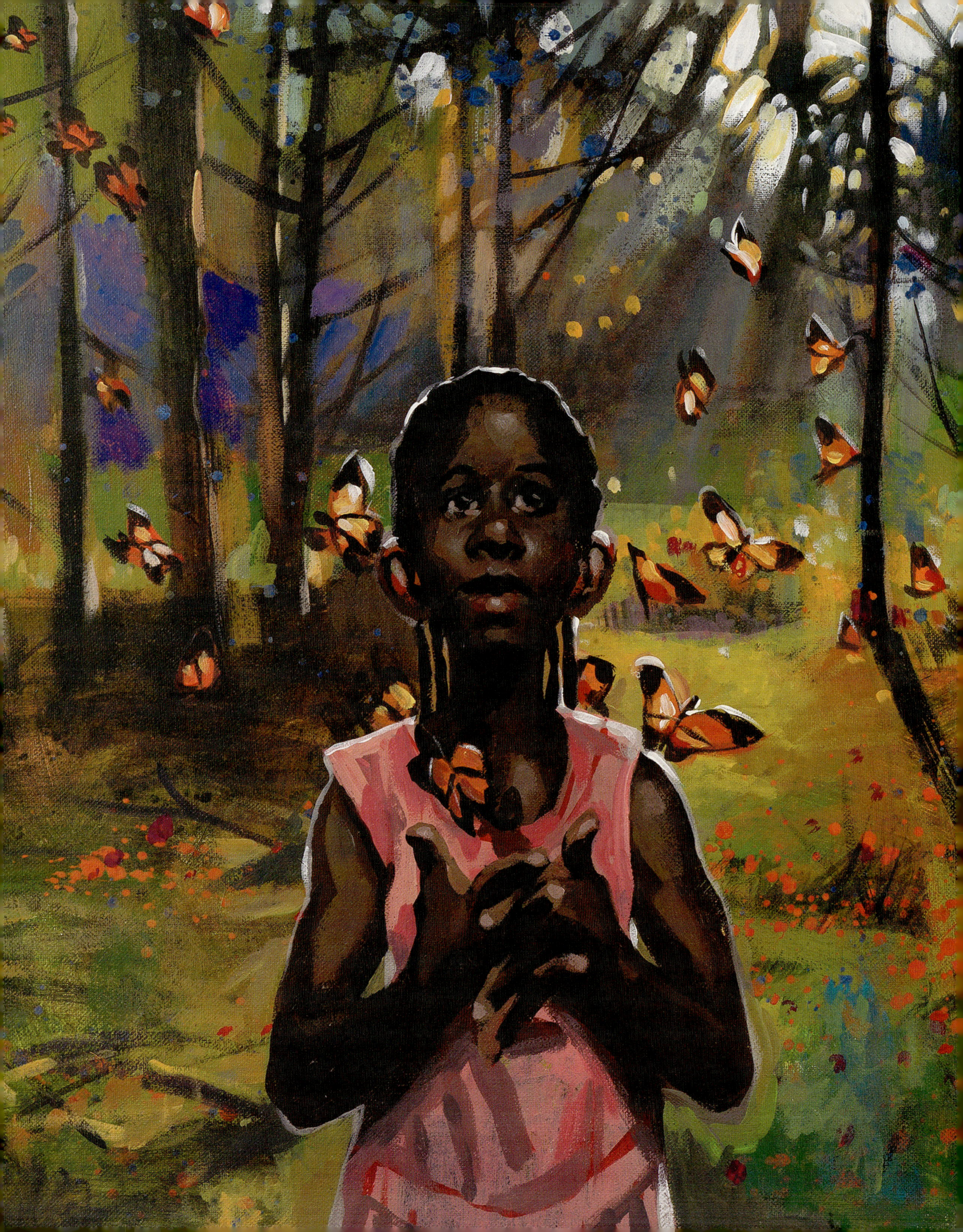

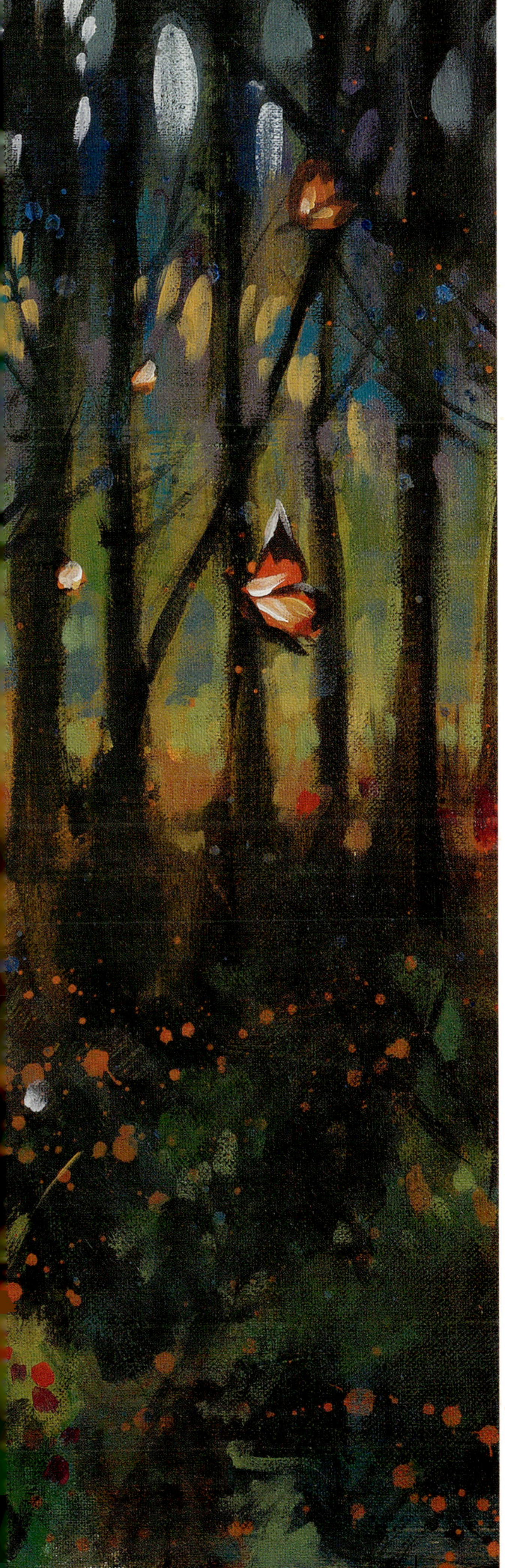

FAIRIES

By Langston Hughes |
From *The Brownies' Book*, January 1921

Out of the dust of dreams,
Fairies weave their garments;
Out of the purple and rose of old memories,
They make rainbow wings.
No wonder we find them such marvelous things!

THE LAMENT OF A VANQUISHED BEAU

By Langston Hughes | From *The Brownies' Book*, August 1921

Willy is a silly boy,
Willy is a cad.
Willy is a foolish kid,
Sense he never had.
Yet all the girls like Willy—
Why I cannot see,—
He even took my best girl
Right away from me.

I asked him did he want to fight,
But all he did was grin
And answer, "Don't be guilty
Of such a brutal sin."

Oh, Willy's sure a silly boy,
He really is a cad,
Because he took the only girl
This I 'most ever had.

Her hair's so long and pretty
And her eyes are very gay;
I guess that she likes Willy
'Cause he's handsome, too, they say.
But for me he's not good looking;
And he sure has made me mad,
'Cause he went and took the only girl
That I 'most ever had.

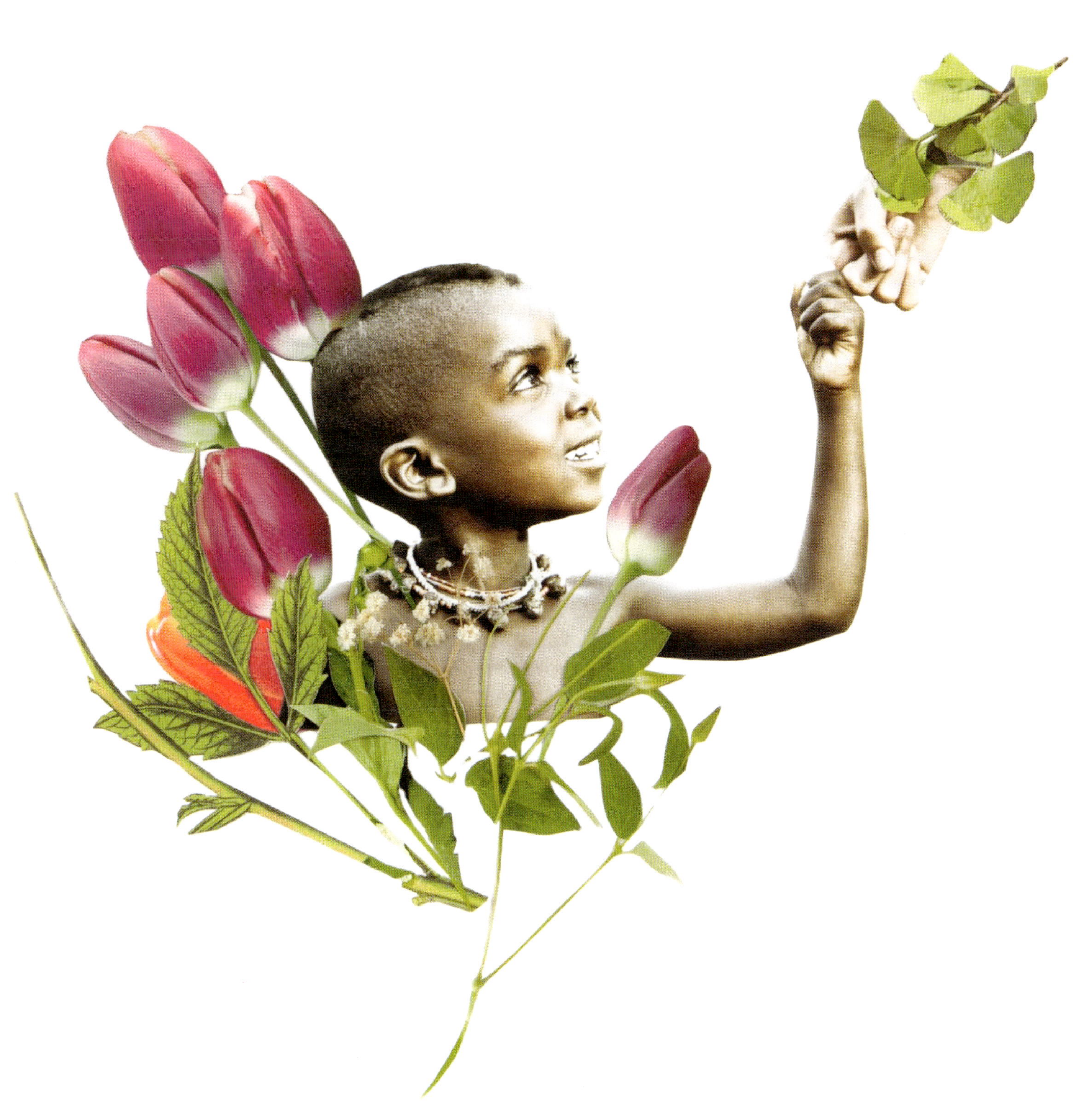

Marryam Moma, *Legacy of Hope*
(Paper collage)

MISTER SANDMAN

By Langston Hughes | From *The Brownies' Book*, August 1921

The Sandman walks abroad tonight,
With his canvas sack o' dreams filled tight.

Over the roofs of the little town,
The golden face of the moon looks down.

Each Mary and Willy and Cora and Ned
Is sound asleep in some cozy bed,

When the Sandman opens his magic sack
To select the dreams from his wonder pack.

"Ah," says the Sandman, "To this little girl
I'll send a dream like a precious pearl."

So to Mary Jane, who's been good all day,
A fairy comes in her sleep to play;

But for Corinne Anne, who teased the cat,
There's a horrid dream of a horrid rat,

And the greedy boy, with his stomach too full,
Has a bad, bad dream of a raging bull;

While for tiny babes, a few days old,
Come misty dreams, all rose and gold.

And for every girl and every boy
The Sandman has dreams that can please or
   annoy.

When at pink-white dawn, with his night's
   work done,
He takes the road toward the rising sun,

He goes straight on without a pause
To his house in the land of Santa Claus.

But at purple night-fall he's back again
To distribute his dreams, be it moon light or rain;

And good little children get lovely sleep toys,
But woe to the bad little girls and boys!

For those who'd have dreams that are charming
   and sweet,
Must be good in the day and not stuff when
   they eat,

'Cause old Mister Sandman, abroad each night,
Has a dream in his sack to fit each child just right.

AN APRIL
RAIN SONG

By Langston Hughes |
From *The Brownies' Book*, April 1921

Let the rain kiss you.
Let the rain beat upon your head
With silver liquid drops.
Let the rain sing you a lullaby
With its pitty-pat.
The rain makes still pools on the sidewalk.
The rain makes running pools in the gutter.
The rain plays a little sleep tune
On our roof at night,
And I love the rain.

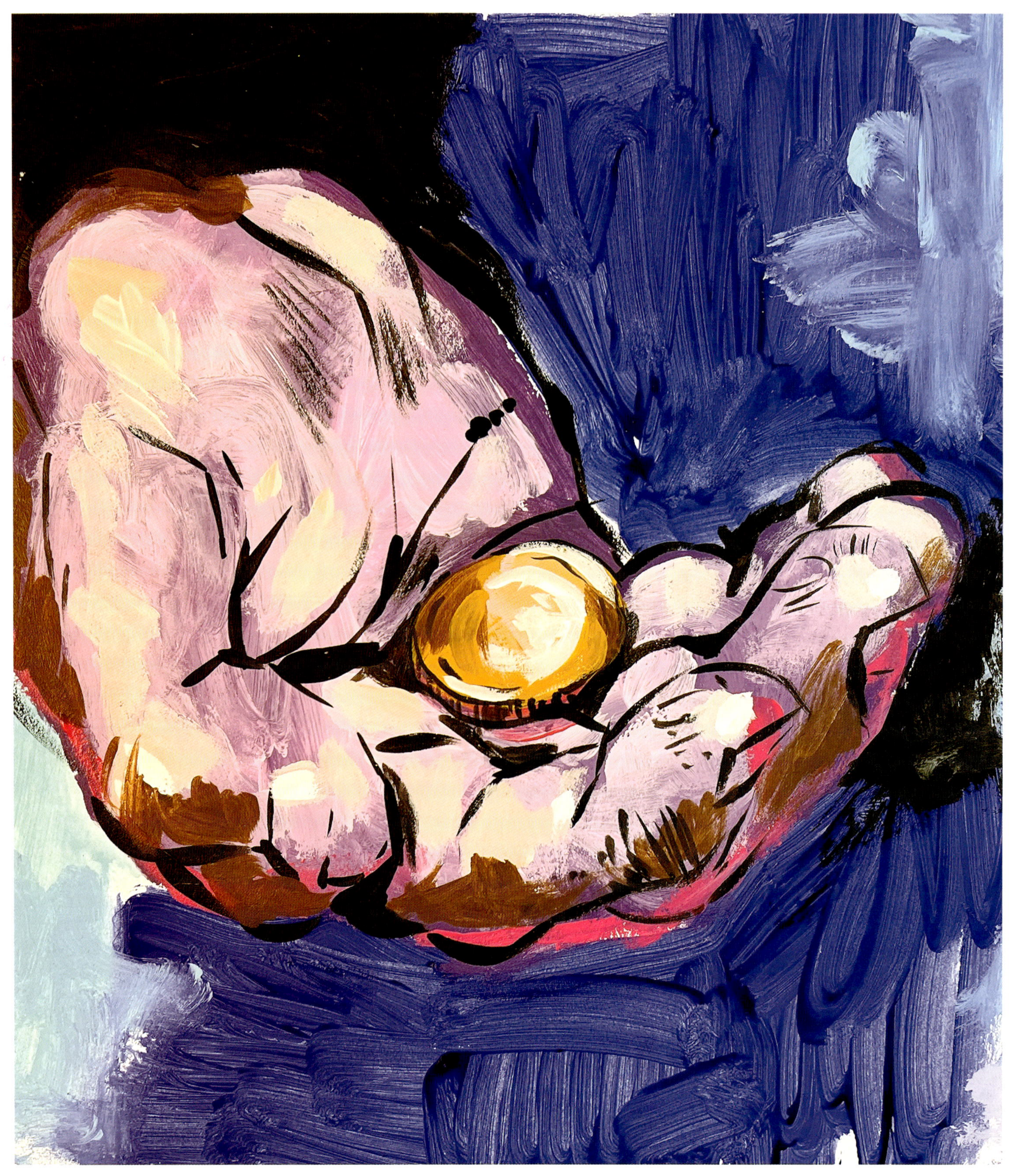

Charly Palmer, *Gold Piece*
(Acrylic on canvas)

THE GOLD PIECE:
A PLAY THAT MIGHT BE TRUE

By Langston Hughes | From *The Brownies' Book*, July 1921

Characters:
A Peasant Boy,
A Peasant Girl, his wife,
An Old Woman.

Scene

The interior of a hut by the roadside. It is twilight. A boy and a girl are lying before the fireplace, a gold piece on the floor between them. There is a door at the right of the fireplace and a window at the left. During the play the twilight deepens into darkness.

THE GIRL (Looking at the coin)—Just to think that this bright gold piece is ours! All ours! Fifty whole loren!

THE BOY (Smiling happily)—The ten old pigs were fat ones, Rosa, and brought us a fine price in the market.

THE GIRL—Now we can buy and buy and buy.

THE BOY—Sure we can. Now we can buy all the things we've wanted ever since we've been married but haven't had the money to get.

THE GIRL—Oh! How good, Pablo! It seems we've been waiting an awfully long time.

THE BOY—We have, but now we shan't wait any longer. Now we can get the wooden clock, Rosa. You know—the one that we've wanted since we first saw it in the old watchmaker's window. The one so nicely carved, that strikes the hours every day and runs for a whole week with a single winding. And I think there is a cuckoo in it, too. It will make our little house look quite elegant.

THE GIRL—And now you can buy the thick brown boots with hob nails in them to work in the fields.

THE BOY—And you may have the woolen shawl with red and purple flowers on it and the fringe about the edges.

THE GIRL—O-o-o! Can I really, Pablo? I've dreamed of it for months.

THE BOY—You surely can, Rosa. I've wanted to give it to you ever since I knew you. It will make you look so pretty. And we'll get two long white candles, too, to burn on Sundays and feast days.

THE GIRL—And we'll get a little granite kettle for stewing vegetables in.

THE BOY—And we'll get a big spoon to stir with.

THE GIRL—And two little blue plates to eat from.

THE BOY—And we'll have dried fish and a little cake for supper every night.

THE GIRL—And-but Oh! Pablo! It's wonderful!

THE BOY—Oh! Rosa! It's fine! ▶

THE GIRL AND THE BOY (Rising and dancing joyously around and around the little gold piece which glistens and glitters gaily on the floor before the open fire as if it knew it were the cause of their joy)—Oh! How happy we are! Oh! How happy we are! Because we can buy! Because we can buy! Because we can buy and buy and buy!

(Just then an old woman's figure passes the window and there is a timid knock at the door. The dancing stops. The boy picks up his shining gold piece and clutches it tightly in his hand.)

THE GIRL (With a little frown of annoyance)—Who's there?

(The door opens slowly and a bent old woman leaning on a heavy stick enters.)

THE BOY (Rudely)—Well, Grandmother, what do you want?

THE OLD WOMAN (Panting and weak)—I've come such a long way today and am very tired. I just wanted to rest a moment before going on. (THE GIRL brings her a stool and she sits down near the fireplace.)

THE GIRL (Sympathetically)—But surely, Old Woman, you aren't going any further on foot tonight?

THE OLD WOMAN—Yes, I am, child, because I must.

THE GIRL—And why must you, Old Lady?

THE OLD WOMAN—Because my BOY is in the house alone and he is blind.

THE GIRL—Your BOY is blind?

THE OLD WOMAN—Yes, for eighteen years. He has not seen since he was a tiny baby.

THE BOY—And where have you been that you are so late upon the road?

THE OLD WOMAN—I've been into the city and from sunrise I have not rested. People told me famous doctors were there who could make my blind boy see again and so I went to find them.

THE GIRL—And did you find them?

THE OLD WOMAN—Yes, I found them, but (Her voice becomes sad) they would not come with me.

THE GIRL—Why would they not come?

THE OLD WOMAN—Because they were great and proud. They said, "When you get fifty loren, send for us and then perhaps we'll come. Now we have no time." One who was kinder than the rest told me that a simple operation might bring my BOY's sight back. But I am poor. I have no money and from where in all the world could a worn-out old woman like me get fifty loren?

THE BOY AND THE GIRL (Quickly)—We don't know!

THE BOY (Keeping his fist tightly closed over the gold piece)—Why, we never even saw fifty loren!

THE GIRL—So much money we never will have.

THE BOY—No, we never will have.

THE OLD WOMAN—If I were young, I would not say that, but I am old and I know I shall never see fifty loren. Ah! I would sell all that I have if my BOY could only see again! I would sell my keepsakes, my silken dress that I've had for many years, my memories, anything to bring my BOY's sight back to him!

THE GIRL—But, Old Lady, would you sell your dream of a wooden clock, a clock that strikes the hours every day and need not be wound for a whole week?

THE OLD WOMAN—Yes, child, I would.

THE BOY—And would you sell your wish for white candles to burn on feast days and Sundays?

THE OLD WOMAN—Oh! BOY, I would even sell my labor on feast days and Sundays were I not too weak to work.

THE GIRL—And would you give up your dream of a woolen shawl with red and purple flowers on it and fringe all around the four edges of it?

THE OLD WOMAN—I would give up all my dreams if my son were to see again.

(There is a pause. THE GIRL, forgetting for a moment her own desires, begins to speak slowly as if to herself.)

THE GIRL—It must be awful not to know the sunshine and the flowers and the beauty of the hills in springtime.

THE BOY—It must be awful never to see the jolly crowds in the square on market days and never to play with the fellows at May games.

THE GIRL—And the doctor says that maybe this BOY could be made well.

THE BOY—And the Old Woman says that it would cost but fifty loren.

THE GIRL (Suddenly)—I have no need of a gay shawl, Pablo.

THE BOY—We have no shelf for a wooden clock, Rosa.

THE GIRL—Nor vegetables to cook in a granite kettle.

THE BOY—And a big spoon would be such a useless thing.

THE OLD WOMAN (Rising)—Before the night becomes too dark, I must go on. (She moves toward the door.)

THE BOY—Wait a moment, Mother. Let us slip something into your pouch.

THE GIRL—Something bright and golden, Mother.

THE BOY—Something that shines in the Sunlight

THE GIRL—Something from us to your BOY. (They open THE OLD WOMAN's bag and the boy slips the gold piece into it. THE OLD WOMAN does not see what they have given her.)

THE OLD WOMAN—Thank you, good children. I know my boy will be pleased with your toy. It will give him something to hold in his hands and make him forget his blindness for a moment. God bless you both for your gift and—Good-Bye.

THE BOY AND THE GIRL—Good-Bye, Old Woman.

(The door closes. It is dark and the room is lighted only by the fire in the grate.)

THE GIRL—Are you happy, Pablo?

THE BOY—I'm very happy. And you, Rosa?

THE GIRL—I'm happy, too. I'm happier than any wooden clock could make me.

THE BOY—Or hob-nailed shoes, me.

THE GIRL—Or me, a flowered shawl with crimson fringe.

(They sit down before the fireplace and watch the big logs glow. The wood crackles and flames and lights the whole room with its warm red light. Outside through the window a night star shines. THE BOY AND THE GIRL are quiet while the Curtain Falls.)

IN A MEXICAN CITY

By Langston Hughes | From *The Brownies' Book*, April 1921

Toluca sits in the highest plateau of Mexico at the foot of the old and long extinct volcano "Xinantecatl," which is said to be named after one of the ancient Indian kings. All around us there are mountains and our valley is broad and fertile. Here the climate is cool and often cold, but the poor folks never have shoes to wear nor do the rich use stoves in their houses. In summer it is the rainy season and every day brings long showers and misty clouds that hide the mountains. In winter the sky is clear and the sun shines warm at mid-day, but in the shade it is always cool.

The house where I live faces a little plaza or park and from my window I can see many interesting things. Every morning a bare-footed old woman in a wide straw hat and long skirts drives a little flock of white sheep down the street, and sometimes she has a tiny baby lamb in her arms. They go to the country to graze all day and in the evening they come back again. Often I see a funeral procession passing through the plaza on the way to the Panteon and as they do not have hearses here, the men carry the casket on their shoulders while the mourners walk behind them. On Sundays the park is full of black-shawled women and men wrapped in *serapes* or blankets who come in the early morning to say mass in the quaint old church in front with its pretty tower and its most unmusical bells.

There are many churches here and all of them are very old. Some were built before the Independence, when Mexico was still under Spanish rule, and have beautiful domes and tall, graceful towers. Practically every one is Catholic and they keep many feast days. On the day of the Innocent Saints there is a custom that reminds one of our April Fool. On this date things should never be loaned and if you forget, the article is sure to be sent back by the joking friend who borrowed it, accompanied by a tiny box full of tiny toys and a note calling you a "poor little innocent saint." On the second of November, which is a day in honor of the dead, they sell many little cardboard coffins and paper dolls dressed as mourners, and if a person meets you in the street and says "I'm dying," you must give him a gift unless you have said "I'm dying" first; then, of course, he has to treat you to the present. On a certain day in January the people take their animals to be blessed and in the church-yard one sees everything from oxen to rabbits. Each is wearing a bit of gay colored ribbon and they wait patiently for the priest to come.

The houses here from the outside all look very much alike and are but a succession of arched doors and windows with small balconies facing the sidewalk. They often have lovely court-yards and verandas but these are hidden from the passers-by behind high walls, and the fronts of the houses never tell anything about the beauty that may be within them. When one enters a house the door usually leads directly into the court-yard or sometimes into the long open corridor from which every room has its entrance. In the *patio* or court-yard there are flowers the year round and if it is a large one, there may be a garden or trees. On the railing of the long veranda, too, there are many pots of red and pink geraniums and fragrant heliotrope. Inside the house there will probably be little furniture. Only a few of the well-to-do people have a great deal, so most of the homes use chairs as their principal space fillers. In a friend's parlor I counted twenty-seven one day and the only other articles of furniture were two small tables. Most of the parlors of the middle-class folk show the same emptiness but perhaps it is a good idea, for on holidays there is plenty of room to dance without moving anything out.

The kitchens here are very different from American ones, for they do not use stoves or gas ranges. The fuel is charcoal and the stoves are made of stone or brick, built into the wall like a long seat, except that they have three square grates on top for the fire and three square holes in front for removing the ashes. Some are prettily built and covered with gaily colored tiles. To make the fire several splinters of pine are lighted in the grate and then the black pieces of charcoal piled on top. Then one must fan and fan at the square holes in front until the charcoal on top begins to blaze, and in a little while you have a nice glowing fire ready to cook with.

The shops here in the portals, which is Toluca's "uptown," are much like the American stores, but in the little *expendios* in the side streets one can buy a penny's worth of wood or a tablespoonful of lard or a lamp full of oil. The poor here do not have much money. These little shops paint themselves all sorts of colors and have the funniest names. One I know is called "The Wedding Bouquet." Others are "The Light Of America," "The Big Fight," "The Fox," and so on, and one tinner's shop is even called "Heart of Jesus."

The last store on the edge of town, where the road leads off to San Juan, has the very appropriate name of "Farewell." One who did not know Spanish could acquire a whole vocabulary just by reading the store names which are painted in large colored letters across the front and are often accompanied by pictures or decorations to illustrate their meanings. For instance, the meat market called "The Bull of Atenco" has the animal's picture on one side of the door and a bull-fighter's on the other, painted over a background of bright blue.

Friday is market-day in Toluca and the square outside the market-house is one sea of wide Mexican hats, as buyer and trader jostle and bargain. The surrounding streets are lined with Indians from the country who squat behind their little piles of vegetables, or fruit, or herbs, which they have to sell and which they spread out on the ground before them. One old woman will have neat little piles of green peppers for a cent a pile. Another will have beans and another wild herbs for seasoning soup or making medicine. The fruit sellers, of course, always have a most gorgeous and luscious display. Under a canopy created from four sticks and some sort of covering to make a spot of shade are piled all sorts of strange, delicious fruits. There one finds creamy alligator pears and queer-tasting mangoes; red pomegranates and black zapotes; small, round melons and fat little bananas and the delicately flavored granada, which feels like a paper ball and has a soft seedy pulp inside. Then there are oranges that come up to us from the hot country, along with limes and juicy lemons that are not sour like the ones we know up North.

Here people never buy without bargaining. If the price asked for a thing is two cents, they are sure to get it for one. These price arguments are always good-natured and the merchant, knowing that he will have to come down, usually asks more than he should in the first place. Everyone going to market must carry his own baskets and sacks and even the paper for his meat, as everything is sold without wrapping.

A market-day crowd is composed of all sorts of people. A rich senorita with her black scarf draped gracefully about her shoulders is doing the family buying, while the servants carrying baskets follow behind. Indian women with sacks of vegetables on their backs; others with turkeys or chickens in their arms; little ragged brown boys seeking a chance to earn a few cents by carrying a customer's basket; and beggars, numberless beggars, blind, lame, and sick beggars, all asking patiently for pennies or half-rotted fruits; these are the folks one sees on market-day pushing and elbowing their way through the crowd which is so thick that nobody can hurry.

On one side of the plaza are the sellers of hats and the large yellow mats that the Indians spread down on the floor at night for sleeping purposes. The Mexican straw hats have wide round brims and high peaked crowns and, though cheap, most of them are prettily shaped. The Indian, upon buying a new hat, will not take the trouble to remove his old one, but puts the new one on top and marches off home with his double decked head gear. Sometimes a hat merchant, desiring to change his location, will put one hat on his head, and as each peaked crown fits snugly over the other, he then piles his whole stock on top of himself and goes walking down the street like a Chinese pagoda out for a stroll.

Here everything that people do not carry on their backs they carry on their heads. The ice-cream man crying *nieve* balances his freezer, and the baker-boys carry a shallow basket as big around as a wagon wheel. This basket has a crown in the center and when filled with bread it fits over the head like a very

wide Mexican hat, while its wearer underneath is as insignificant as the stem of a mushroom.

Sometimes we see fruit sellers, too, with great colorful mounds of fruit piled upon their wooden trays and balanced gracefully on their black-haired heads. When a thing is too heavy or too unwieldy to put on the head, then it is carried on the back, and the Indians bear immense burdens in this way. Men, women, and even small children are often seen with great loads of wood or charcoal, or sacks of grain, on their backs, and the only carriage that the little Indian baby ever knows is its mother's back, where it rides contented all day long, tied in her *rebosa* or shawl.

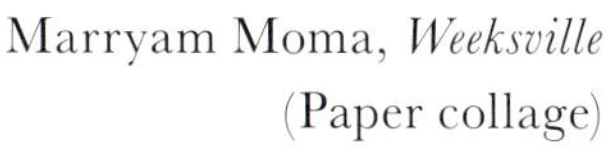

Marryam Moma, *Weeksville*
(Paper collage)

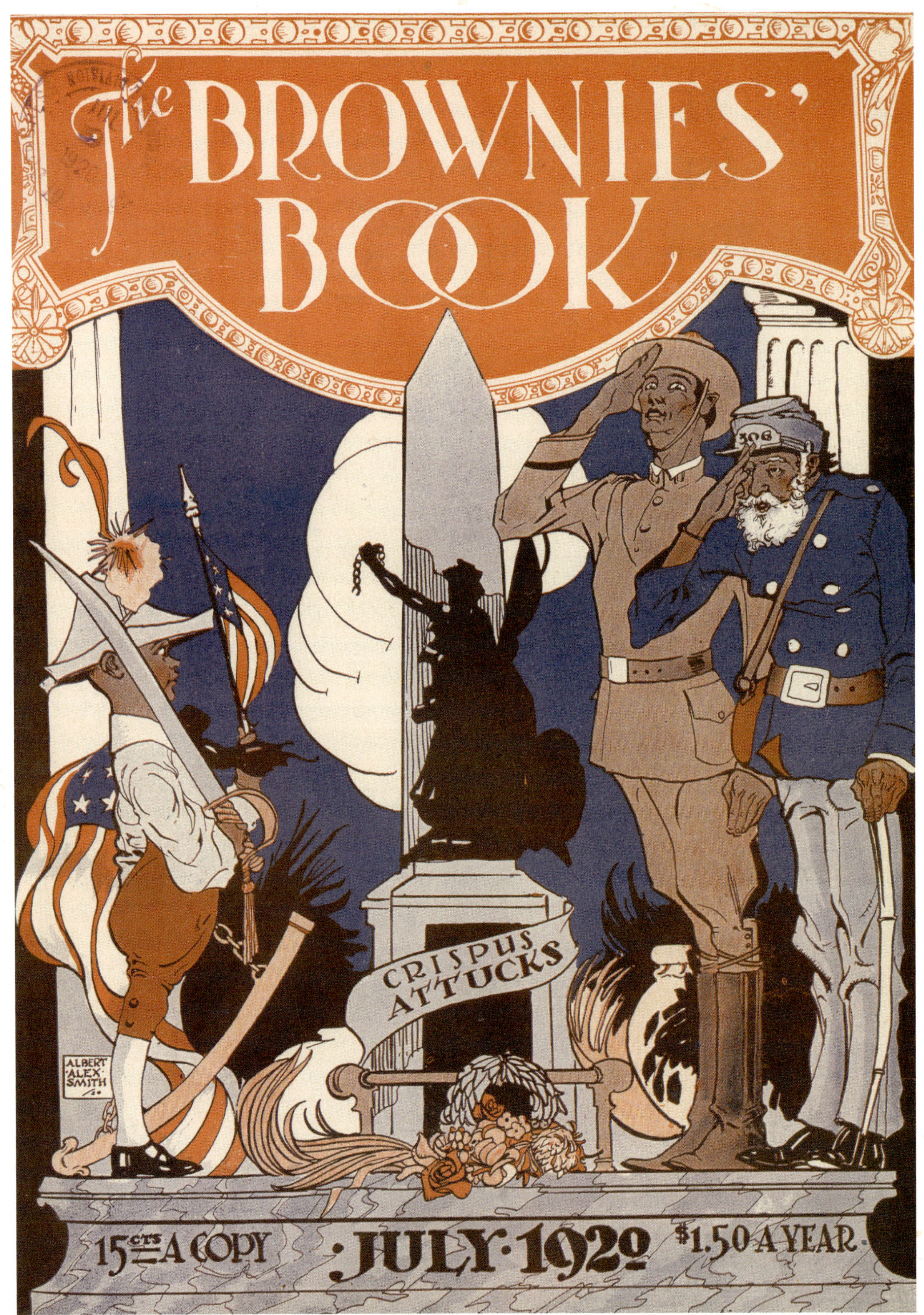
The BROWNIES' BOOK
CRISPUS ATTUCKS
ALBERT ALEX SMITH
15 CTS A COPY
·JULY·1920·
$1.50 A YEAR

POEMS

Little Moon Dancer

EULALIE SPENCE

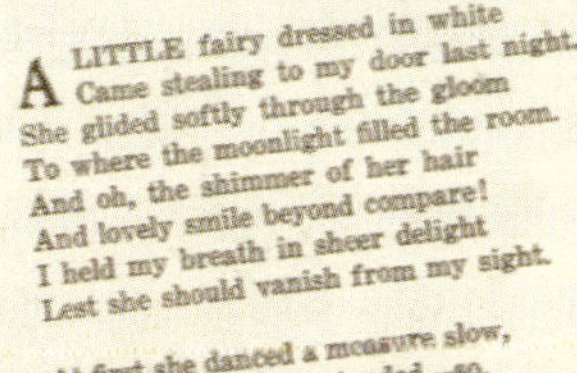

A LITTLE fairy dressed in white
Came stealing to my door last night.
She glided softly through the gloom
To where the moonlight filled the room.
And oh, the shimmer of her hair
And lovely smile beyond compare!
I held my breath in sheer delight
Lest she should vanish from my sight.

At first she danced a measure slow,
With gauzy wings extended—so.
Then next her feet tripped fast and faster
And where I lay, I hugged my laughter;
Oh, what if she should disappear
Before I've asked her name, or sphere!
Alas; she guessed my thought too soon,
And floated upward to the moon!

To Our Mother

MADELINE G. ALLISON

AS dawn peers through the western sky,
To you our radiant visions hie;
Then silent stars steal to their home,
And to you all our dear dreams roam.

The Strawberry

MARY EFFIE LEE

THE strawberry's my fav'rite fruit;
And why's not hard to say:
No other fruit is half so good
Or tastes in that same way.

It is rose-red and has gold eyes,
And grows low on the ground
On bushes green, whither I steal
When mother's not around.

The Grasshopper

MARY EFFIE LEE

O HAPPY little grasshopper
In shirt of lettuce-green,
With wings as thin as isinglass
And sprightly legs and lean!

O little leaping grasshopper,
I watched you spring and pass,
And found that though your name sounds
You don't just jump on grass.

You sped right by Parnassus grass
To land on daddy's knee;
Then made my tie a boulevard,
As we sat by the tree.

I saw you pass some fox grass once
And light—snap!—on a rose:
So, after all, one's not known by
The name one's parents chose.

Tomboys

ANNETTE CHRISTINE BROWNE

LITTLE maids, what joy is yours!
Children of the great out-doors!

Nature's forces, every one
Join in hand to give you fun.

She her carpet green has spread
For your play and for your bed.

You may play up in the trees,
Or chase the butterflies and bees.

You may heed the water's call,
Being yet so young and small.

When I was a child like you
I could wade in water, too.

Childhood days pass quickly by.
Live them fully as they fly.

When you enter grown-ups' ways
Oft you'll long for bare-foot days.

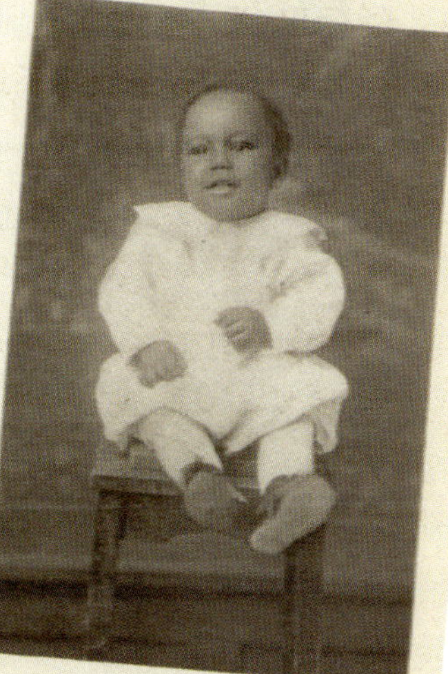

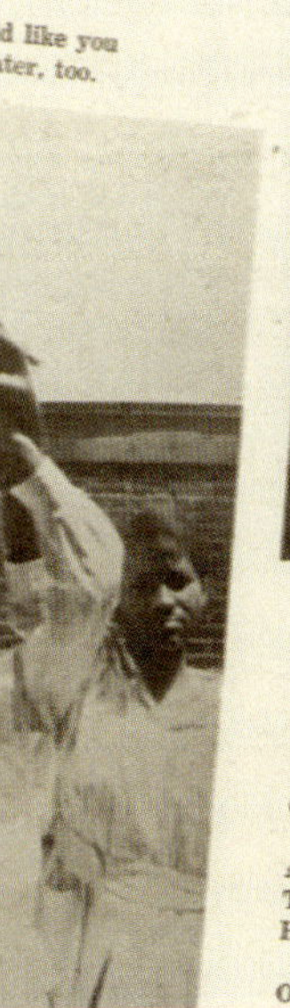

The Baby Boy

WILLIS RICHARDSON

WITH little dimpled hands and feet,
He sits in summer garments neat,
Of lace, all lily white;

And when through lattice-work of green
The sun's invading rays are seen,
His eyes are trebly bright:

Or if while sitting there at play
Some golden beams that drift astray,
Upon his feet alight,

He gazes at them steadily,
Then claps his hands in highest glee
Enraptured at the sight.

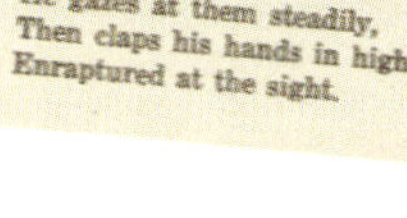

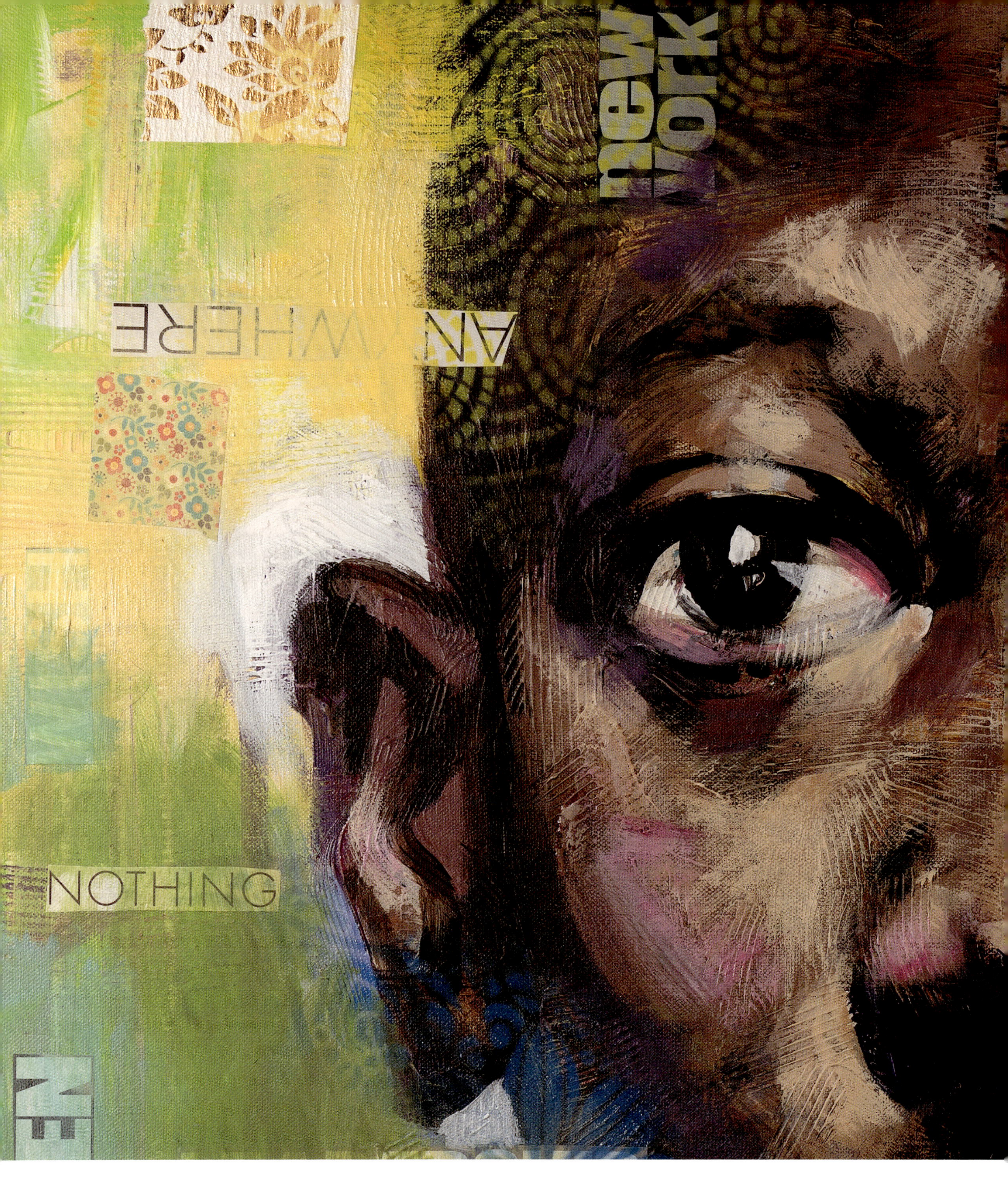

new york
ARTWHERE
NOTHING
NE

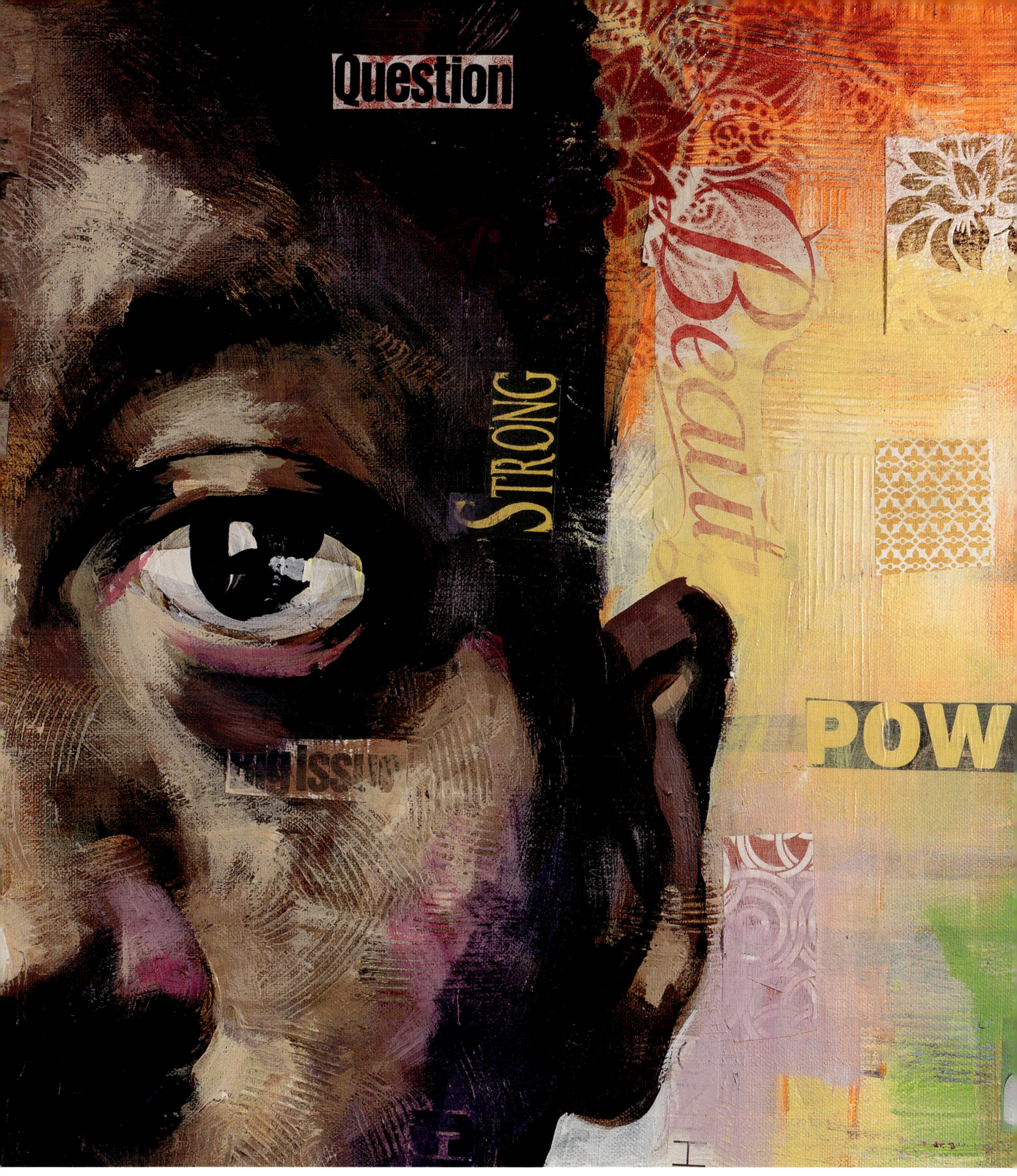

Charly Palmer, *Kalief Browder*
(Acrylic on canvas)

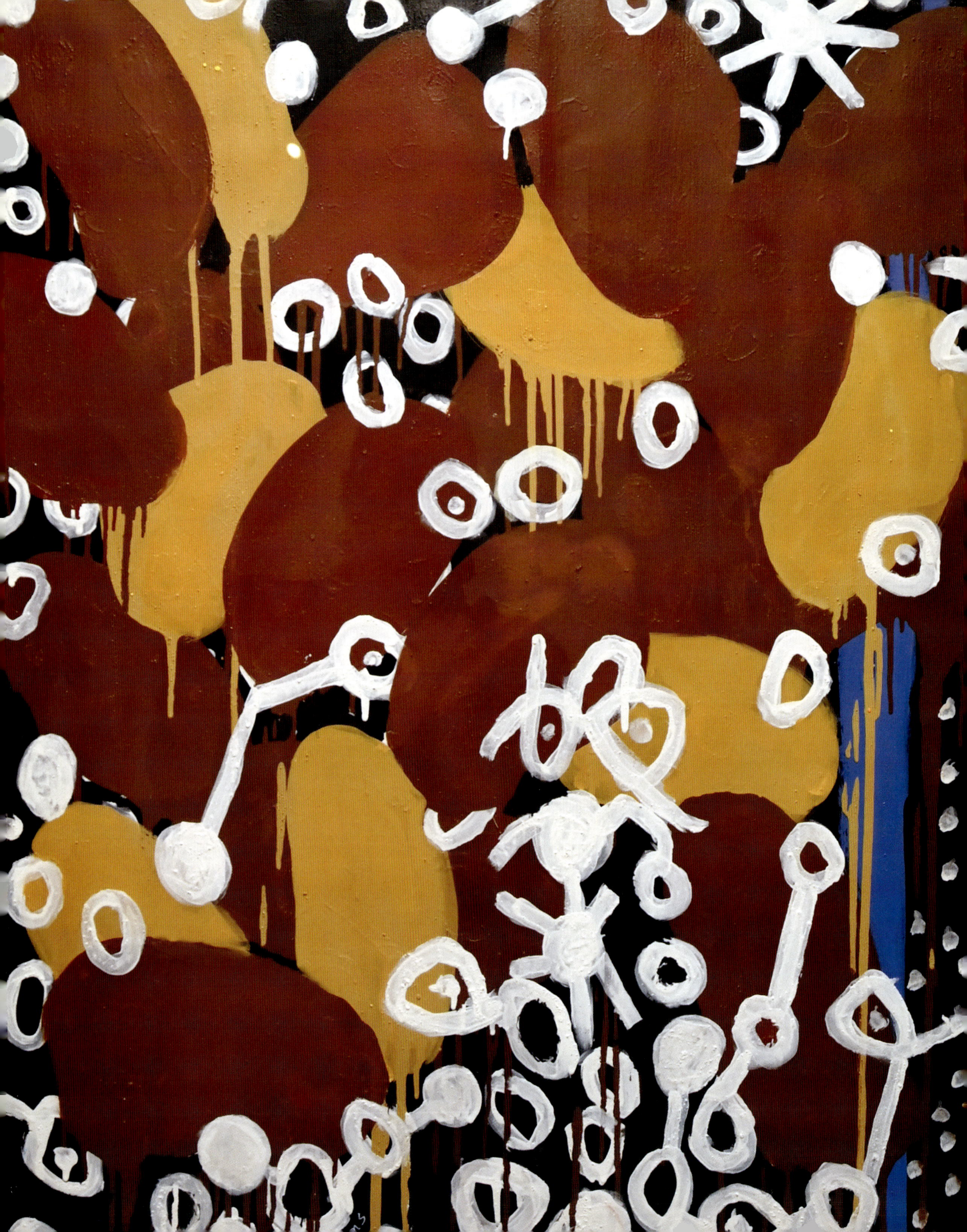

WINTER SWEETNESS

By Langston Hughes |
From *The Brownies' Book*, January 1921

The little house is sugar,
Its roof with snow is piled,
And from its tiny window,
Peeps a maple-sugar child.

Chapter 4

WE WERE
KINGS

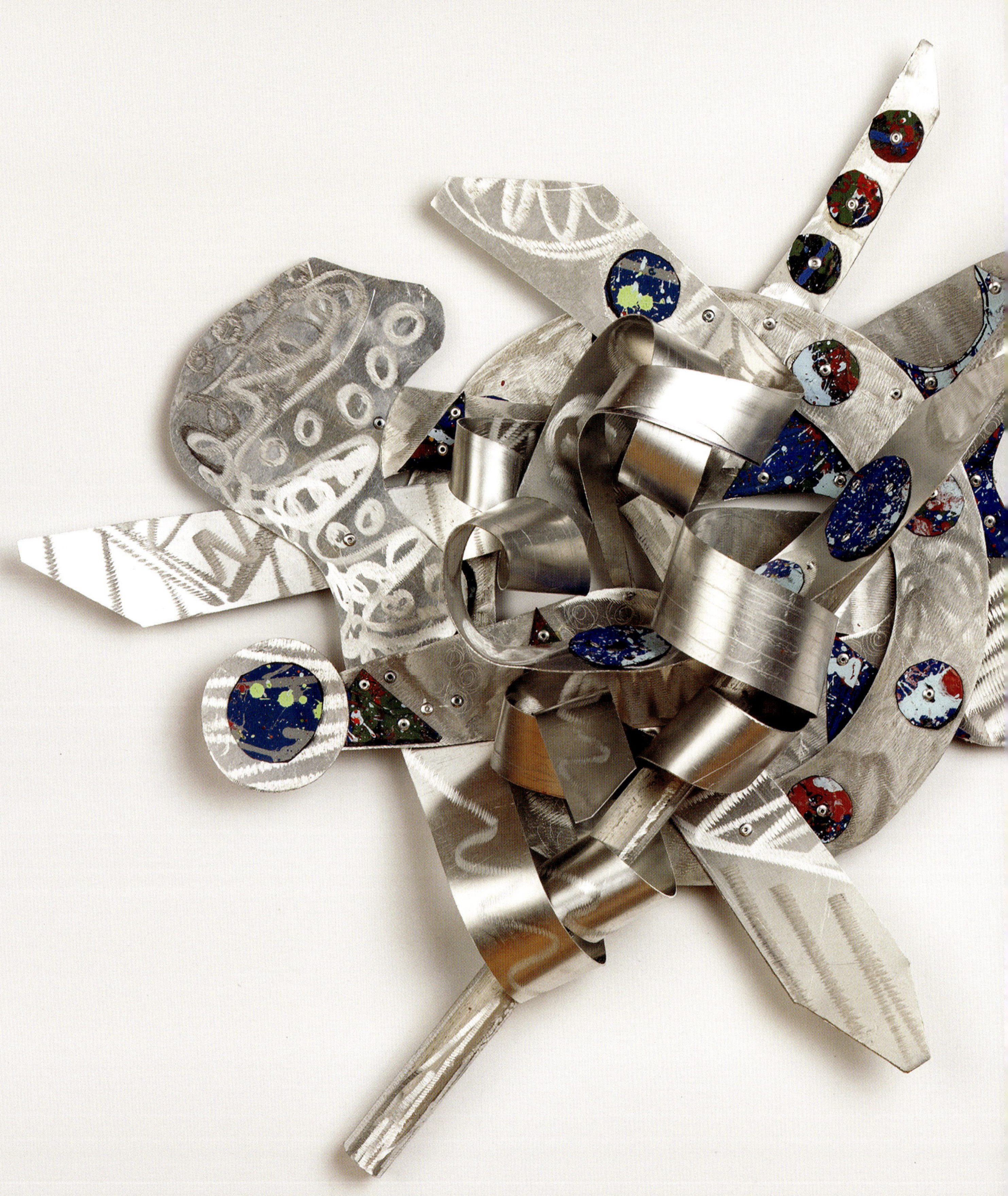

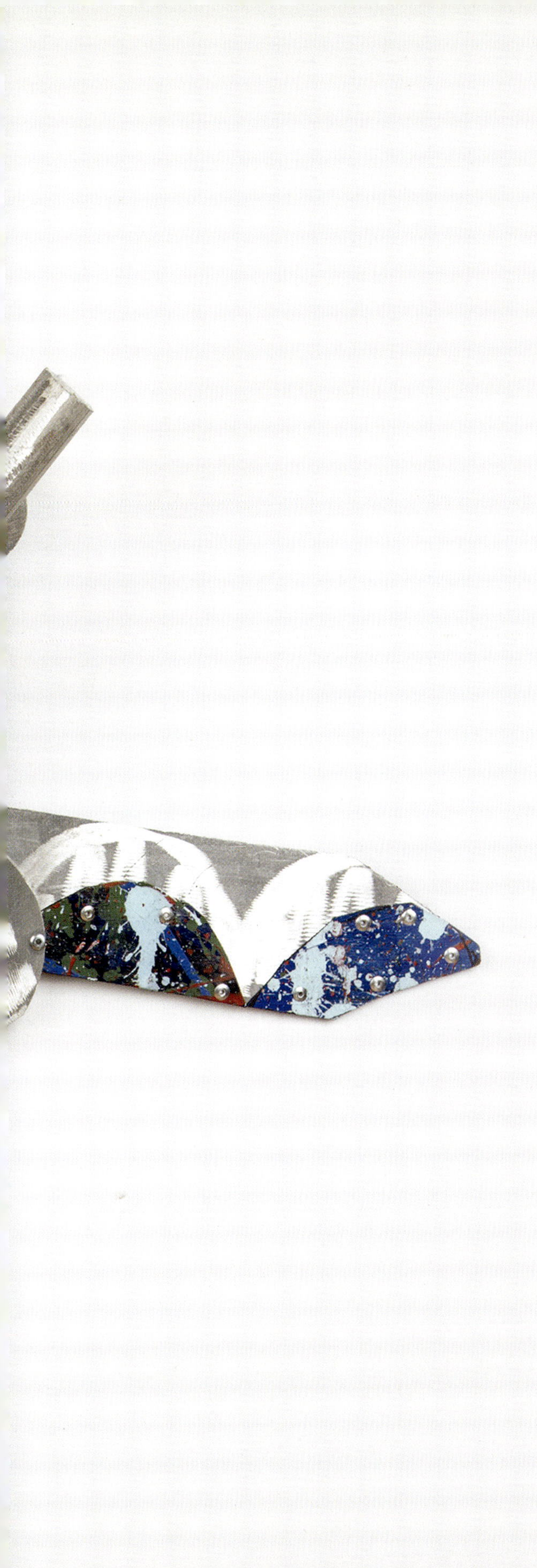

A LETTER TO THE KID WHO EVENTUALLY BREAKS MY WORLD RECORD OF

"Most Bite-Sized Snickers Eaten by a Twelve-Year-Old in a Thirteen-Minute Span While Waiting Between Pickup Basketball Games at Mellon Park"

By Damon Young

The thing about records is that they have rules, right? First, you need an established standard. And then you need a witness or two to watch you break it. And then your mark is written in some book somewhere as *the* record. For instance, this man named Robert Wadlow is the tallest person who ever lived. He grew to be eight feet eleven inches tall—and he was still growing when he died! But he's only the record holder because people knew him and saw him and measured him against the old standard.

But then sometimes records work . . . differently. Like if you, right now, got up from wherever you're sitting, stood on the chair, and then said, "PITTSBURGH COOTIES BOOTY BUTT!"

seventy-four times in a row, I'm *certain* you would have just set the world record for "Most Times Saying PITTSBURGH COOTIES BOOTY BUTT! in a Row While Standing on a Chair." It probably won't make any record books, but you'll be able to call yourself a world record holder. My bite-sized Snickers record—well, *your* bite-sized Snickers record now—follows the same rule.

I'm one hundred thousand trillion percent certain that no twelve-year-old had ever eaten eleven bite-sized Snickers in a thirteen-minute span while waiting between pickup basketball games at Mellon Park before I did. So many random things had to come together for me to even be able to complete that task. I needed to be:

A) twelve years old

B) playing basketball at Mellon Park

C) hungry enough between games to eat eleven bite-sized Snickers in a thirteen-minute span, and (most importantly)

D) in possession of eleven bite-sized Snickers.

A, B, and C were pretty easy, but D was only possible because it was the day after Halloween, and I'd taken a bag of bite-sized Snickers to school to pass out to my classmates in homeroom, but I was so distracted by Dorian Jenkins making me laugh when saying our homeroom teacher, Mr. Winslow, smells like shark teeth that I forgot. And I still had the bag with me when I went to hoop.

Anyway, I don't know how you came to break my record. I assumed it was unbreakable—I thought eleven bite-sized Snickers was the limit of between-hoop-game Snickers consumption, until I learned you somehow ate seventeen (!!!)—but I guess I was wrong. So congrats to you.

Unfortunately, I don't have any trophies or plaques or anything for you. I apologize if you were expecting one. I can, however, give you some advice. It's been thirty years since I set the record, and here's some of what I've learned in the time since.

1. If you're already playing pickup games at Mellon Park at twelve years old, you must be a serious ballplayer, like I was. So I'll give you some serious basketball advice. I remember this one time, when I was around your age, and I was feeling myself and my game. So I asked my dad what I still needed to work on—since I had so very obviously mastered so many skills. I was expecting him to say something like, "Well, your lefty floater could use more arc." But instead he looked at me real funny, smirked, paused, and then said, "Um . . . *everything.*"

You want your game to be as well-rounded as possible. That means always working on your handle, your jimmy, and your hawk so you can be flexible and nimble enough to handle whatever and whoever comes at you. If they take away your strong hand, then it ain't nothin' because, surprise, both your hands are strong. If they play your drive, well, hands down man's down because your j is wet. You just don't want to fall into the trap so many of us do of assuming your work is done, 'cause it never is. There's always room to grow, expand, and evolve. Always a new journey. Always a new adventure. Always a new challenge. Will you be prepared for it when it comes?

2. Every fifty-seven years or so, Mickey D's drops this sandwich called the McRib. It's basically the Halley's Comet of fast food. What is a McRib, you ask? Well, it's a barbecue rib–like substance, but on a sandwich. Duh.

Anyway, if this happens while you're alive, eat one, because they're delicious. But stop there, because two or more will kill you.

3. One of the things I've always appreciated about pickup ball at a public park is that it's free and open to anyone, which means you'll be on the court with all types of people. Some younger than you, some older than me. Some short, some tall. Some with round bodies. Some built like Macy's mannequins. And then you'll also have all the different skill sets and playing styles. Cats with real funny form, who shoot a hoop rock like they're throwing an axe at a squirrel. Cats who say "Buckets" each time they shoot, even if they don't be making nothin'. Cats who can't dribble. Cats who can *only* jump real high. Cats who come to hoop in actual $200 NBA uniforms, like if rocking a Ja Morant Memphis jersey means you're gonna play like him too. Cats who call foul each time they miss. Football player–ass cats who *never ever ever ever* call foul but be fouling the heck out of you and expect you to never call it. And cats who can't hoop at all and are just out there for cardio or something.

Thing is—and this took me a looooong time to realize—everyone out there is valuable, in their own way. Just because someone is smaller or slower or less skilled than you doesn't mean that they don't have the same right to be on the court as you do. And yeah, you got to be as good as you are through hard work and perseverance. All them days and nights by yourself, working on your game, sweatin' through your shirts, scraping your knees, callusing your hands, practicing with puddle-splashed wet balls on them triflin'-ass double rims—nothing can take that away from you!

But what if you ain't have the time to put in that time because you had a little brother to take care of after school each day because your mama worked nights? Or what if you were born with all the heart in the world and none of the height, hops, or hand-eye coordination? Or what if you had chronic asthma that stopped you from training as hard as you wanted to?

My point is that you just never know what advantages you have that others just ain't ever had. That don't mean you need to feel bad or whatever about what you have. That's wack. But just don't act like your s**t don't stink, 'cause it do. (Especially after all them bite-sized Snickers.) And also, like, if you want to be the best player you can possibly be, and you're the one with skill advantages, it's up to you to help get the best out of your less talented teammates.

And for real for real, there will be times you're the youngest or the slowest or the weakest out there too. Unless your name is LeBron, it happens to us all. (And even LeBron ain't always been LeBron, you know?) Do you want your bigger, older, stronger, and better teammates to act like you don't belong? That you don't matter? Or do you want them to value you and help you succeed?

(Yeah, I thought so.)

4. So, a few years ago, I went to my twenty-year high school reunion, because I'm *OLD*. I saw some old friends, stunted on some new haters, and ate some red velvet cake. It was a good time. One thing I'll always remember about that night,

though, was how some of the people . . . dressed. I graduated high school in 1997, and at that time, super baggy jeans, oversized sports jerseys and Polo rugbys, and multicolored Timberland boots were hot. Fashion changes though, and those types of clothes have gone out of style. But . . . some of the guys there were still dressed like it was 1997. It was like I was in a Karl Kani time machine. (Google him.)

Now, I don't want to gear-shame anyone. Dress however you want. These guys were clearly still more comfortable in those dated threads—or perhaps they just couldn't afford to stay up with trends. Either way, it's fine.

But—do you know what an analogy is? It's when you compare two seemingly unrelated things and find the similarities between them to make a point. Like, if I said, "My Aunt Jean is the Beyoncé of chili," that means my Aunt Jean makes bomb-ass chili. (And *not* that she makes her chili while dancing in a leotard. She probably could though, because my Aunt Jean has skills!)

Anyway, back to the guys at the reunion. You don't want *their clothes* to be *your brain*. What I mean is that the world has changed so much since I was your age. There was no internet, no electric cars, no cell phones (unless you were richer than Scrooge McDuck), no almond Snickers bars, no

popular Canadian rappers, no GPS in cars—we had to use these big-ass, printed-out, foldable-globe-sheet things called "maps" to know how to get places—and TVs used to be as heavy and wide as IKEA couches are. And the world will continue to change, and I want you to continue to evolve and change with it. The career you eventually decide to pursue *might not have even been invented yet*. Shit, *you* might invent it yourself. Crazy, right?

Look, I'll admit that when I first heard about the record, I was pissed. And the last thing I wanted to do was actually *talk* to the kid who broke it. But then I remembered who I was back then, and how annoyed I'd be at the oldheads who acted like I ain't know anything just because I was young. I want to be better than them. And I want you to be better than me. You're already off to a great start, breaking one of my records. Let's see if you can break some more. I'm also the world record holder for "Stankest Post-Nap Breath on a December Saturday" and "Most Consecutive Times Forgetting the Lyrics to 'Lift Every Voice and Sing' but Still Singing Like They Know Them Anyway."

(Actually, maybe you don't need to break those two.)

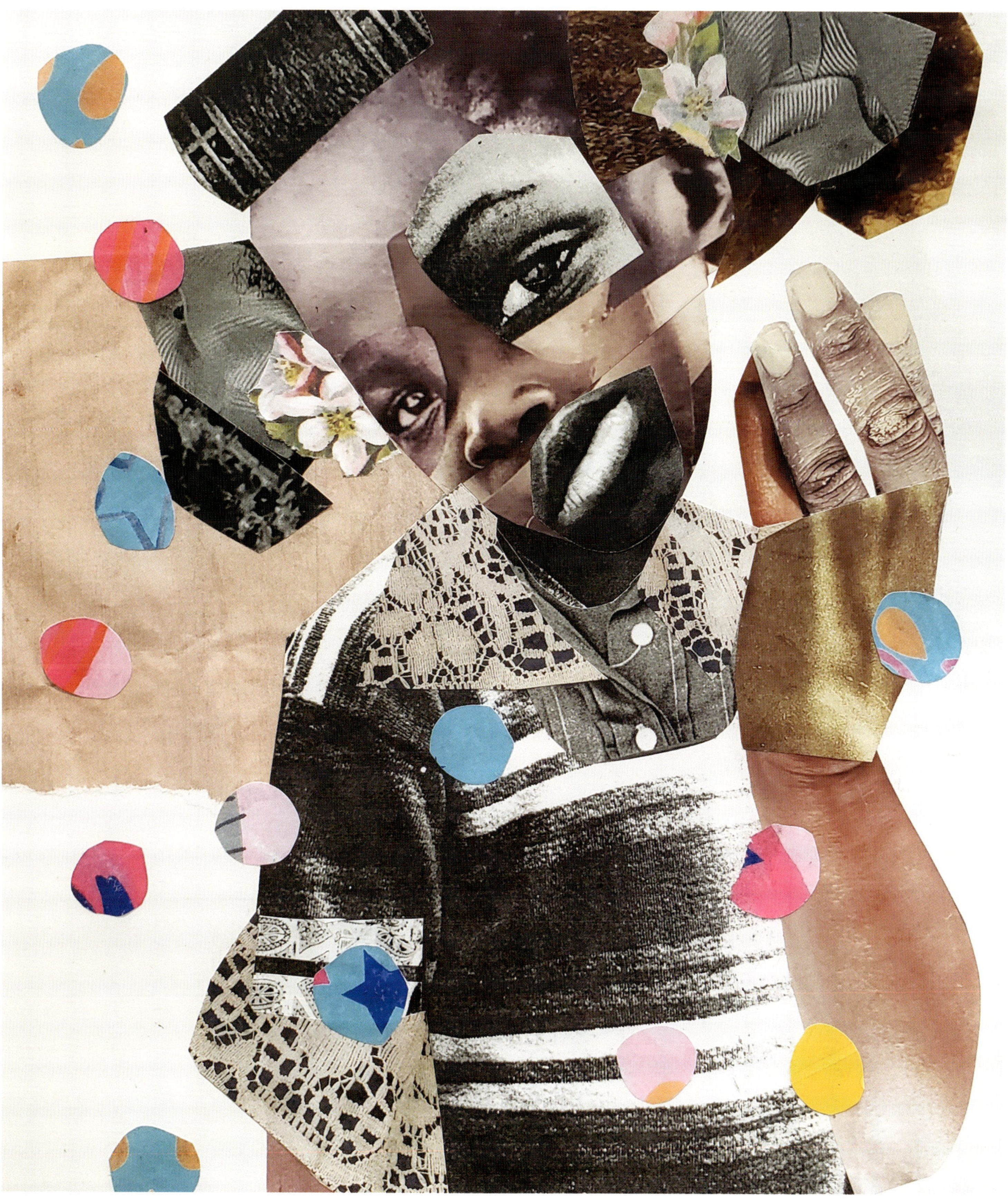

Lynthia Edwards, *Sassy Mouth*
(Paper collage)

A HOUSE FOR A KING

By Magana J. Kabugi

As the summer of 1944 drew to a close, Alberta Williams King and Martin Luther King Sr. had started to notice a change in their fifteen-year-old son. During his earliest years growing up on Auburn Avenue in the heart of Black Atlanta, Martin Luther King Jr. had been shielded from the harsh realities of racism. But as he got older and started to venture outside his upper-middle-class bubble, he started to ask more questions—questions about why things were the way they were, why Black people were mistreated and disrespected, and what he could do about it.

In April 1944, a few months after Martin had turned fifteen, he went with his teacher, Mrs. Sarah Grace Bradley, and some of his classmates to compete in a statewide oratorical contest hosted by the Elks Lodge in Dublin, Georgia. Martin won first place with his speech, which was called "The Negro and the Constitution." He brought the audience to their feet with his closing words: "My heart throbs anew in the hope that inspired by the example of Lincoln, imbued with the spirit of Christ, they will cast down the last barrier to perfect freedom. And I with my brother of blackest hue possessing at last my rightful heritage and holding my head erect, may stand beside the Saxon—a Negro—and yet a man!" Though Martin's words brought tears of joy to the audience's eyes, the world outside the oratory hall had different ideas. On the bus, Martin and Mrs. Bradley were yelled at by the white bus driver for not getting out of their seats quickly enough for a group of white passengers. Despite Martin's protests, he and Mrs. Bradley were forced to stand in the aisle during the entire ninety-mile trip back to Atlanta while the white passengers sat comfortably.

That same year Martin and some of his classmates got a summer job on a tobacco farm in Simsbury, Connecticut, outside of Hartford. On the trip north he was surprised to see the lack of Jim Crow signs noting separate facilities for Black and white people. In a letter he wrote to his father, Martin said he could eat in the finest restaurants, and he wasn't made to sit in the kitchen either.

He and his Black friends could enter movie theaters through the main entrance. In church, though he and his classmates were the only Black people in the congregation, he was offered the chance to serve as the religious leader over a group of 107 white boys. In his words, he felt "an exhilarating sense of freedom." However, as he crossed back into the South, he was made to sit behind a curtain in the train's dining car. He felt, as he later told the historian Lerone Bennett Jr., "as if the curtain had been dropped on my selfhood."

Martin's parents realized that their ability to explain the world to their son had reached its limitations. The elder King decided to send his son to another "house"—specifically, Morehouse College, Atlanta's historically Black college for men. Though Martin was only fifteen, his parents felt he was ready. He took a college entrance exam and passed, and he enrolled at Morehouse that fall.

For young Martin, the road to becoming a Morehouse Man had many bumps and steep curves. Because many Black college-aged men were away fighting in the Second World War, Morehouse filled the enrollment gap by recruiting high schoolers like Martin. Though he had other peers on campus, he still felt disconnected from the majority of students there, who were much older than him. He was also indecisive and a bit scattered. Before finally deciding to major in sociology, he briefly flirted with being a lawyer and then a physician. Over the course of four years he received only one A, which he got in a biblical studies course in the spring semester of his junior year. In class, Martin was shocked to find that his reading was only at an eighth-grade level. This pushed him to develop his public speaking skills.

Martin also found inspiration in faculty members and administrators at Morehouse, including the president, Dr. Benjamin Mays. Students were required to attend Mays's Tuesday morning lectures, which covered topics ranging from religion to racism to the importance of education for Black men. The more Martin listened, the more he felt comfortable enough to engage and debate with Mays.

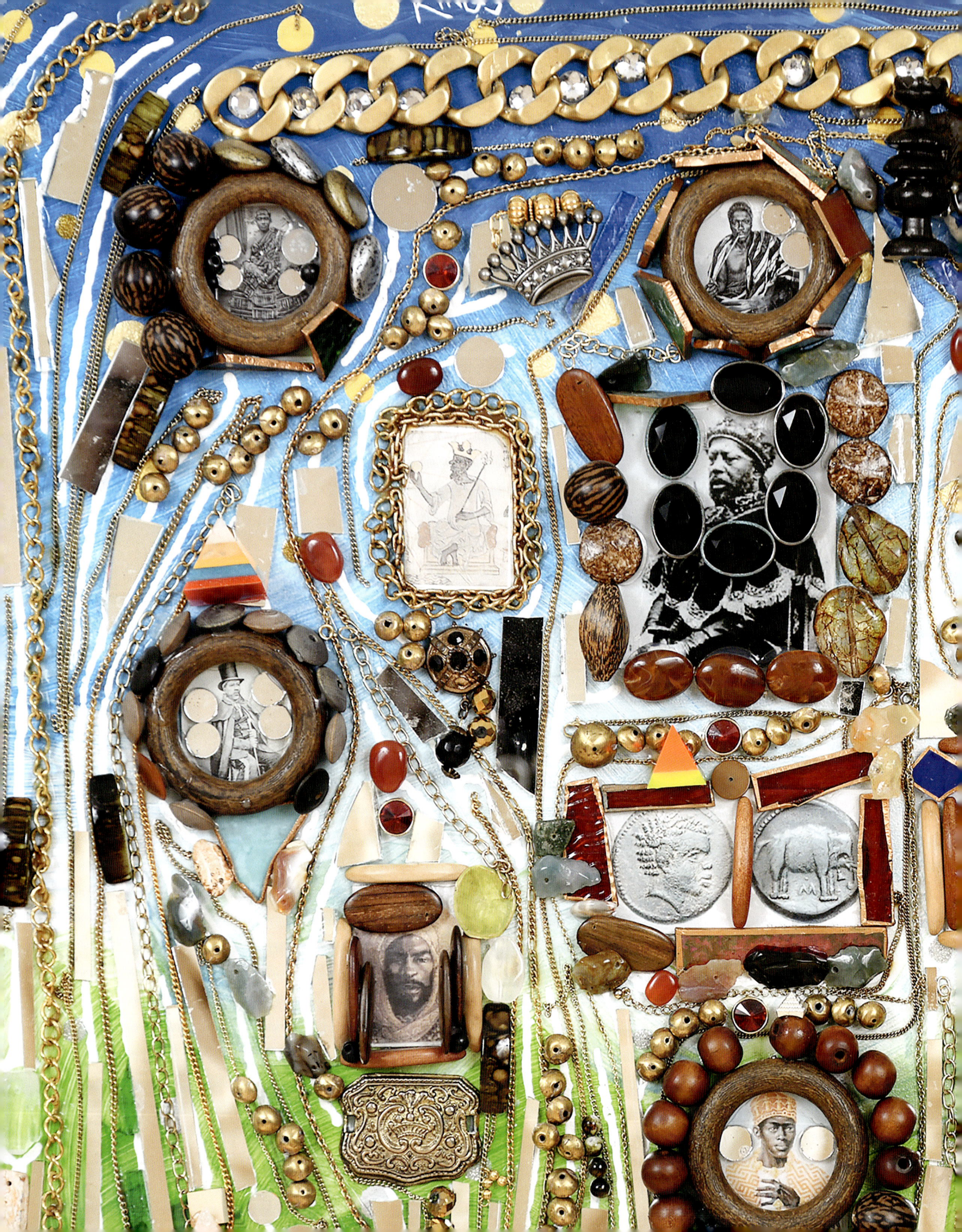

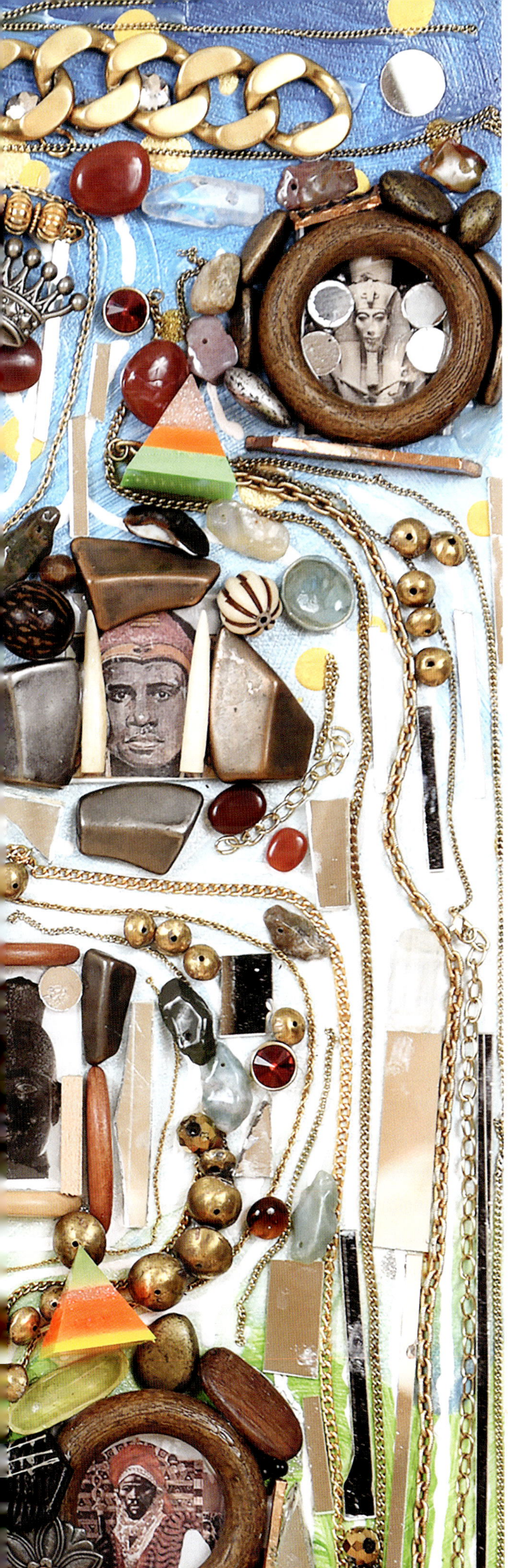

Eventually a friendship developed between the two, and Mays would invite King to his home for debates over meals. As an English minor, Martin counted among his favorite professors Gladstone Lewis Chandler, a Caribbean American literary scholar known fondly as "GLC" by students. Professor Chandler often taught using word games, and he created a "word bank" in which students would deposit new words on slips of paper into a box, pull out words of their own, and use the words in everyday conversation. The writing skills Martin learned in Chandler's classes would serve him well. In Morehouse's campus literary journal, *The Maroon Tiger*, Martin published an essay titled "The Purpose of Education" in which he argues that education should have two objectives: "We must remember that intelligence is not enough," he wrote. "Intelligence plus character—that is the goal of true education."

In spring 1948 Martin graduated from Morehouse alongside his sister Christine, who graduated from Morehouse's sister school, Spelman College. As he walked across the stage and shook hands with his mentor, Dr. Mays, little did Martin know what a powerful impact he would have on the world. He would live true to the words spoken by the Baptist preacher Howard Thurman, also a Morehouse graduate: "Over the heads of her students, Morehouse holds a crown that she challenges them to grow tall enough to wear."

LIL' KINGS

By Frank X Walker | From *Affrilachia*, Old Cove Press, 2020

what if
the good revren doctah
mlk jr
was just marty
or lil' king
not a pastor
but a little faster
from the streets
quoting gangsta rap
not Gandhi

was not dr. king
but king doctah
or ice-k
his peace sign on a gold tooth
or gleaming 14 karat like
from around his neck

what if somebody
screaming "nigger"
hit 'im in the head
with a brick
and he pulled out a nine
and squeezed off
one or two rounds
not tears
praying
only that he
not miss
sported mlk
on phat brass knuckles
and a lefthanded
diamond pinky ring
walked the streets
with his home boyz

spray painting
let freedom ring
and I had a dream
on bus stops
and stop signs

got arrested for
conspiring to incite riots
disturbing the peace
and resisting arrest

didn't preach from
no pulpit
but on a microphone
behind turntables
mixin' and scratchin'
listenin' to dr. dre

wu tang
and the notorious b.i.g.

pants down to his hightops
hat on backwards
eyes on a prized new voice
not no bel
no peace
of nothin'
that just rings
when it's hit
a voice that
hits back

could he still
be king?

GIVE THE BALL TO LISA

By Alice Faye Duncan

Lisa Leslie, WNBA Superstar.
Born and raised in Southern California, Lisa Leslie is an American Hall of Fame basketball star.
As a member of the Los Angeles Sparks, she became the first player to dunk in a WNBA game. Lisa led the Sparks to two WNBA championships. She won three MVP awards and made eight All-Star teams.
Playing center position, she participated in four summer Olympic Games, and with her American team she won four Olympic gold medals from 1996 to 2008.
Lisa Leslie was inducted into the Naismith Memorial Basketball Hall of Fame in 2015.

From season to season and year to year,
change consumed a little girl's growing body.
Lisa Leslie's arms grew into graceful tree branches.
Her limber legs grew into long tree trunks.

And with exercise and dribbling drills,
chiseled muscles strong like granite
consumed her slender frame.

The teenager towered over friends in the
  neighborhood.
She towered above teachers at school.
It was rare to see a girl stand six-foot-five.
Some nights—she prayed to shrink or vanish like
  a genie.

Lisa's brooding soon abated, and feelings turned
  to pride,
when she gave herself to basketball and found her
  SUPERPOWER.
She joined her high school basketball team—it was
  good to be tall.
She lorded over center court dropping twos like
  "Wilt the Stilt."

Persistent practice with Cousin Craig made her
  sparkle and shine.
And at every school game—the coach would
  wave and shout . . .
"Give the ball to LISA!"

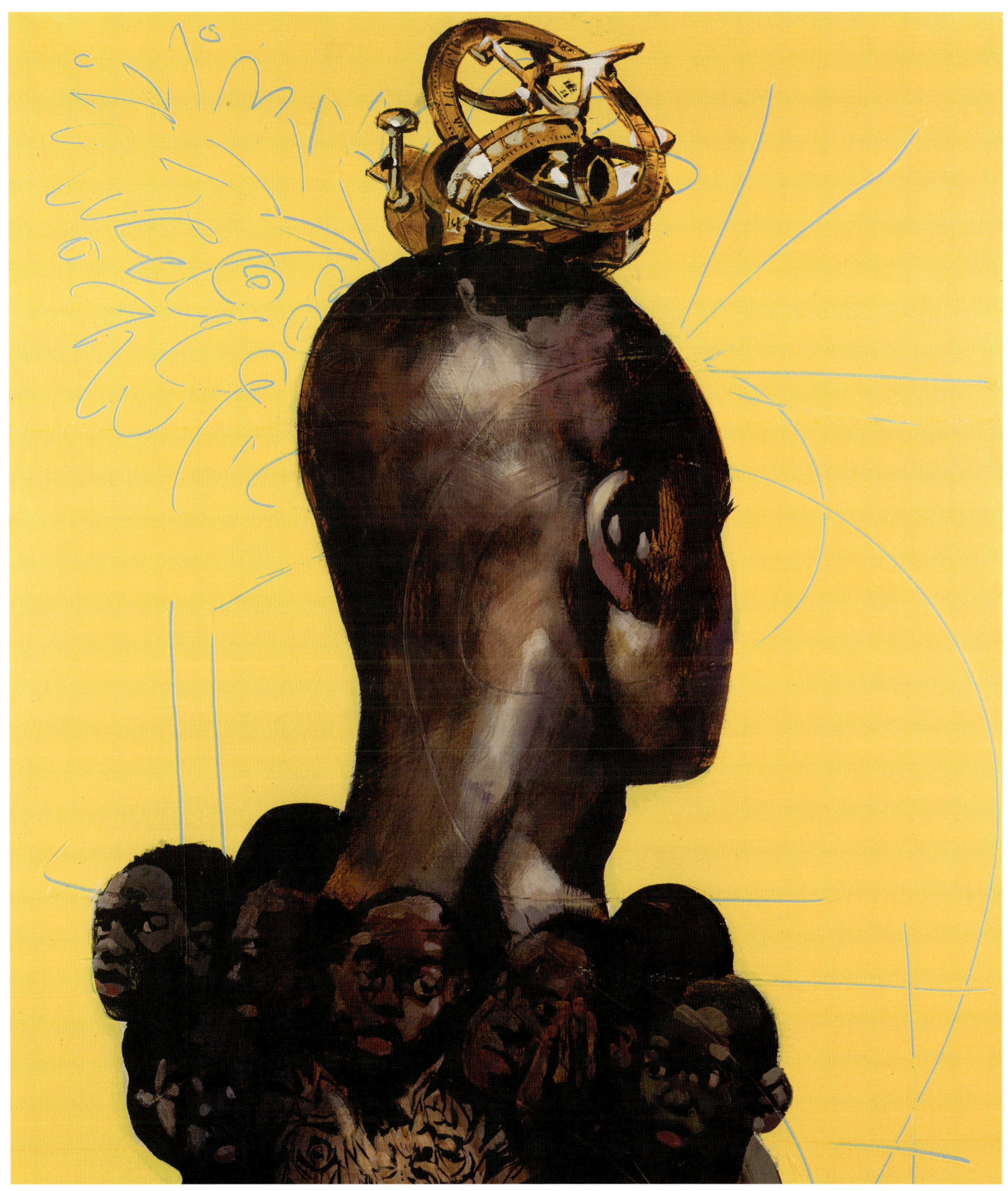

Charly Palmer, *Navigator*
(Acrylic on canvas)

Chapter 5

SCHOOL DAZE

HISTORICALLY BLACK COLLEGES AND UNIVERSITIES

By Karida L. Brown

Dear Reader,
Do you know what an HBCU is? The term stands for Historically Black Colleges and Universities. There are 107 of them in the United States, and they are a very special kind of school. This is because HBCUs are sources of beaming pride, infinite accomplishment, and deep legacy for Black people in America and across the African diaspora. The Higher Education Act of 1965 defines an HBCU as "any historically black college or university that was established prior to 1964, whose principal mission was, and is, the education of Black Americans." Today HBCUs serve students of all races and ethnicities, from the United States and from countries around the world.

Many of the most accomplished Black Americans in the world attended an HBCU. Notable alumni of HBCUs include sociologist, activist, and organizer W. E. B. Du Bois; Supreme Court judge Thurgood Marshall; Civil Rights Movement activists Diane Nash, Reverend Dr. Martin Luther King Jr., and Congressman John Lewis; media mogul Oprah Winfrey; actors Chadwick Boseman and Taraji P. Henson; Oscar-winning film director Spike Lee; astrophysicist Dr. Jedidah Isler; and vice president of the United States, Kamala Harris, to name a few.

Here are the names and locations of ten HBCUs for you to look up: Fisk (Nashville), Howard (Washington, DC), Spelman (Atlanta), Florida A&M (Tallahassee, Florida), Xavier (New Orleans), Morgan State (Baltimore), Lincoln (Lincoln University, Pennsylvania), Wiley (Marshall, Texas), Norfolk State (Norfolk, Virginia), and Tougaloo (Tougaloo, Mississipi). Can you name ten more?

W. E. B. Du Bois himself attained his undergraduate degree from Fisk University in 1888. There he served as the editor of the school's newspaper, *The Fisk Herald*, and spent his summers teaching children to read in rural Black communities outside Nashville. Continuing Du Bois's legacy, his daughter Yolande also attended Fisk University— you will see some of her writings about her time in college reprinted here.

The contributions that follow include *Brownies'* "Love Letters" penned by Fisk University undergraduate students, current and past, just for YOU!

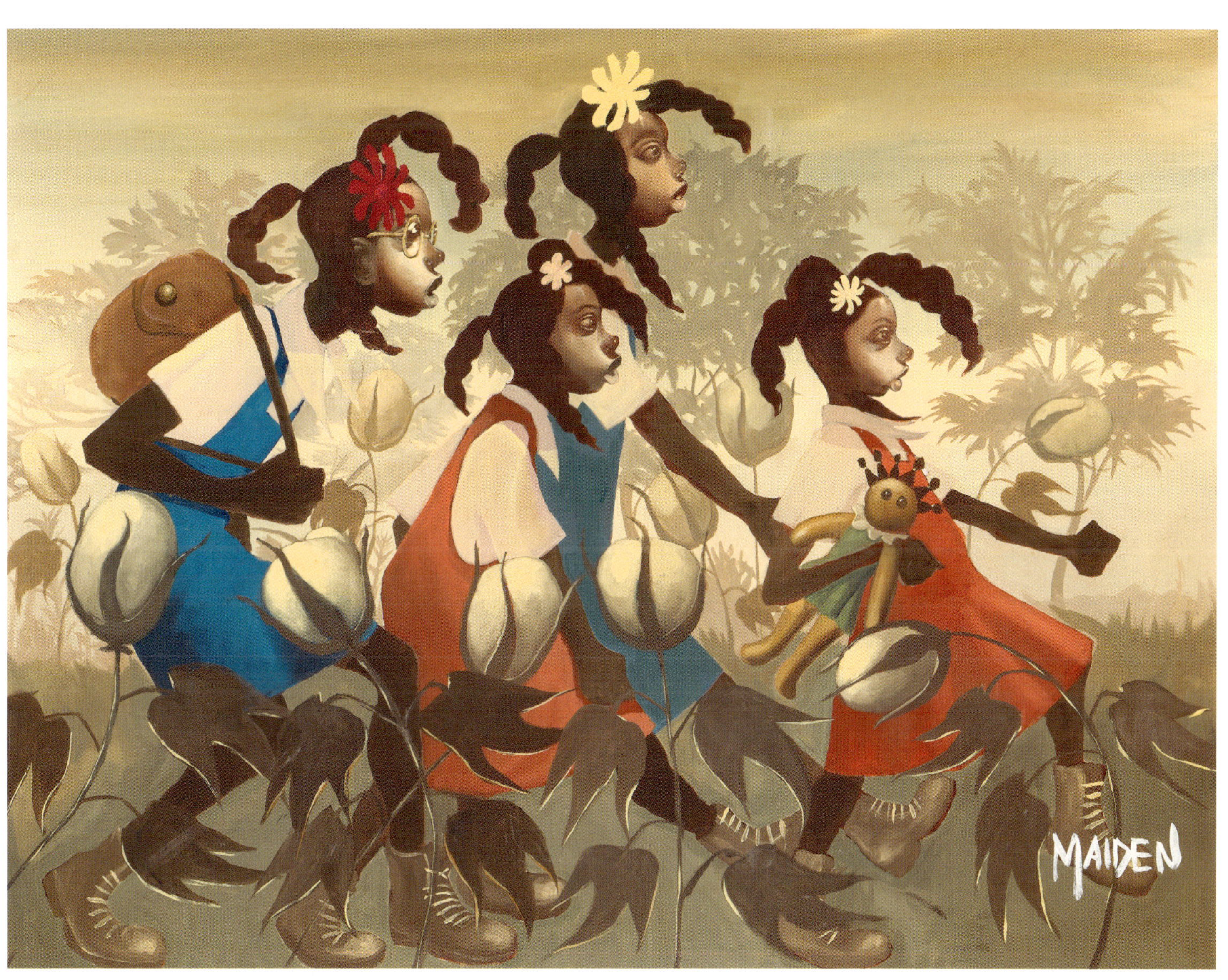

Leonard Maiden, *School Girls*
(Oil on canvas)

OUTSIDE OF HARLEM: THE RENAISSANCE

By Jasmine Mitchell | Fisk University, Class of 2023

In the aftermath of the abolishment of slavery in the United States, Black Americans worked tirelessly to write and illustrate their own culture and heritage into the American art and literary worlds. Historically Black Colleges and Universities (HBCUs) were established to provide an education for the four million formerly enslaved American citizens and helped cultivate an interest in the cultural heritage and contributions of Black people. Events such as World War I propelled African Americans to yearn for positive cultural affirmations within the intellectual conversations. For example, when African American soldiers who fought in World War I, known as the Harlem Hellfighters, returned to their homeland of America, they were still working against racism, prejudice, and Jim Crow segregation. This feeling of exclusion from the "American dream" inspired African Americans across the nation to write and sing their stories into the cultural fabric of the United States. African American intellectuals Anne Spencer, W. E. B. Du Bois, Jessie Redmon Fauset, Langston Hughes, and Arna Bontemps were significant influences on the legacy of the Harlem Renaissance, and much of their work happened outside of Harlem.

This is a historical play set in the garden Edankraal, which belonged to Anne Spencer in Lynchburg, Virginia, and where W. E. B. DuBois, Jessie Redmon Fauset, Langston Hughes, and Arna Bontemps would stop by for friendly conversations.

SCENE 1

Anne Spencer: Willie! Will you hand me those shears sitting on the garden table over there?

W. E. B. Du Bois: Sure, Anne. You've always had the most beautiful roses in your garden. You know, it's very peaceful here. I pondered about what you said last time I was visiting while I was away in Africa.

Anne Spencer: What a great experience that must have been! I love reading Langston's story of how he felt arriving in Africa. How was your trip?

W. E. B. Du Bois: Yes, *The Big Sea* is a great one. I went to Ghana in West Africa on business. Hearing the birds sing there felt like my first time hearing Bessie Smith at the 81 in Atlanta. I've always enjoyed listening to the birds freely sing. That is why it brings me much pleasure to be in your garden that is so beautiful it attracts the Billie Holiday of birds. *(Helps Anne Spencer pick up a fallen rose and places it in the flower bucket)*

Anne Spencer: You are too kind. They give me the sweetest blues when I'm writing my poetry.

W. E. B. Du Bois: Ah yes, that is what I was thinking about. While I was away, you sent me a letter about women's issues with getting published and the education of our youth.

Anne Spencer: Yes, I did. *(She takes roses and places them in a basket and neatly ties them with a piece of yarn)*

W. E. B. Du Bois: Gender equality and education are important issues and I am happy you brought them up.

Anne Spencer: Thank you for letting me say this. *(She and Du Bois walk down the garden pathway)* As a woman who works in the library, I have noticed that the material is too advanced for the children. I love the idea of your *Brownies' Book*! No one can be taught preciousness, self-worth, and beauty after their maturity. And also, the woman is a great person to give a platform right now.

W. E. B. Du Bois: Oh, I agree, Anne! I had it on my mind to bring it up next time I came through town. I wanted to ask you if you wanted to contribute to *The Brownies' Book* one of your beautiful poems. I wanted to introduce you to my dear friend and colleague Jessie Redmon Fauset. She helps me with *The Crisis* magazine, especially when I am not in New York. *(Anne Spencer looks at him as if he just told a tale)*

Anne Spencer: Helps?

W. E. B. Du Bois: Alright *(he admits),* she does take care of a lot for me while I'm out working with the NAACP. I'm hoping she could do the same for you if you would be willing to contribute, perhaps for *The Crisis* magazine if not *The Brownies' Book*.

Anne Spencer: You sound like a busy man! I would love the opportunity to put my pen to poetry and publish my work in *The Brownies' Book*.

W. E. B. Du Bois: Great! She should be visiting town after a while. How about I send her by for you two to become acquainted?

Anne Spencer: Set it up for a tea in my garden. I'd be delighted to host Ms. Fauset!

W. E. B. Du Bois: That brings me much pleasure, Anne. *(Both stop at the end of the garden trail)* You know I always love stopping by to catch up. I brought something back from West Africa for you and your garden. *(Edward Spencer walks into the garden rolling a cart with a gift from Du Bois)*

Anne Spencer: How beautiful!

W. E. B. Du Bois: Igbo's bust—it is the mask of an African prince. I also included a letter I wrote when I first picked it up.

Edward Spencer: It is a beautiful gift, Anne. *(She walks up to the sculpture in admiration)*

Anne Spencer: We should place it at the focal point, by the edge of the garden pool. But Willie, don't expect to not receive anything from me! Here, take this arrangement of blue and yellow roses to Yolande. And tell her I said congratulations on her enrollment into Fisk University!

W. E. B. Du Bois: I sure will! Fisk was an important part of my education, and I know it will be a great growing environment for her as well. She is going to love the colors! I'll be heading out now. Be expecting to hear from Ms. Fauset soon! Best wishes to the both of you. *(They all hug and say their final goodbyes)* ▶

Jessie Redmon Fauset: *(Speaking out loud to herself)* This has to be the correct place. William told me all about her beautiful garden. *(She looks over to see the sculpture by the pool and walks over in awe)*

Anne Spencer: What an amazing piece, right? *(She gives a soft smile, admiring the piece as well)* It was a gift from W. E. B. Du Bois's visit to Africa. You must be Ms. Jessie Redmon Fauset.

Jessie Redmon Fauset: *(Stunned by the mellow tone of Anne Spencer's voice)* Why, yes. I am a colleague of W. E. B. DuBois's with *The Crisis* magazine. I read some of your poetry, and I must say it is a fertile subject.

Anne Spencer: Ha ha, the poems are always about thoughts I have on my mind at the moment. Why don't you come sit on the porch over tea and we can chat about it some more? *(She gestures for Fauset to follow her inside the cottage)*

Jessie Redmon Fauset: Yes, that would be great. It is a pretty day. I wanted to show my appreciation for your work and what you submitted to *The Crisis*. You have a talent for being able to reflect on nature and turn it into a needed conversation through poetry. Your poem "Before the Feast of Shushan" was one of my favorites.

Anne Spencer: My story of beauty and brains. *(She grabs the tea kettle and pours tea into two porcelain teacups from China)*

Jessie Redmon Fauset: The use of biblical terms and locations adds much social context to your poem. I believe it can open conversations about the effects of patriarchy as well as how to deal with an educated Black woman. *(Sips tea)*

When I taught summer school at Fisk University, I saw a need for an emphasis on the experiences of not only Black women, but the whole Black community. It pleases me to see women such as yourself putting forth that effort.

Anne Spencer: I was just telling Willie about the literature us Black women have produced but seldom have the platform to share. It is so important to build an authentic story about Black women. That is what I love to do. It helps instill self-awareness in our children in this isolating world.

Jessie Redmon Fauset: I agree and would like to do my part in providing a platform for us women to speak for ourselves. Even the charming Arna Bontemps's *St. Louis Woman* is from a male's perspective. Your writing, however, is so pure and gentle. I would love to invite you to include your poem in *The Crisis*.

Anne Spencer: I appreciate your kind words. When Willie said you would be coming to visit, I couldn't help but to read every word you've ever put out. I love building relationships with other people who want to uplift our community. And Arna is my great friend! He should fall in here soon; he said he'd be visiting.

Jessie Redmon Fauset: It's such a small world! He is a great friend of mine as well. We crossed paths while he was the librarian at Fisk University.

Anne Spencer: We met while attending a conference for librarians in the southern region. *(Arna Bontemps and Langston Hughes enter the garden gates while laughing about who was a better writer)*

SCENE 3

Arna Bontemps: I knew my ears weren't itching for nothing!

Langston Hughes: Hey, I thought I felt something too!

Anne Spencer: *(In joy, she goes to meet them at the gate)* Well look what the cat drug in! It brought a bird too! What a wonderful sight to see. Please come in! *(Hughes laughs with open arms to greet Anne Spencer and Fauset)*

Jessie Redmon Fauset: *(Smiling)* Langston! It's so good to see you!

Langston Hughes: Heyyyy Ms. Jessie, you know I didn't forget about you! This is my good friend, Mr. Arna Bontemps.

Arna Bontemps: Nice to meet you, Ms. Fauset. A pleasure to see you, Mrs. Spencer.

Anne Spencer: What a day I am having! I am so delighted for everyone to be here. What brings you in?

Langston Hughes: Oh, we were just in the neighborhood and I had to stop and check in on you and Spence.

Anne Spencer: In the neighborhood! *(She chuckles with Fauset)*

Arna Bontemps: He knows good and well we just passing through from Fisk to get to Hampton.

Anne Spencer: Yes, I was just telling Ms. Fauset about your librarian position at Fisk University.

Jessie Redmon Fauset: What a great school Fisk is! I taught for a summer there. You must feel honored!

Arna Bontemps: Oh I do! I have met very intelligent students and friendly colleagues. I enjoy the experience of collecting items for our archive to help the students and their research.

Jessie Redmon Fauset: Anne, you have to come visit Fisk sometime! Maybe perform a poem at convocation after the Jubilee Singers perform?

Anne Spencer: Ha ha, maybe one day!

Langston Hughes: I surely would hate to miss that performance. *(He smiles at Anne Spencer)* Well, we have to get back on the road now. *(He gives her a tight, memorable hug)* Anne, you know I'll be thinking about you! And I hope to see you soon, Ms. Fauset. *(He hugs Fauset)* I haven't seen Spence; be sure to tell him I said hi!

Anne Spencer: He's going to love hearing about you!

Arna Bontemps: Alright now, Mrs. Spencer and Ms. Fauset. *(He hugs them both)*

Jessie Redmon Fauset: I'll be heading out behind you. I have an editors' meeting to attend! *(Hugs Anne Spencer)* Keep an eye on the mail—we will be staying in contact.

Anne Spencer: Alright everybody, y'all have safe travels! I can't wait to share my stories! Take a few of these roses with you! *(Langston Hughes, Arna Bontemps, and Jessie Redmon Fauset take the roses and exit the garden)*

Anne Spencer: *(Watches everyone leave until they are out of her sight and then sits at her garden table) (Ponders)* What wonderful people have traveled through Fisk. It must be an eminent environment. *(Writes notes on envelope that enclosed her letter from Du Bois)*

END PLAY

FISK'S HISTORY

By Asante Guzik Bates | Fisk University, Class of 2025

The warm and genial setting sun
The oldest building on campus,
Has gone through changes tremendous.
First known as the Railroad Hospital,
For those fighting in the war needed assistance
   from all vices of medical.
Sometimes these heroes needed an exit to zoom,
So you'll still find one of the tunnels in the girls'
   dressing room.
Then the building turned a page for children
   young and old,
To continue telling stories yet to unfold.
Although it hasn't had much experience with
   Shakespeare,
This little white building is now known as the
   Little Theatre.
Plenty of performances and plays that are on
   display for days.
Lights up the hills with mellow hue
Ding! Ding! Ding!
Is the sound this bell rings.
Stationed next to New Livingston Hall,
is the bell meant to help all.
Back when the KKK was on the attack,
we needed a system to have each other's back.
All it took was a few tugs,
and everyone knew to hide under the rugs.
Today we don't need the bell to hide,
instead it helps light a fire inside.
Meant for celebration for our winners playing
   basketball,
to remind people that Fisk has it all.

Where Fisk our alma mater stands
Fisk's pride and joy isn't a building at all,
it comes from people both short and tall.
Unfortunately as a start-up the school was broke,
and the dreams of Clinton B. Fisk almost went up
   in smoke.
Just when the school thought it was done,
The Jubilee Singers set out on October 6, 1871.
With their professor George L. White,
the singers made sure they were in everyone's
   sight.
Their voices gave everyone a strong sense of
   euphoria,
they even went as far as to perform for Queen
   Victoria.
Nashville is deemed the Music City not because of
   country,
but because of the Jubilee Singers who created the
   industry.

Majestic dear old Gold and Blue
Jubilee Hall,
the grandest building of them all.
Built in 1876,
thanks to the Jubilee Singers' fix.
It's the school's crowning jewel,
and there's no way of removal.
The building has seen weddings, concerts, young
   women, and more,
as it's a landmark for the present to remember
   those from before.
Currently it's strong wooden doors,

for upcoming Black women to live and explore.
Then hurrah and hurrah!
Fisk's standing colors are blue and gold,
reminder that while it stays up to date there's a
  window to the old.
There were two separate rooms,
one for the brides and one for the grooms.
These rooms were labeled the Gold and the Blue,
These spaces hold so much history from all points
  of view.
After preparation by the bride and the groom,
they headed to the Appleton Room.
This is a place of new beginnings, full of artists'
  printings.
One includes a portrait of the school's pride
  and joy,
showcasing a gift from the queen of the Jubilee
  Singers back from their deploy.
A place where students first meet,
all the way up 'til their journey's complete.
Her sons are steadfast, Her daughters true,
Fisk was able to produce some of the greatest
  minds,
leaving strong legacies behind.
W. E. B. Du Bois creates the NAACP,

making him a Black freedom fighter VIP.
Nikki Giovanni is a renowned poet who says
  whatever is on her chest,
letting the world know she's always ready to
  protest.
Judith Jamison is a dancer who has hit the
  Broadway stage,
showing Black women everywhere to break
  from their cage.
Many more legends have moved the tassel from
  one side to the other,
making a path for future sisters and brothers.
Where e'er we be we shall still love thee.
HBCUs are rare,
but it's the students' job to remind the world
  they're there.
Fisk is no exception as it continues to produce,
and the number of those going through the
  pipeline is beginning to reduce.
This university's work is far from done,
and more and more legacies will be made one
  by one.

Fisk our alma mater.

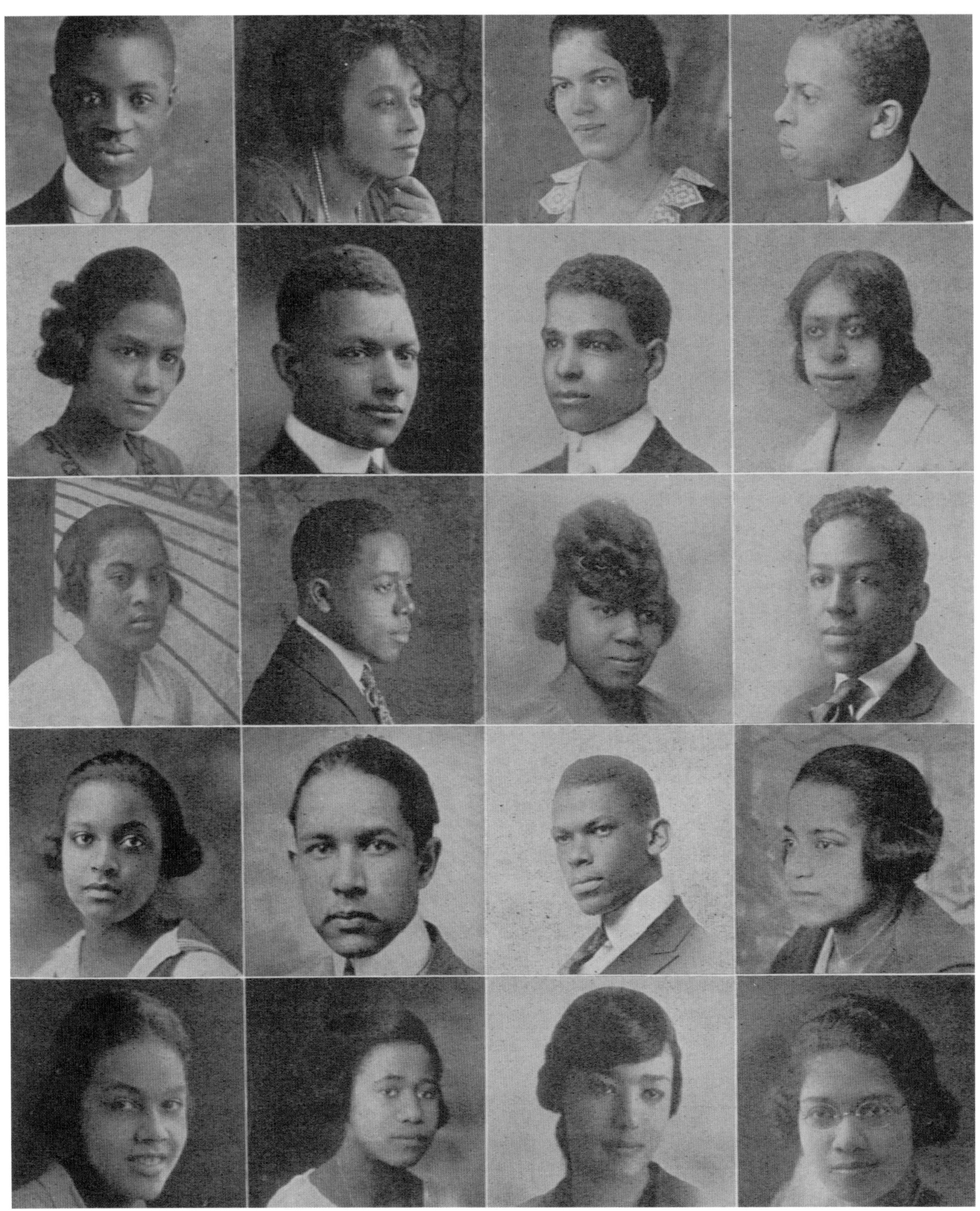

   THE NEW BROWNIES' BOOK

DEAR FISK

By Mekhi Yant | Fisk University, Class of 2023

Dear Fisk,

The experience you have given me has been anything but ordinary. From the extraordinary circumstances of the COVID-19 pandemic and the obstacles to being a thriving student to the financial burden college itself puts on you, I must say that my experience here has not been easy. Some might call it the normal stresses of being a college student. You have helped shape me for life. From the connections you've given me, to the knowledge I've acquired from you, to my personal growth as a young adult, being at Fisk has advanced me far beyond my peers.

The obstacles you have put in front of me, like those facing many other students here, have prepared me well for the obstacles of life. Things like handling the responsibility of financial aid, conducting professional administration meetings, and, of course, the hardships of just living on our own. The multiple challenges you've thrown at us have brought the best out of each and every student under your watch. While it is true the path you have set for me here has been tough, you've blessed me by surrounding me with others that are going through similar things as I am. Being able to be around peers who understand the difficulties I'm going through brings light to each situation I'm faced with. Sharing the college experience with people who look like me, who know what I'm going through, who have faced some of the same struggles as I do, encourages me to keep moving forward and helps me feel at home.

This is all before mentioning the love and rich history you have brought to everyone here. I find pride and encouragement from being able to see my culture in a position where our success is recognized and celebrated. Being able to just see the history of Fisk alumni such as W. E. B. Du Bois, Aaron Douglas, Alfred Coffin, Nikki Giovanni, and Etta Falconer all give me inspiration to thrive as an African American man and as a student. It does the same for other students. As an added bonus, I am able to play the game I love (basketball) in front of a supportive fan base and surrounded by people who want to see me do better. I will be forever thankful for the once-in-a-lifetime moments you have brought to me. From homecoming to orientation week, Jubilee Day to graduation—Fisk University, you will always hold an important place in my life.

Images from "Brownie Graduates," *The Brownies' Book*, Volume 1, Issue 7, July 1920.

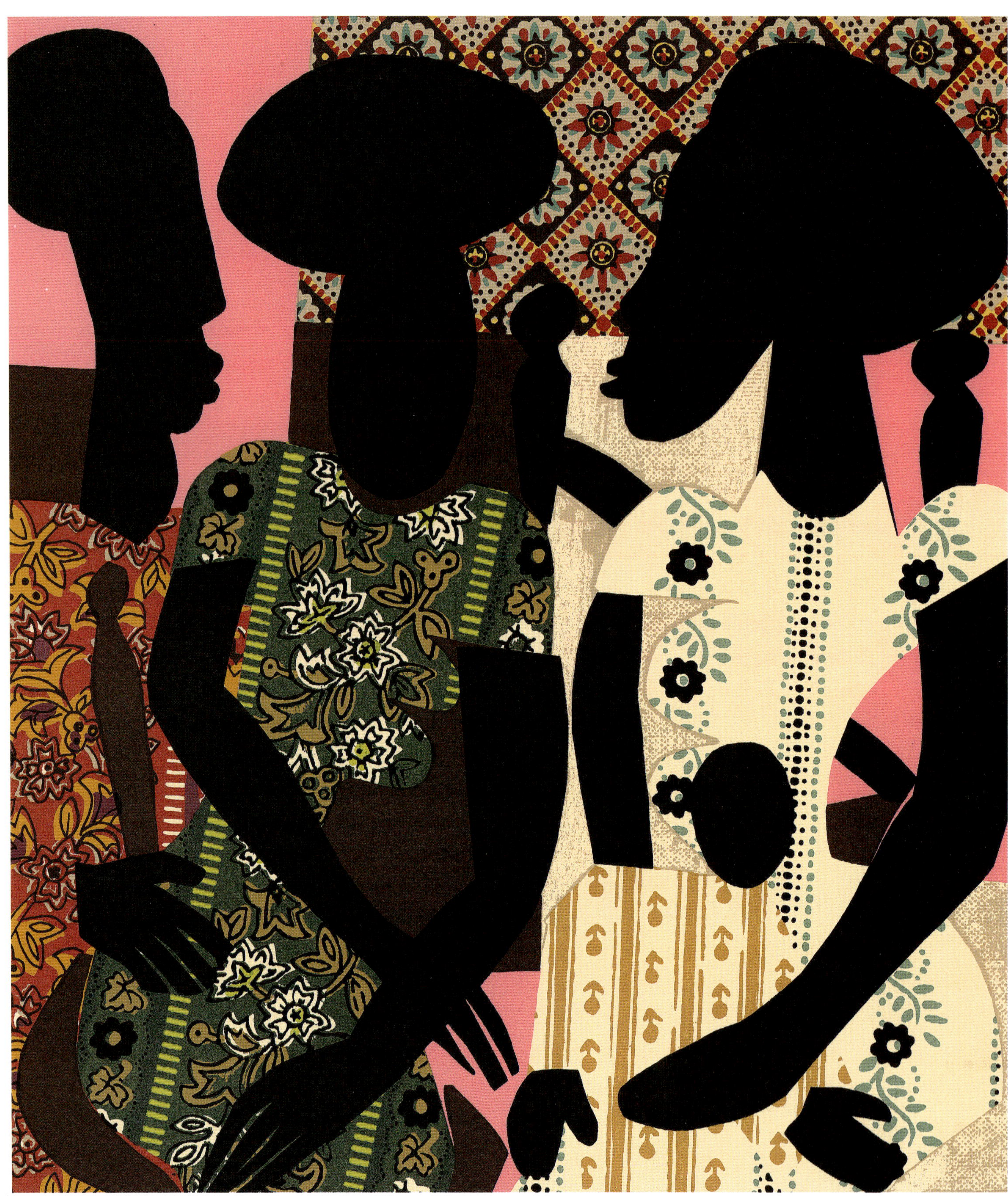

James Denmark, *The Family*
(Collage)

RETROSPECTION

By Yolande Du Bois |

From *The Brownies' Book*, August 1921

I.

THE COLLEGE SPIRIT

If you had stood on our college campus on a certain day last autumn, you might have seen an interesting sight, at least it was a lively one and a happy one to the persons concerned. We, the students of Fisk University, were the persons concerned, and the occasion was a football game with one of our "friendly enemies," a neighboring college.

Down the shaded walk came the boys, perhaps two hundred of them, led by the school band playing a very lively march. When the boys reached the steps of the girls' building they paused to wait, for of course there would have been no fun without the girls. However, they didn't wait long before the girls appeared, laughing, jumping and running down the broad stone steps; clad mostly in sport sweaters and short, wide skirts, they resembled a flock of children all set for mischief. In a way known only to themselves they formed fours behind the band and eagerly awaited the signal to start. This was given as soon as the boys had placed themselves behind the girls, and we all set off across the hilly streets of the town. The homes for blocks around rang with our college yells. Only you who have been to college can know what a wonderful feeling it is to follow your team, your boys, to do battle for you. And as for you who have never been to college, you'll never know how much of all that is worthwhile in life you have missed. ▶

Of course, needless to say, we won by a drop kick, and did we mob the fellow who made that kick? I'll say we did! Back through the town we marched, hilariously happy but still keeping step with the band in front. At last we reached again the broad white steps of the girls' building, just as the sun was touching the distant pines, and with much laughing and waving of pennants the column of boys swung back across the campus through the trees. Those of us who were fortunate enough to have front rooms curled up in the windowsills to watch them out of sight. But what was the matter? At the entrance to the long walk they had stopped; the yells had died down and the band was still. For a moment absolute silence prevailed and the deepening twilight added a certain spirituality to the motionless figures by the gate. Then suddenly came a clear tenor voice—alone for a moment, then the others joined in swelling the sweet sound across the grass. Clearly I could hear the words—*I'm gonna lay down my heavy load down by the riverside, down by the riverside, I'm gonna lay down my heavy load, ain't gonna study war no more.*

Again they sang, still more vigorously—*made my vow to the Lord and never will turn back; I will go, I shall go see what the end will be*—following this by the plaintive words—*Way down yonder by myself, I couldn't hear nobody pray.* As these words died away it became absolutely dark, and in the shadows one could just discern the moving figures. When they had almost

> **" JUST AT THIS MOMENT A SOUND FROM THE INSIDE OF THE BUILDING ATTRACTED ME. "**

disappeared among the trees, the faint, sweet strains of "Mandy Lou, My Mandy Lou" rose on the night air, combining in its melody all the love songs of their race. I had thought all day that at last I had felt the F.U. Spirit, but that night among the hills of Tennessee, as I listened to the strange, weirdly sweet music of my people, I knew that the true Fisk Spirit was only a phase of the World Spirit and the Brotherhood of Man.

And through the harmony of "Mandy Lou" came the words of Whitman: "All the past we leave behind, Fresh and strange the world we see, World of labor and the march, Pioneers, O Pioneers!"

II.
VOICES

Out of the past—into the future they creep—voices, insistent and clear. So I am sure that when at length I stand at the end of the road and earthly shadows fall across my path, my eyes will grow dim, but far ahead the veil will lift, and beyond that I shall hear again—even as of old—the sad, sweet music of the ancient songs of my people. Glad songs, sad songs, songs of sorrow, across the years we will hear them again, we who are singing today. From time immemorial they have been learned and sung by the slaves groping blindly for the light through the hot summer nights.

These the voices, these are our heritage, in them we hear the struggles, the tragedy, the wonderful faith and destiny of a race. With new voices, steady and true, we carry on the old melody to strengthen us, to guide us in our small share of service—each in his own way, some with our hands, some with our minds, some with our lives, and then "They also serve who only stand and wait." And of those, who shall come after, they also shall hear my sad voices, plaintive voices, blessed voices.

III.
SHADOWS

The storm broke fiercely against the walls of Jubilee, crashing among the ancient trees. Alone in a deserted part of the building I lay, broken in spirit, spent with pain. Then at last, as though under a gentle hand, the storm abated and I only heard the patter of the raindrops against the pane. It seemed as if I heard the Singers of Jubilee saying, "I know the Lord has laid His hands on me," for when we are bowed in brief and pain and the shadows close about us, aye and we walk in the valley of the shadow of death, then do our weary, stumbling feet turn towards Our Father. And out of that hopelessness of bodily pain, out of the darkness of the Gethsemane, which leaves its mark on us all; from the edge of eternity comes a wonderful summons, a message of hope.

For we have become as little children and He hath said unto us, 'Suffer little children to come unto Me." Then in the silent cathedral of the night come the angel voices chanting, "I am the Resurrection and the Life." A few moments before it seemed as though the very heavens wept in sympathy with my anguish, but after the fury of the storm was stilled— the rain that fell in Tennessee was tender as a prayer.

IV.
PEACE ON EARTH

I did not awake—I just glided gently from the hand of sleep back to the world. At first I lay perfectly still, wondering what had awakened me. Glancing across the room I could see that my roommate was sound asleep, so I quietly slipped out of bed and climbed up in the window. The world was bathed in moonlight and across our valley to the distant hills was a carpet of pure snow, gleaming crystal clear in the fantastic light. Not a sound could be heard, and as I raised my eyes I noticed a particularly brilliant star; then I remembered. It was Christmas Eve and the Star of Bethlehem shone steadily over the waiting world. Just at this moment a sound from the inside of the building attracted me, and tipping to the door I opened it a crack. Down the dim corridor came what seemed to me to be a column of angels—slim, white-robed figures— and they were singing "Joy to the World." Near they came and passed—fading, fading into the mystic shadows of the far corridors. As I listened I noticed that the room got lighter as though with an eternal light and, hurrying back to the window, I beheld a faint glow in the East. Above, the Star of Bethlehem shone steadfast and true. As I watched the deepening rose in the East, there appeared far below several figures in the snow. After a moment they began to sing. It was the F.U. boys bringing "Merry Christmas" to the girls of Jubilee. Clear and appealing across the snow came their message to us and to you—"In the beauty of the lilies Christ was born across the sea, With a glory in His bosom that transfigures you and me; As He died to make men Holy let us die to make men free." ▶

V.

MAYTIME

In Tennessee among the Cumberland Hills there is a valley. During the autumn and winter it sleeps quietly, but in the spring balmy breezes blow up from the Southland, birds make sweet music in the barren trees, and the silent valley begins to awaken. The walks and the lawns are dotted with trees which gradually become enveloped in a cloud of delicate green tracery. Upon the smooth swells of lawn below they shed the same soft shades of green. Then on the distant hills one can also see terraces of shaded green foliage. Here and there a single pine rises tall and stately, rises against the deep blue and the sky. Here in this beautiful valley I have spent my happiest hours. In the golden sunshine of an afternoon in May you may catch fleeting glimpses of multicolored ruffles as the girls wander in the shade of the wide-spreading trees. The blossom-laden bushes and the pastel colors of the girls' dresses give touches of color to the scene. Then, lastly, you raise your eyes above the trees and you can see the gables and chimneys of the vine-clad buildings which have looked down in quiet dignity on the children of Fisk through the ages.

> **THE BLOSSOM-LADEN BUSHES AND THE PASTEL COLORS OF THE GIRLS' DRESSES GIVE TOUCHES OF COLOR TO THE SCENE.**

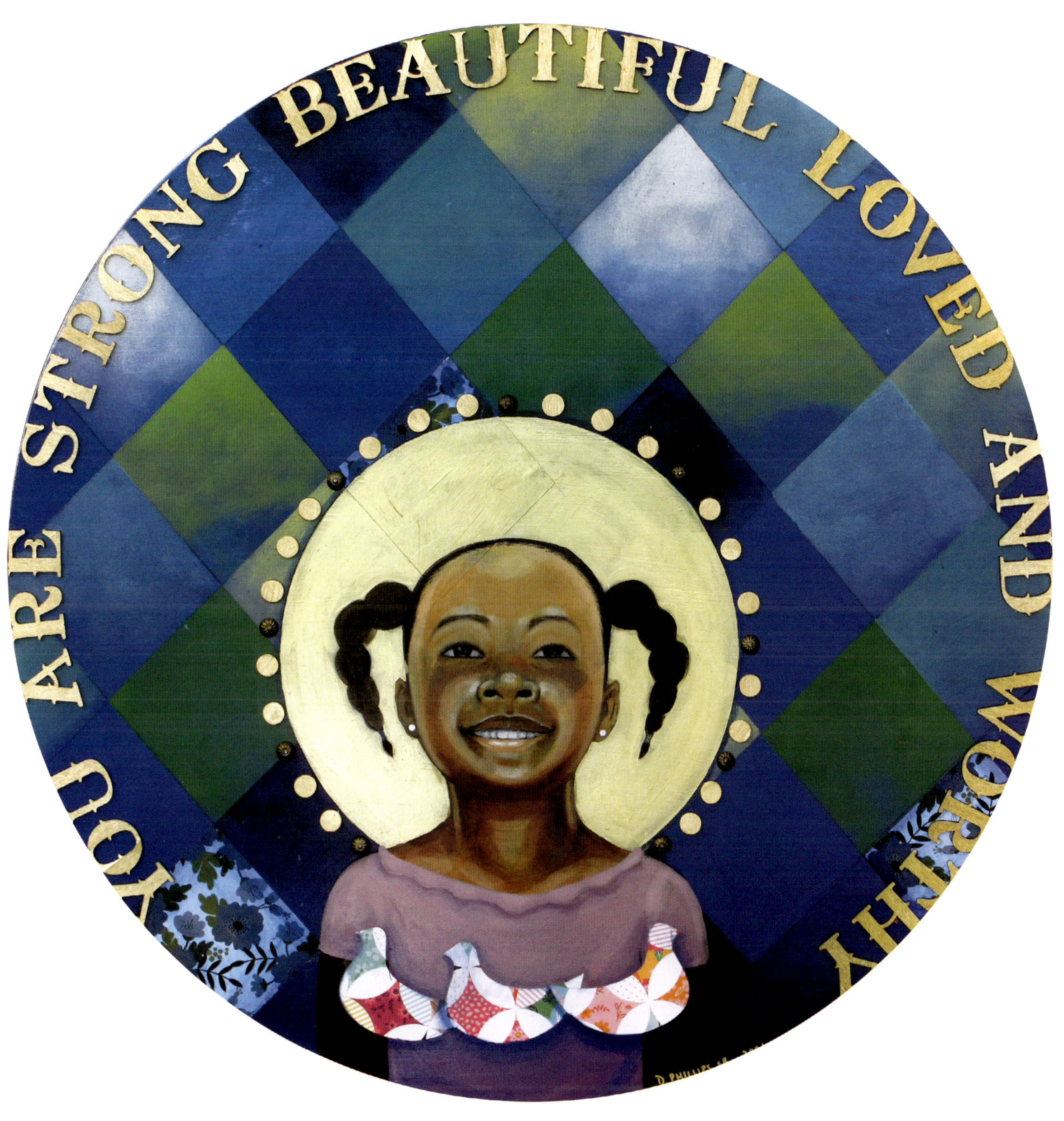

Derrick Phillips, *You Are 2021*
(Wood and acrylic paint)

THE MAKINGS OF A FISK WOMAN

By Amber Curtis | Fisk University, Class of 2022

As a first-generation college student, I was not sure what to expect when I arrived at Fisk. I came from a low socioeconomic background, and both of my parents only have a high school diploma. I did not feel good enough for college, let alone financially prepared. My mom could not afford to take out loans, and the chronic fear of not being able to afford my dreams nearly paralyzed me. Imposter syndrome—a nagging sense of self-doubt and feeling like a fraud—held me back from submitting my application to Fisk up until three days before the deadline.

Since I had walked through the Thomas F. Eagleton Courthouse in St. Louis, I knew I wanted to be a judge. In high school I researched Historically Black Colleges and Universities and that's what led me to Fisk. The university's rich legacy of producing social justice leaders such as John Lewis, W. E. B. Du Bois, Diane Nash, and Nikki Giovanni awakened my passion for fighting for social justice for the marginalized and oppressed. I wanted to soak up the culture and environment of social justice warriors that have left a legacy to be admired and advanced. I wanted to be a Fisk woman that was developed and molded into the powerhouse I knew I could be, taking my place in the world.

My aspirations became a reality when I received my acceptance letter and scholarship.

My first day at Fisk was a downpour. The campus was flooded with an onslaught of rain and mist. Unequipped, I stood in the doorframe of the historic Jubilee Hall, my new home, overlooking the campus. At that very moment, a realization happened; I was home. This was home. From that day on, I knew I belonged and that my journey was awaiting me. I found a family formed of students, professors, faculty, and staff that lifted me and poured into me. Over the last four years, through trials and tribulations, through grit and sacrifice, I can proudly call myself a Fisk woman. My experiences at Fisk have enabled me to stand toe-to-toe with the best in the nation, holding my head high with the knowledge that Fisk has prepared me to stand in any room and know I belong.

After graduation I will work as a litigation paralegal at the prestigious Cravath, Swaine & Moore LLP in New York to gain experience on the road to law school. On the last day that I moved out of Shane Hall, Fisk University's upperclassmen dormitory, a familiar downpour took place. The campus was once again filled with rain and mist, signifying the end of my time at Fisk.

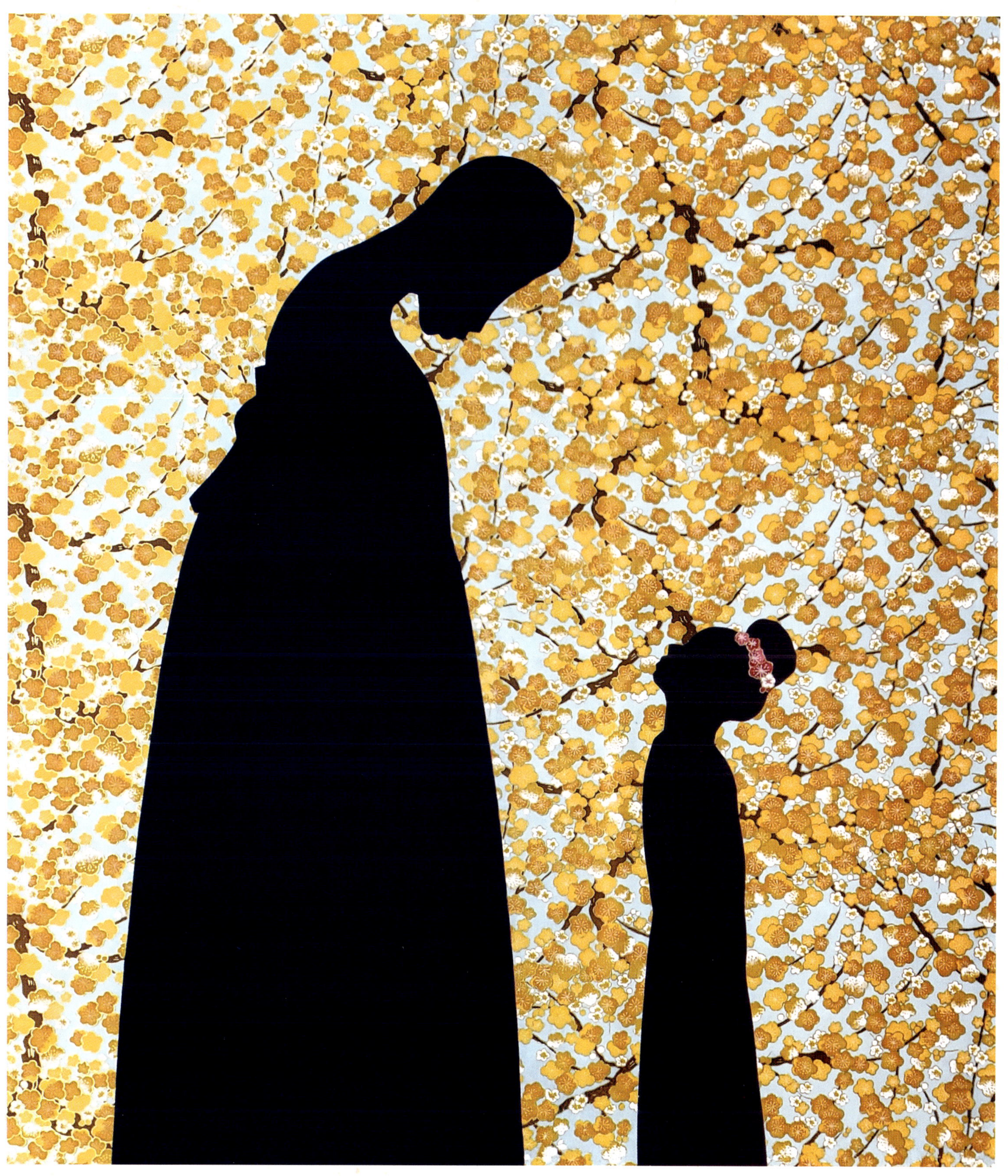

Tracy Murrell, *You Are My Spring* | *I Am Your Fall*
(Paper cut and resin pour)

A THOUSAND WORDS

By Daikerra Sweat | Fisk University, Class of 2023

It has been said that a picture is worth a thousand words. Well, here are a few thousand words that show Nashville, Tennessee, Fisk University, and the community of empowered people empowering people.

I have selected these photos because they speak to the many generations that have contributed to the Black community in some way, shape, or form.

The photo of students in Fisk University sweatshirts: The group of students were HBCU Battle of the Brain participants (including myself). On March 9, 2022, Fisk-ites flew to Austin, Texas, to represent Fisk University at the weeklong HBCU Battle of the Brains Competition at SXSW, majorly sponsored by the National Football League (NFL). Fisk emerged first out of thirty colleges, winning more than $80,000. The students participated in a twenty-four-hour technology-and-problem-solving competition (hack-a-thon), which lasted from 7 a.m. on Friday to 7 a.m. on Saturday. They invented an innovative solution (and built an app!) that connects HBCU student talent to opportunities in the sports industry.

The Fisk University Historic Marker: This speaks volumes in helping those who may not be familiar with Fisk understand the history and importance of the illustrious Historically Black College and University.

The picture with the students on the stairs: This image represents students leaving the dawn dance. The Fisk University Easter dawn dance was a dance for Fisk-ites to gather and celebrate life.

The image of Nashville: This image was taken at the Nashville Black Market, also known as the New Black Wall Street. This is an event that happens every first Friday of the month on Rosa L. Parks Boulevard. This event highlights and showcases Black talent and Black businesses and gives the Black community a chance to be creative in spaces that are made for them.

The image of William Edward Burghardt Du Bois: This bronze statue of W. E. B. Du Bois is located on the grounds of Fisk University. The civil rights activist was a student at Fisk from 1885 to 1888 and went on to become a cofounder of the NAACP.

The image of the Jubilee Singers: The Fisk Jubilee Singers are vocal artists and students who sing and travel worldwide. The original Fisk Jubilee Singers introduced "slave songs" to the world in 1871 and were instrumental in preserving this unique American musical tradition known today as Negro spirituals, raising funds to keep Fisk University alive and thriving.

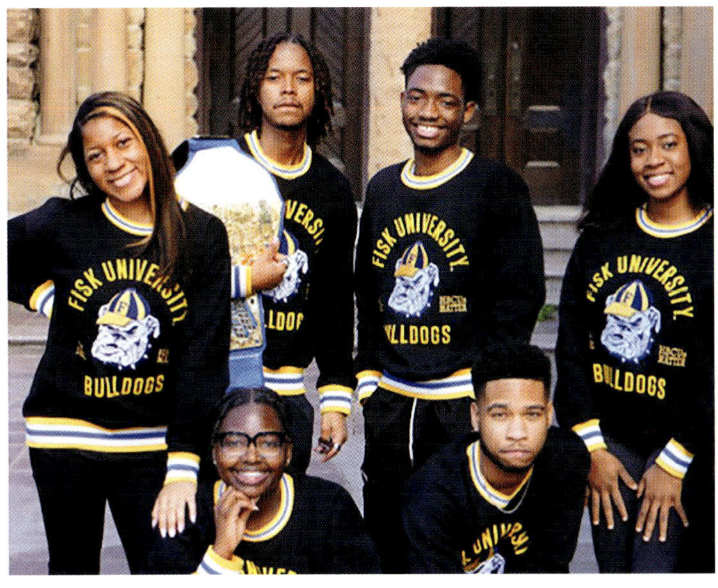

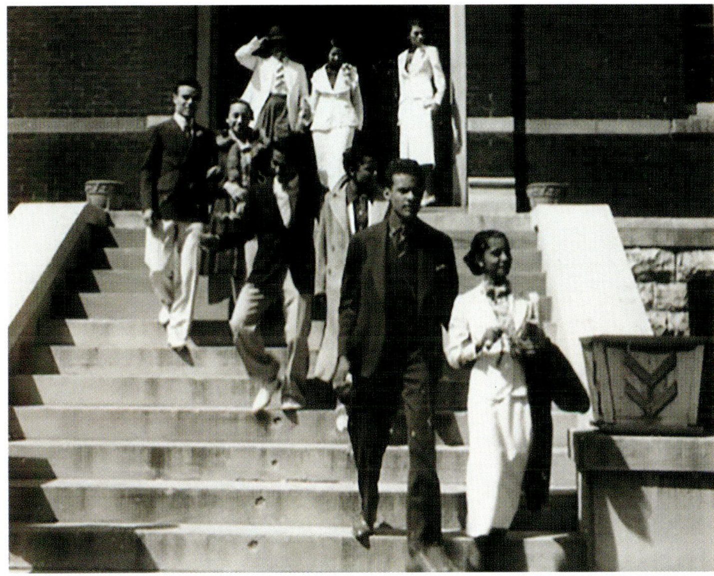

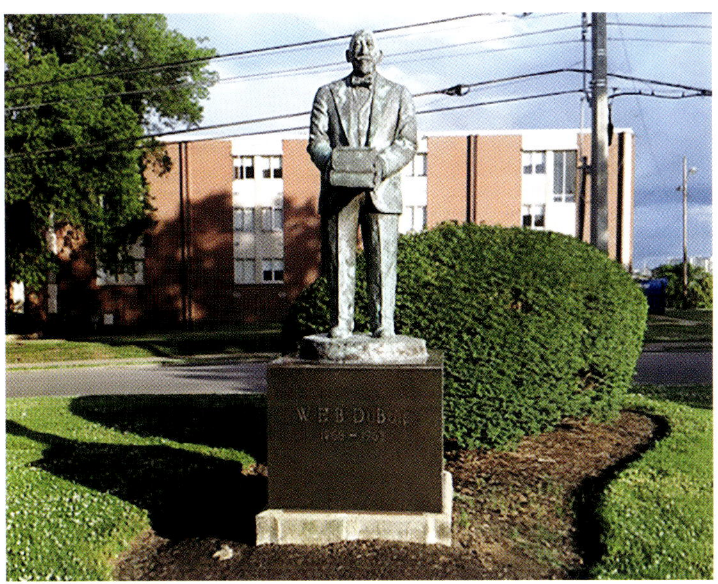

W.E.B. DuBois
1868 - 1963

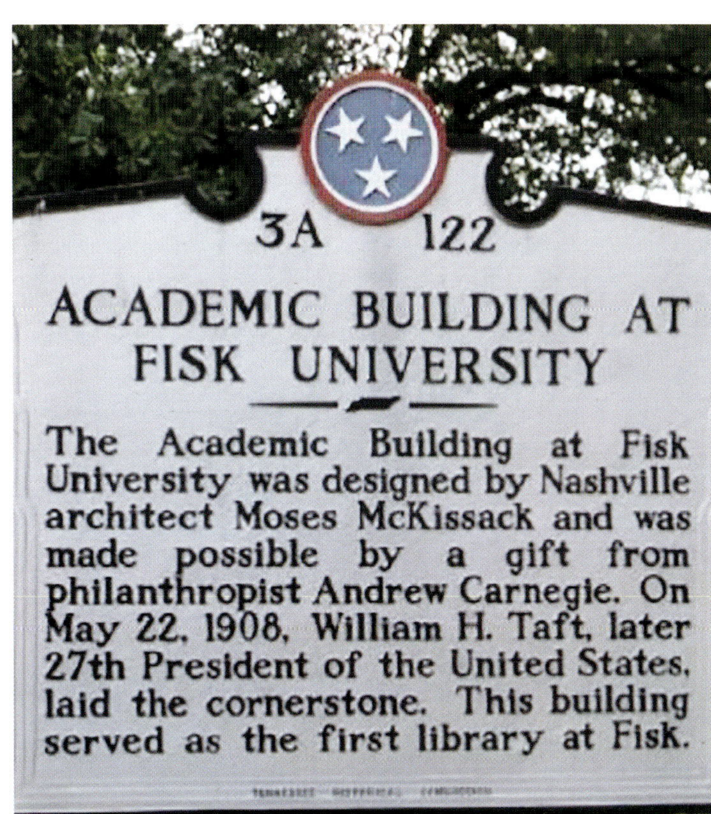

3A 122
ACADEMIC BUILDING AT FISK UNIVERSITY
The Academic Building at Fisk University was designed by Nashville architect Moses McKissack and was made possible by a gift from philanthropist Andrew Carnegie. On May 22, 1908, William H. Taft, later 27th President of the United States, laid the cornerstone. This building served as the first library at Fisk.

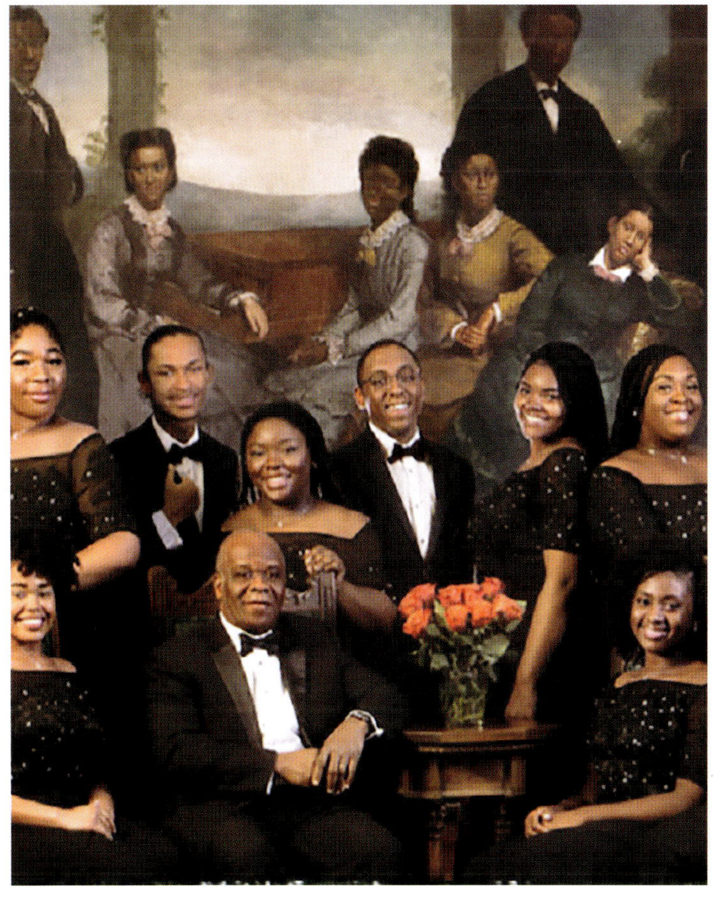

SHE'ROES

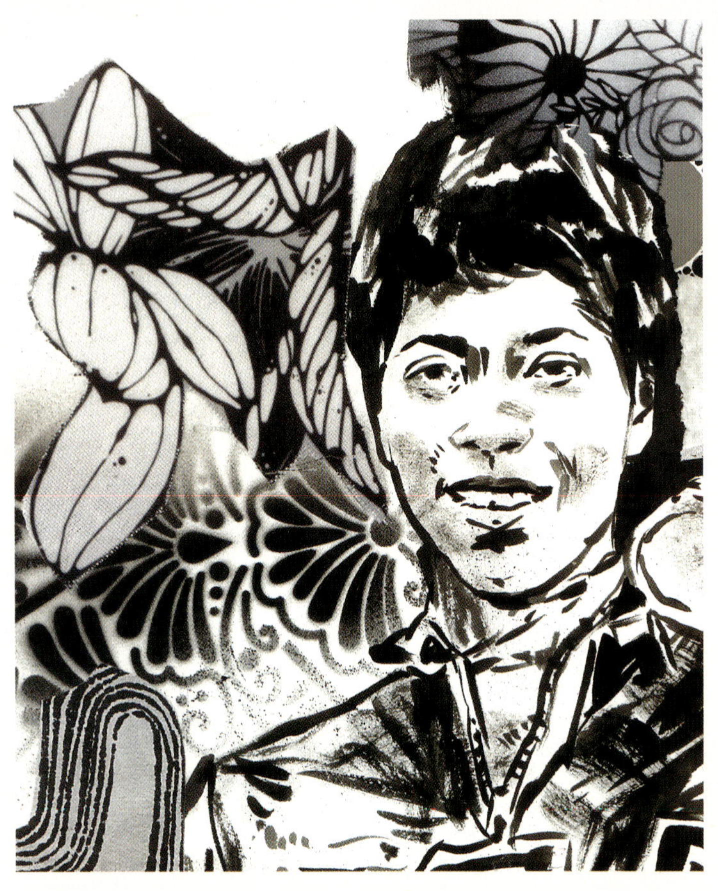
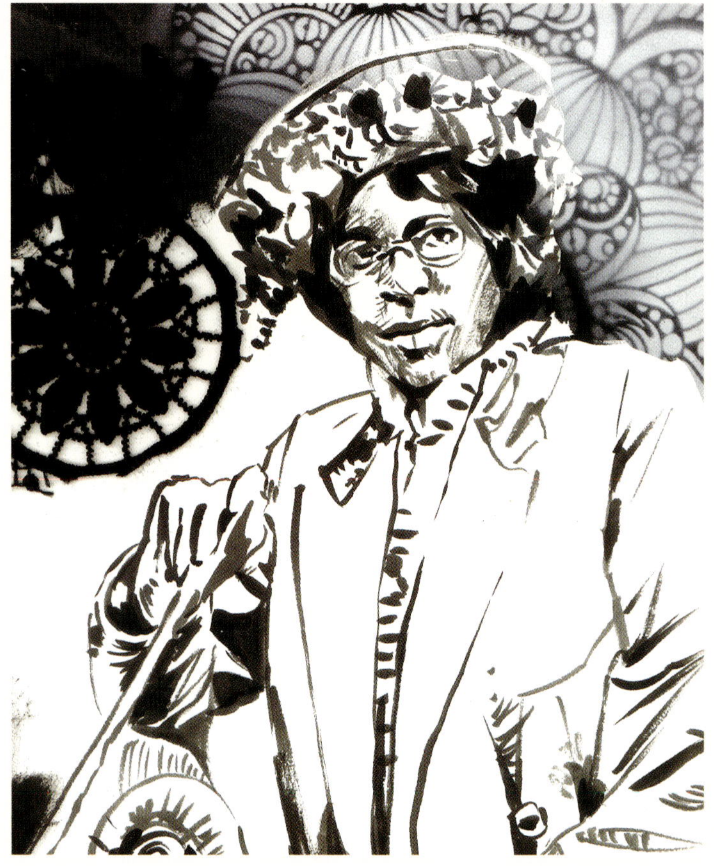
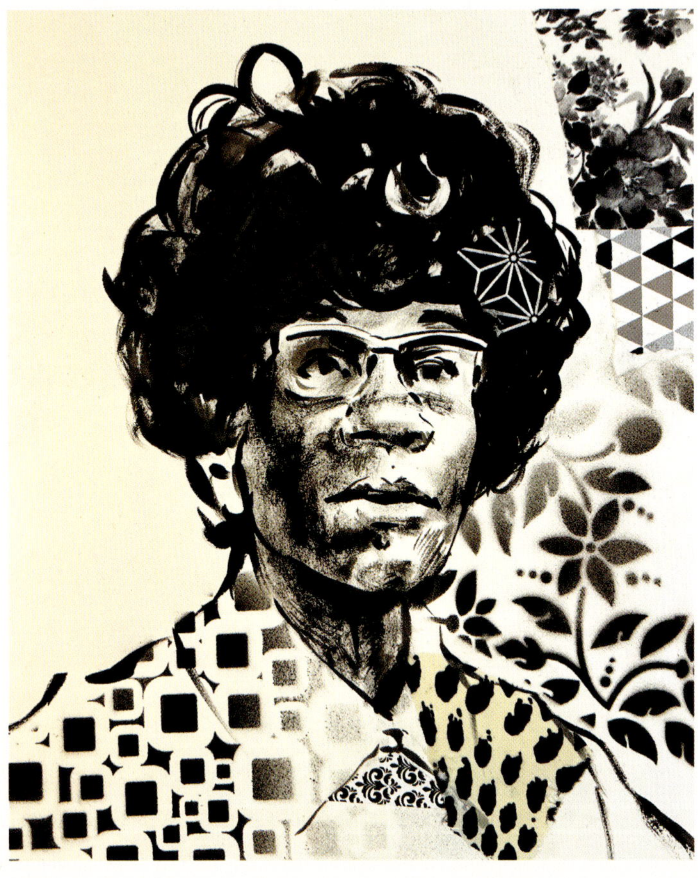
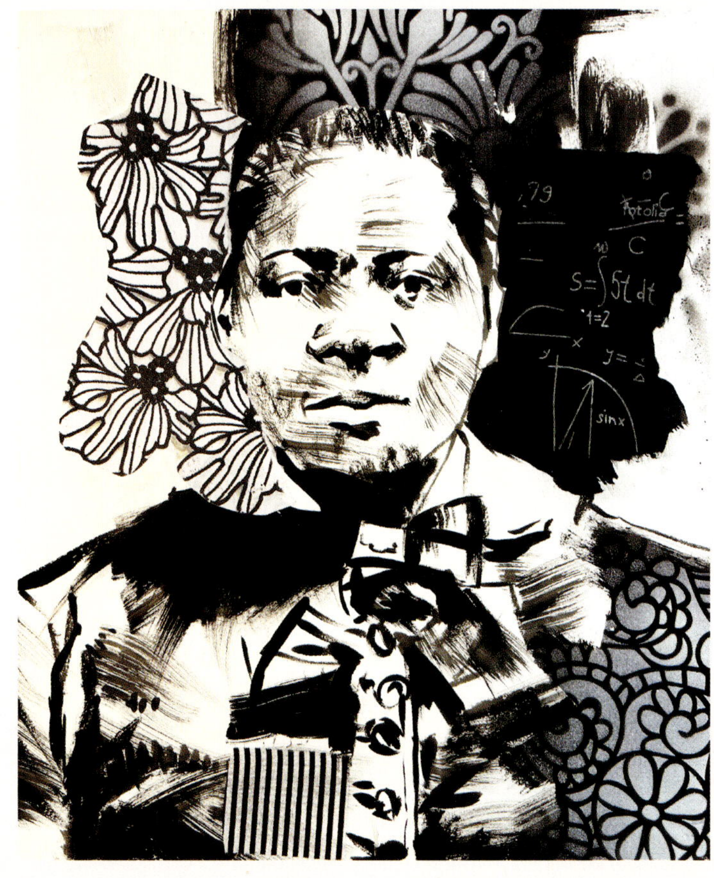

PORTRAITS AND BIOGRAPHIES

Written by Karida L. Brown | Artwork by Charly Palmer

Wilma Rudolph
(1940–1994)

Wilma Rudolph was born in Saint Bethlehem, Tennessee, in 1940, and contracted a disease called polio at the age of five. She lost strength in her left leg and wore a medical brace until she was twelve years old. Nevertheless, she became one of the greatest athletes in history! Rudolph began training in track and field events as a teenager. After winning a bronze medal in the 1956 Olympic Games, Rudolph won three events at the 1960 Olympics in Rome, Italy, making her the first American woman to win three or more gold medals at a single Olympics.

Shirley Chisholm
(1924–2005)

Shirley Chisholm was born in 1924. Despite facing discrimination throughout her life due to her race and gender, she never gave up on her mission of pursuing justice through politics. She rose to become the first Black congresswoman in American history! Chisholm's ambition served as an example for those around her. She was the first woman and the first Black American to run for president as a Democrat. She developed a comprehensive platform of social justice initiatives, ranging from education reform to better protections for low-income citizens. And she published an acclaimed autobiography, *Unbought and Unbossed*, which told the story of her time in office.

Charlotte Hawkins Brown
(1883–1961)

Charlotte Hawkins Brown was born in Henderson, North Carolina, in 1883 and moved with her family to Boston, Massachusetts, as a child. As an adult, Brown dedicated her life to educating Black children in the South. In 1902 she opened the Palmer Memorial Institute in Sedalia, North Carolina, and provided quality education for African American children—a rarity due to Jim Crow laws and racial prejudice. Brown's passionate pursuit of education made her a leader in her community as she worked to provide every child with opportunities for learning and growth.

Biddy Mason
(1818–1891)

Enslaved at birth in 1818, Biddy Mason overcame adversity to become a successful real estate mogul, nurse, midwife, and philanthropist. Brought to Los Angeles by her "owner," Mason learned that slavery was illegal in California and successfully petitioned the Los Angeles court system to declare her and her children free. Mason was an impressive entrepreneur and a generous leader. She worked as a nurse and midwife, delivering thousands of babies, and invested her savings in real estate; she then donated the land for the first African Methodist Episcopal church in the city and set aside another parcel for an elementary school for African American children.

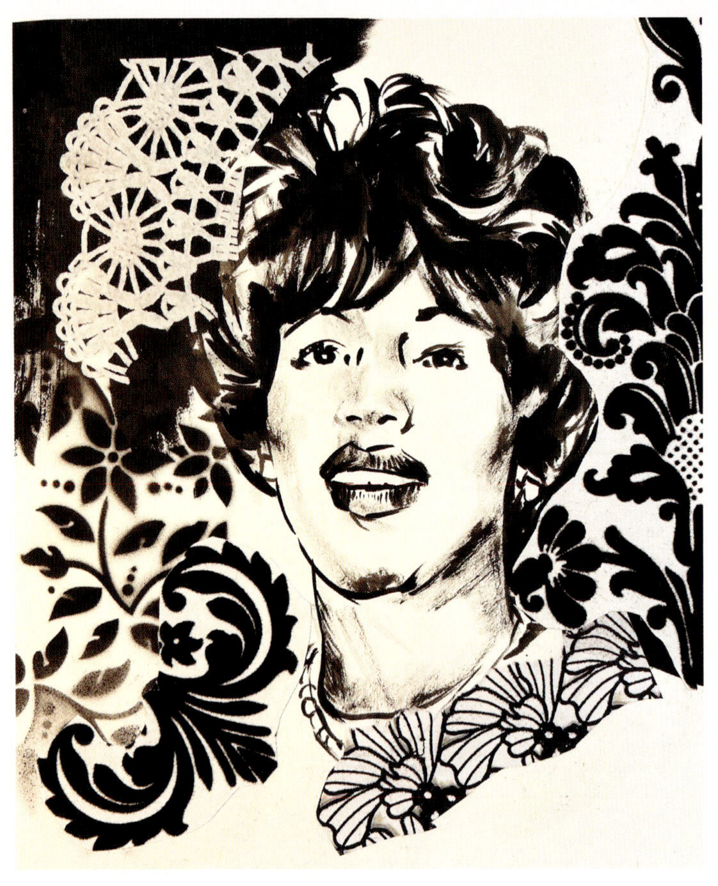
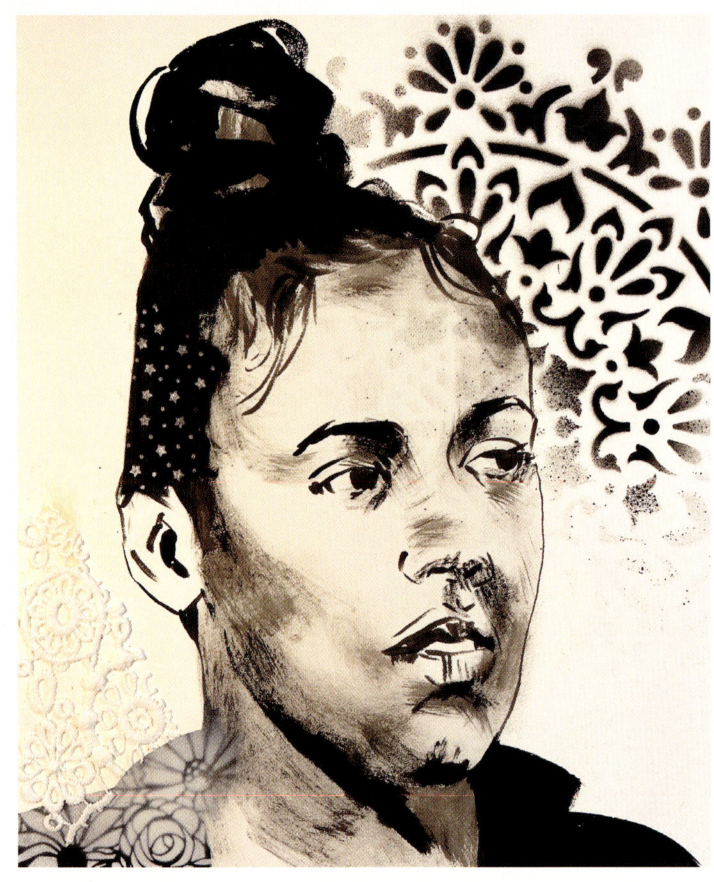
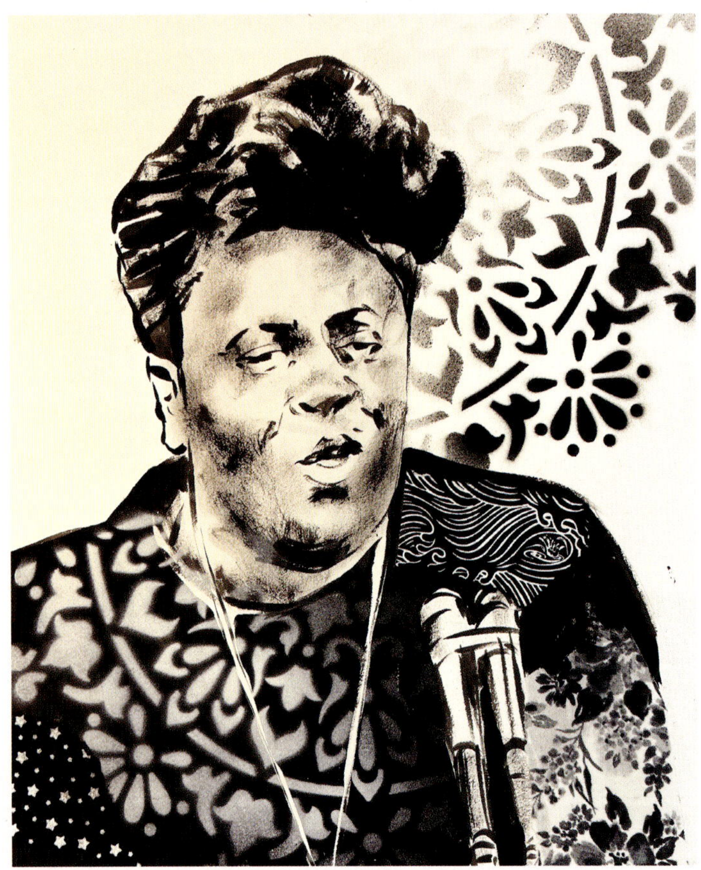
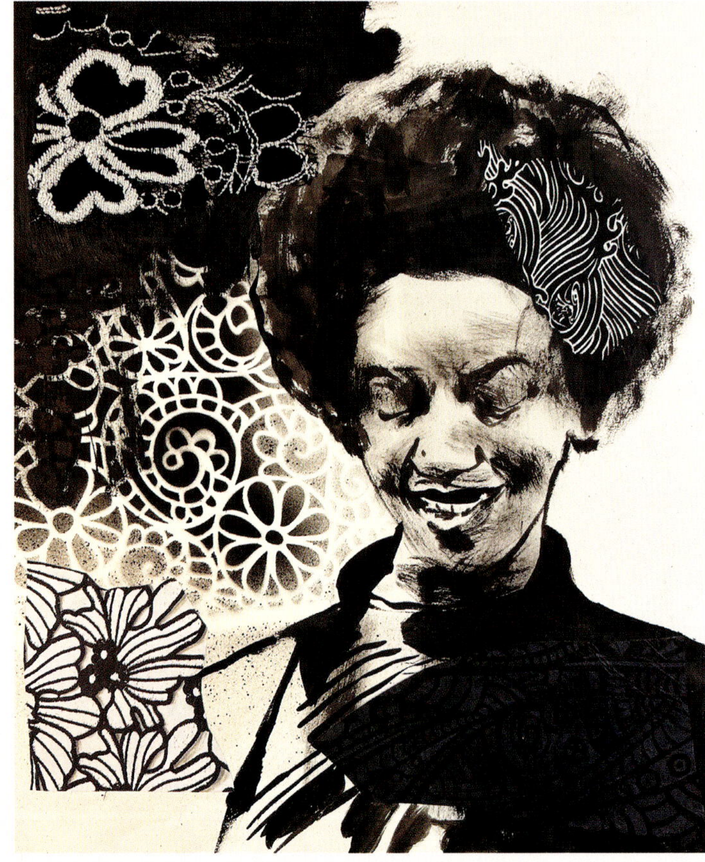

Vivian Malone Jones
(1942–2005)

Born in Mobile, Alabama, Vivian Malone Jones was a Civil Rights Movement trailblazer. Prior to 1963, the University of Alabama refused to admit Black students. Jones broke that barrier; she and James Hood were the university's first Black students. They faced extreme racism and intimidation on campus, including a public protest led by segregationist Alabama governor George Wallace. That did not stop Vivian Malone Jones. In 1965 she became the first African American person to graduate from the University of Alabama. After graduation Jones earned a master's degree in public administration from George Washington University. She worked for the federal government in many roles, including as the Director of Civil Rights and Urban Affairs and Director of Environmental Justice.

Fannie Lou Hamer
(1917–1977)

Fannie Lou Hamer was born in rural Mississippi in 1917. She became an activist in the Civil Rights Movement, fighting tirelessly for Black citizens' right to vote and to receive equal treatment under the law. She became a member of the Mississippi Freedom Democratic Party and made history by challenging the Mississippi Democratic Party's all-white delegation at the 1964 Democratic National Convention. Fannie Lou Hamer's powerful voice and tireless advocacy helped to ensure that the issue of voting rights was brought to national attention. Her speech at the convention, in which she talked about being beaten and jailed for standing up for her rights, remains one of the most powerful addresses in American political history.

Elaine Brown
(1943–)

Born in 1943, Elaine Brown is an American activist, author, and singer-songwriter. Throughout her life, she passionately pursued Black liberation. She was chair of the Black Panther Party from 1974 to 1977, during its most turbulent years, when it battled repression at home and sought diplomatic recognition abroad. Brown also wrote several books about the Black Panther Party and her experiences as a Black woman in America. Through her commitment to speaking truth through political organizing and activism, Elaine Brown demonstrates the strength of our communities when we stand together against oppression and strive for collective liberation from all forms of injustice.

Nikki Giovanni
(1943–)

Nikki Giovanni is an African American poet, fiction writer, and social critic. She was born in 1943 in Knoxville, Tennessee, and raised in Cincinnati, Ohio. She is also a proud alumna of Fisk University in Nashville, Tennessee. Giovanni has always been passionate about writing. Her work, both lyrical and prose, focuses on the struggles and desires of Black women. Her books have earned her international acclaim over the course of her career, in addition to commercial success—three of her poetry collections have been *New York Times* bestsellers. She uses her platform to stand up against injustices—such as poverty, racism, and sexism—while also creating works of art that celebrate the beauty and joy of Black womanhood.

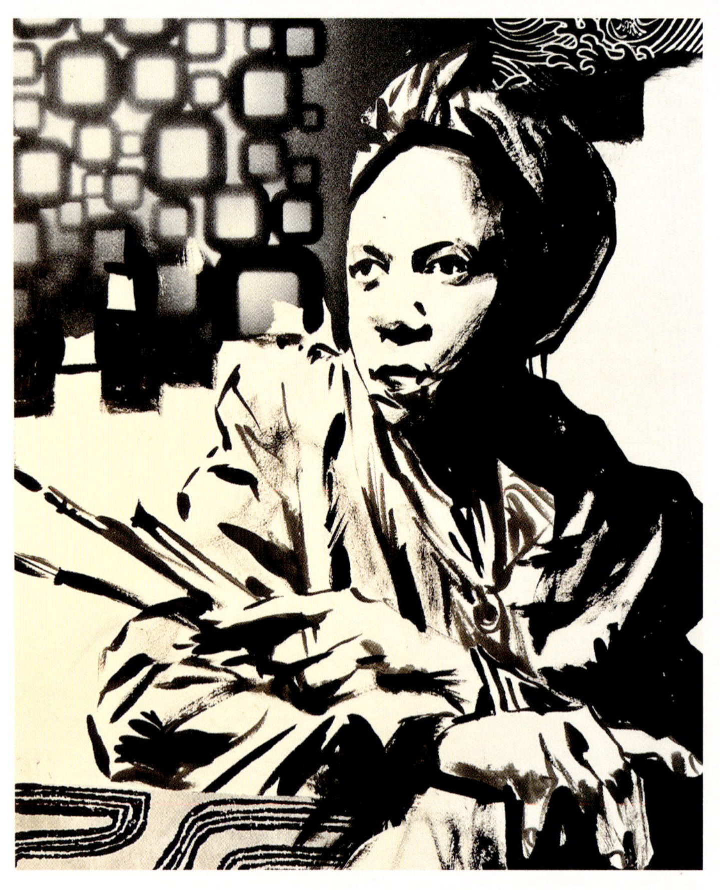
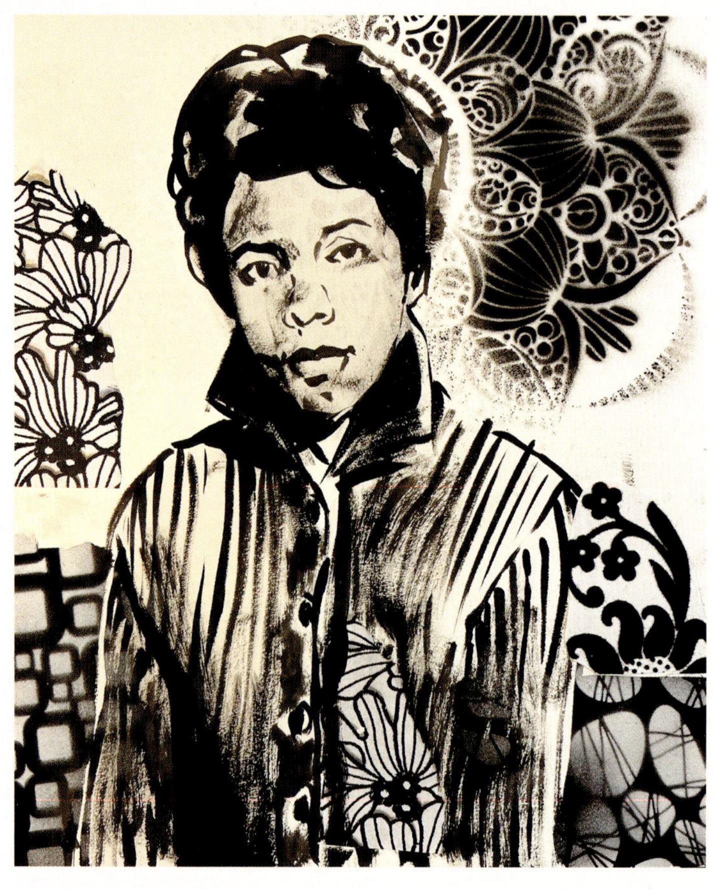
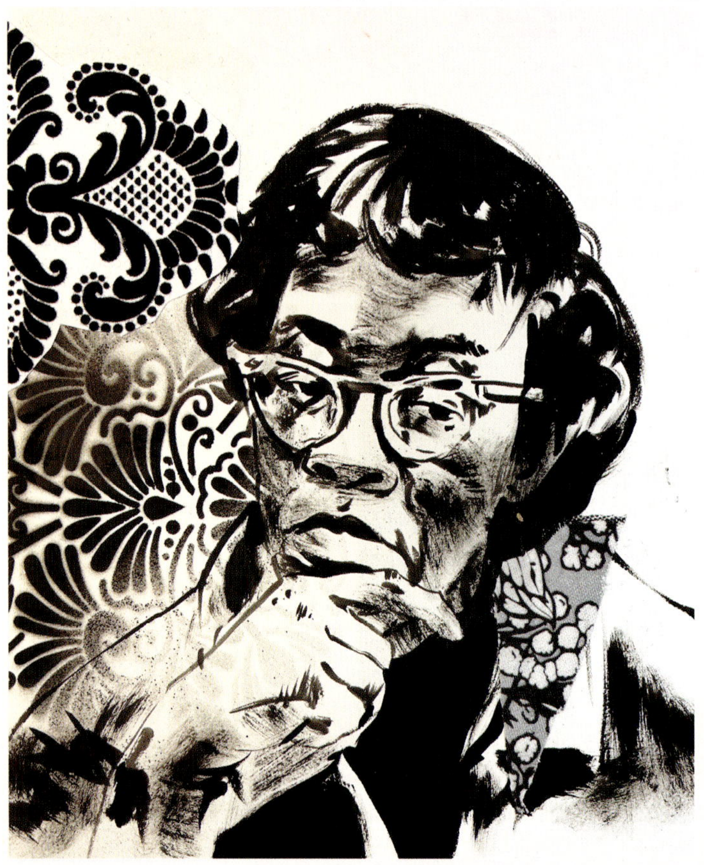
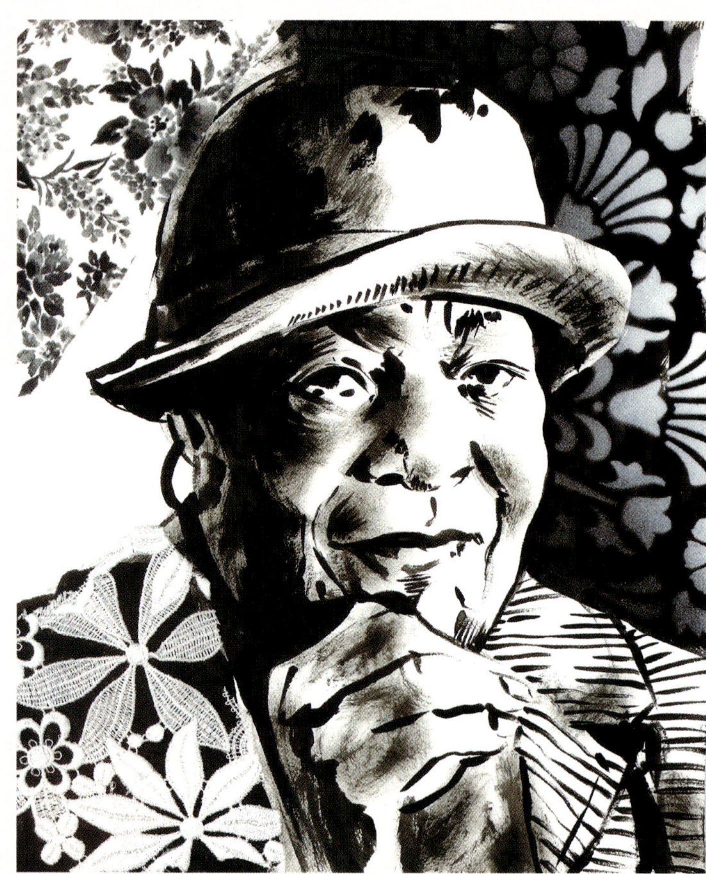

Margaret Taylor-Burroughs
(1915–2010)

Margaret Taylor-Burroughs was born in 1915 in St. Rose, Louisiana. Despite facing discrimination on many fronts, she steadfastly pursued her passion for the arts and culture, lifting up the work of her community. An artist herself, she dedicated much of her time to creating opportunities for other Black artists whose works were often overlooked or excluded from mainstream museums, galleries, and art programs. In 1961 she cofounded the Ebony Museum of Negro History and Art (now the DuSable Black History Museum and Education Center) in Chicago, an acclaimed center for Black art and history. Burroughs's lifelong mission to introduce Black art into the mainstream art world opened many doors for young artists and art professionals.

Gwendolyn Brooks
(1917–2000)

Gwendolyn Brooks was a leading poet and writer of the twentieth century. She was born in Topeka, Kansas, in 1917, but when she was only six weeks old, she moved to Chicago, Illinois, where she spent the rest of her life. Brooks created beautiful poetry and prose about everyday Black life in the South Side of Chicago. Brooks's masterpiece *Annie Allen* won the Pulitzer Prize for Poetry in 1950, making her the first Black person to win a Pulitzer. Through this book and her subsequent works, she shared her own story and highlighted the experiences of African Americans throughout history.

Lorraine Hansberry
(1930–1965)

Lorraine Hansberry was an African American playwright. Born and raised in Chicago, Hansberry eventually moved to New York City, where she rose to fame as the first Black woman to have a play produced on Broadway. Hansberry married, and eventually divorced, Robert Nemiroff—but she wrote privately of her romantic relationships with women. She used her platform to stand up against racism while also creating rich works of art that provided insight into the complexities of Black life. Her most notable work, *A Raisin in the Sun*, remains one of the most beloved plays in American history. When Hansberry died of pancreatic cancer at the age of thirty-four, Nemiroff adapted some of her writings into a play, *To Be Young, Gifted and Black*. (The work inspired legendary singer Nina Simone to write a song of the same name.)

Samella Lewis
(1923–2022)

New Orleans–born Dr. Samella Sanders Lewis was a pioneering painter, printmaker, art historian, writer, publisher, curator, and educator with a distinguished career spanning six decades. Lewis is remembered for advocating for equality in the fine art world. In 1975, she founded an arts journal, the *International Review of African American Art*, and the next year she launched the Museum of African American Art in Los Angeles. Throughout her career she taught art history at numerous institutions, including Scripps College, where she went on to become chairperson of the art department. After inspiring thousands of young artists, Lewis passed away peacefully at age ninety-nine.

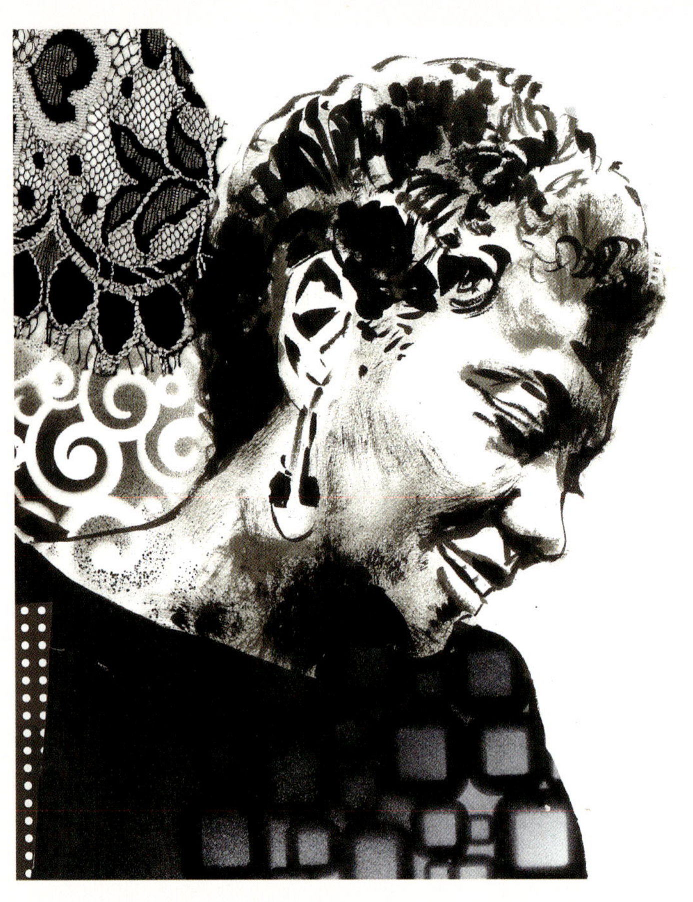
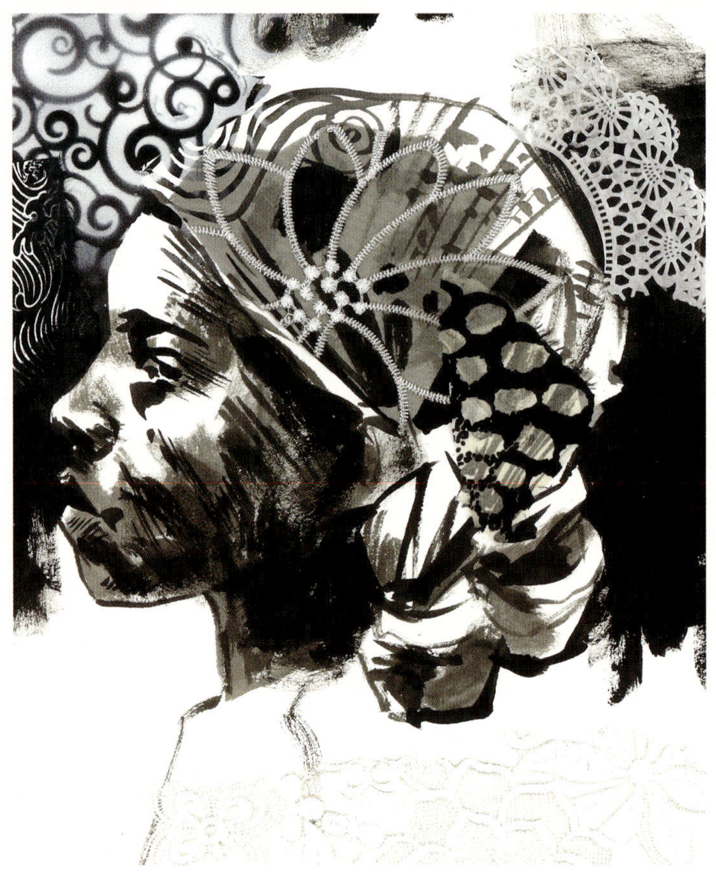
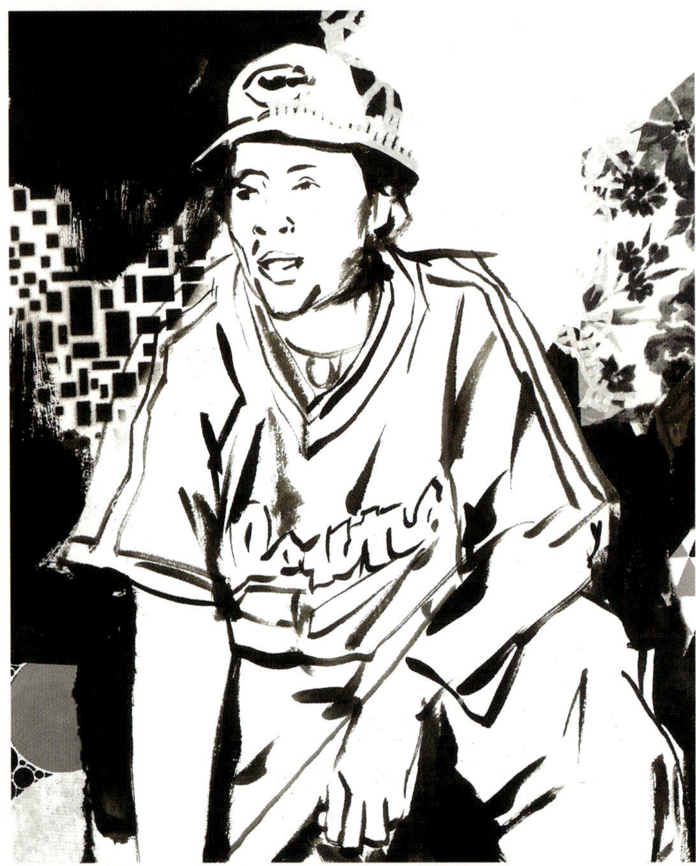
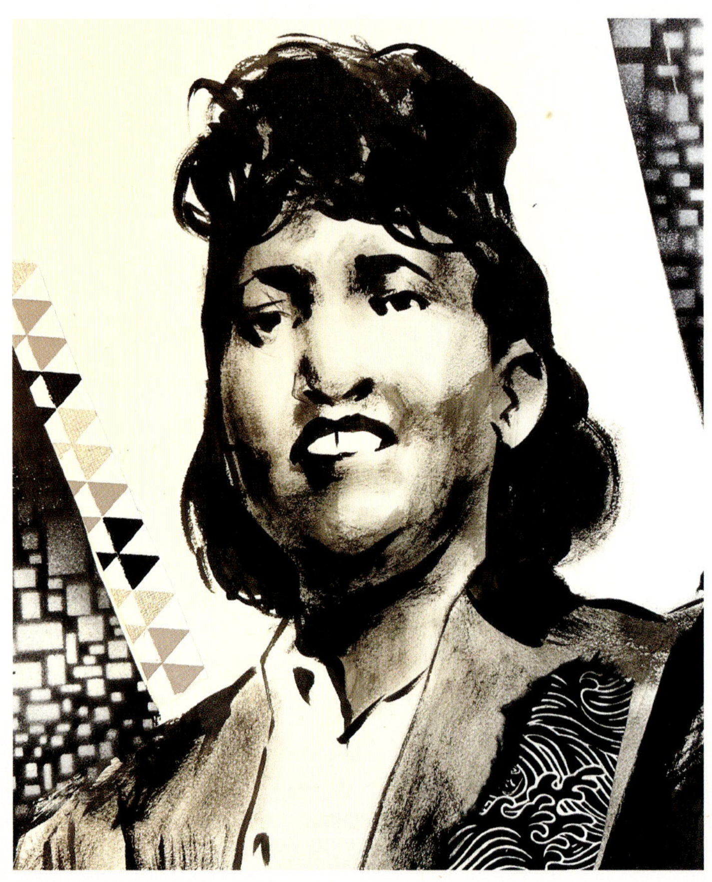

June Jordan
(1936–2002)

June Jordan was one of the most influential Black feminist writers of the twentieth century. The award-winning author and poet wrote about civil rights, race, and gender with a unique blend of intellect and passion. She proudly proclaimed herself to be bisexual in her writing, both poetry and prose. Her work often centered on the African American experience, but she also promoted and solidarity with marginalized people around the world. Born in 1936 to immigrant parents in New York City, Jordan was raised in Brooklyn and earned her bachelor's degree from Barnard College. Throughout her career, she taught writing and literature at numerous institutions, including Yale University and Sarah Lawrence College. In 1988, became a professor of African American Studies at UC Berkeley, where she founded the groundbreaking arts activism program Poetry for the People.

Connie Morgan
(1935–1996)

In the 1950s, Philadelphia native Connie Morgan became the third woman to become a professional Negro American League baseball player. She played for the Indianapolis Clowns, which also employed Toni Stone and Mamie "Peanut" Johnson, for one season before retiring. Morgan spent the remainder of her career at the largest labor union in the United States, the American Federation of Labor and Congress of Industrial Organizations (AFL-CIO). Although she did not stay in the Negro League for long, her contributions to the sport opened doors for generations of women in professional sports. In 1995 she was posthumously inducted into the Pennsylvania Sports Hall of Fame.

Ntozake Shange
(1948–2018)

Ntozake Shange was a dramatist and poet born in Trenton, New Jersey, on October 18, 1948. An ardent Black feminist and an incredible innovator, Shange's poetry and stage productions pushed the boundaries of genre and form. In 1975, she took Broadway by storm with her play *For Colored Girls Who Have Considered Suicide/When the Rainbow Is Enuf.* Shange won an Obie award for the production, which featured seven women actors who combined dance and poetry to great effect. Shange died in 2018, but her life and work continue to inspire artists to take risks, face difficult emotions head-on, and make art on their own terms.

Henrietta Lacks
(1920–1951)

Born in Virginia in 1920, Henrietta Lacks was diagnosed with cervical cancer in 1951. Despite undergoing treatment at Johns Hopkins hospital, she passed away at just thirty-one years old. However, she left behind a legacy that changed the course of modern medicine forever. Lacks's cells were collected without her knowledge and used in the first steps toward developing a cure for cancer. Now known as "HeLa" cells, hers were the first human cells to be successfully grown in a laboratory, and they have been used in countless medical breakthroughs since. Lacks's daughter, Deborah, worked tirelessly to raise awareness of her mother's story, fighting to ensure that her mother was given the recognition she deserved.

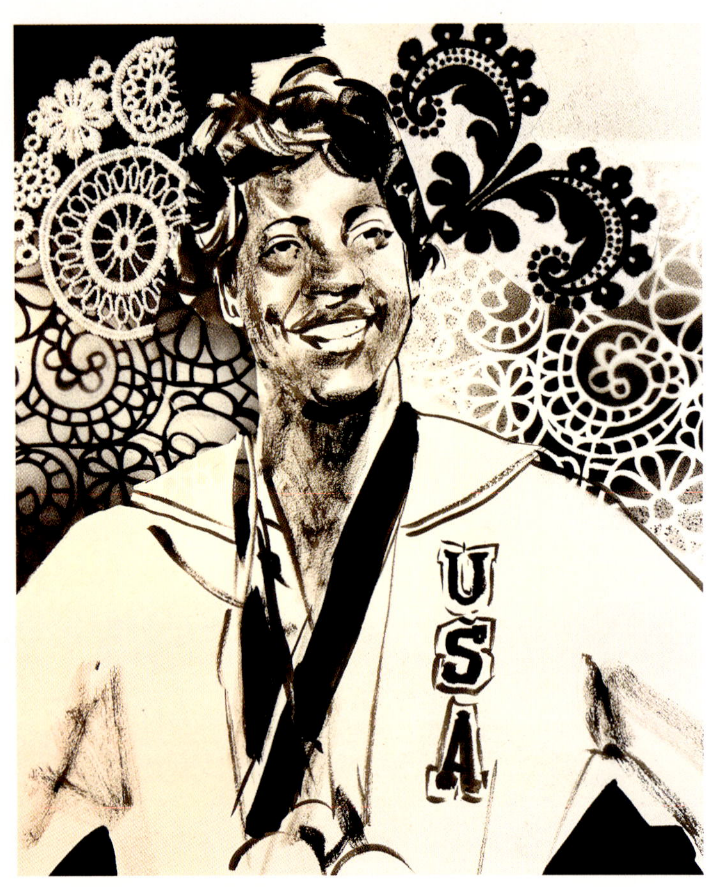
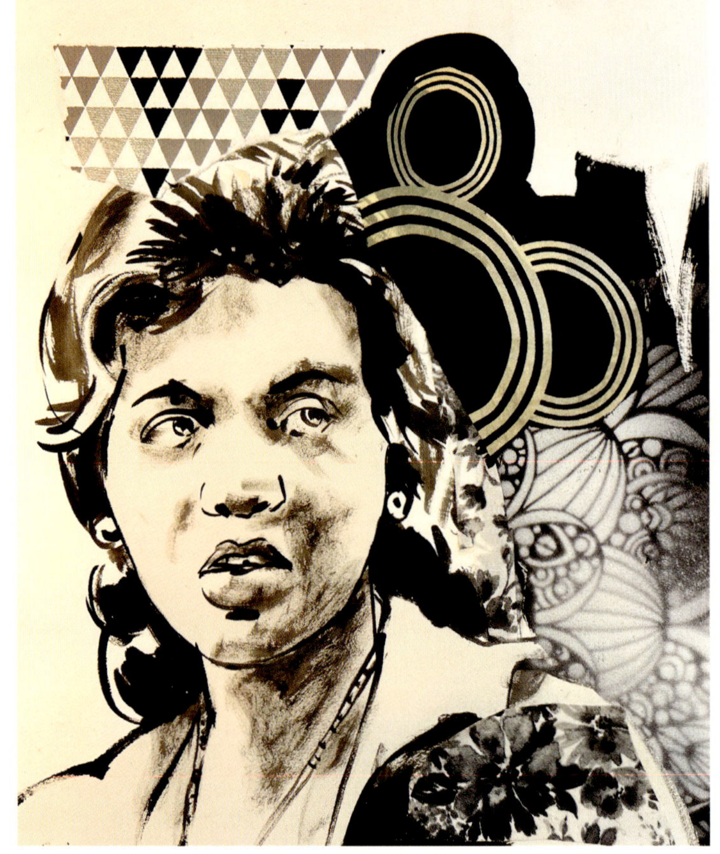
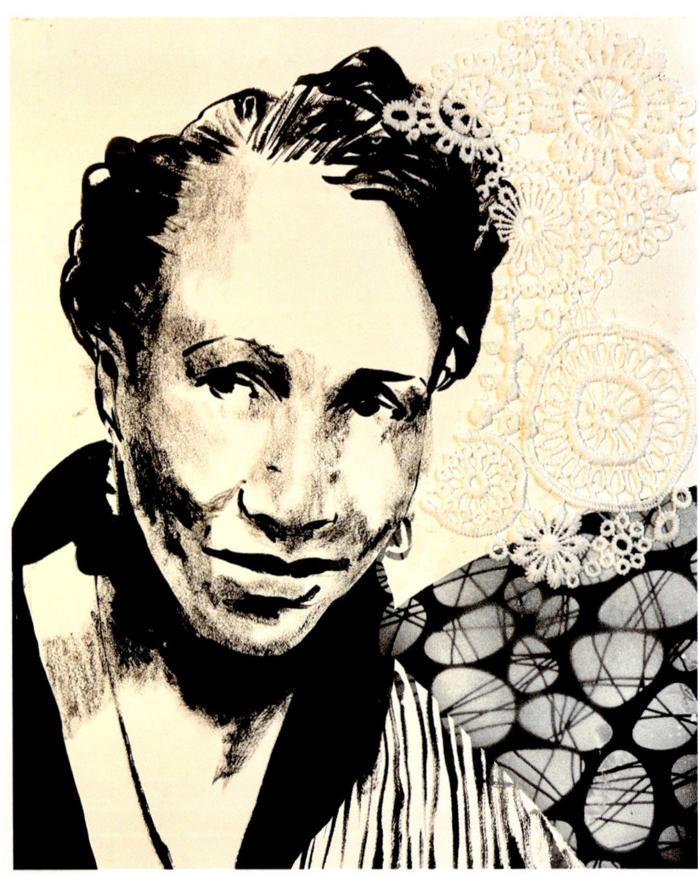
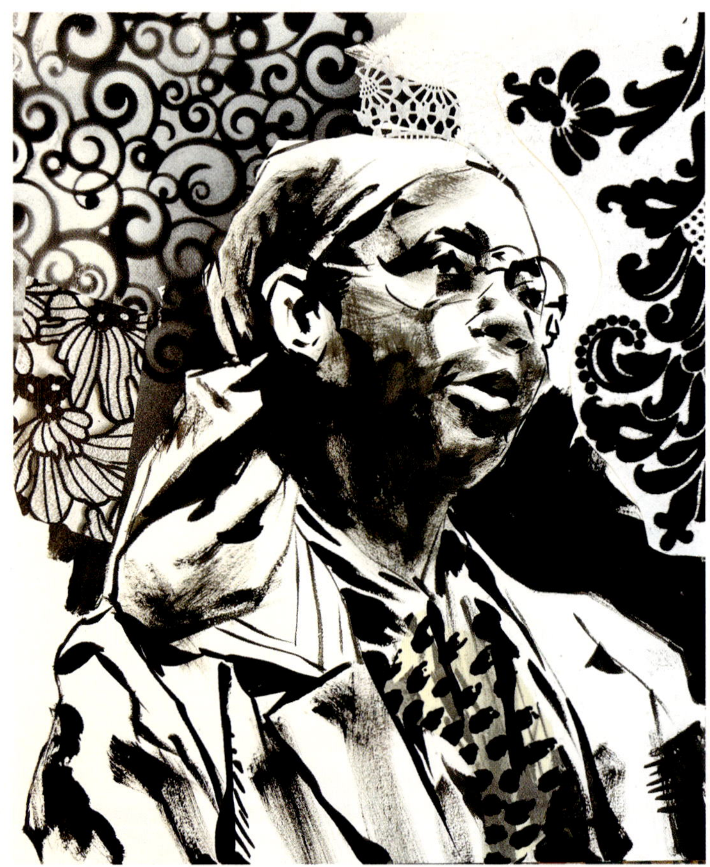

Althea Gibson
(1927–2003)

Althea Gibson was an extraordinary athlete whose courage and determination changed the face of professional sports forever. She was born in 1927 in South Carolina, and she fell in love with tennis at a young age. Despite facing discrimination and racism, she trained hard and excelled at the sport. In 1956 Gibson became the first Black person to win a Grand Slam title. Her victory inspired generations of future Black women tennis players, including Venus and Serena Williams! Gibson's legacy has continued to live on since she passed away in 2003, through the programs established by the Althea Gibson Foundation, which offer tennis-playing opportunities to children who otherwise would not have the resources to participate.

Shirley Graham Du Bois
(1896–1977)

Shirley Graham Du Bois was a composer, playwright, author, and activist. She earned a bachelor's degree from Oberlin College in 1934 and a master's degree in music a year later. She also married none other than W. E. B. Du Bois! While at Oberlin, she produced *Tom-Tom*, the very first opera composed, produced, and performed by Black Americans and later wrote multiple award-winning books for young adults. Du Bois became increasingly involved in political activism, advocating for Black women's rights, racial equality, anti-imperialism, and the denuclearization of the Western world. In 1961, she and W. E. B. Du Bois immigrated to Ghana, where she served as special advisor to the president of Ghana, Kwame Nkrumah, and the inaugural director of Ghana's public broadcasting network.

Diane Nash
(1938–)

Diane Nash is a civil rights icon. Born in 1938 to a middle-class family in Illinois, she attended Fisk University in Nashville, Tennessee, where she became deeply involved in the Civil Rights Movement. She organized sit-ins with fellow student John Lewis, and helped plan the 1961 Freedom Rides, which aimed to end segregation on public transportation. Nash dedicated herself to fighting oppression and injustice as a member of the Student Nonviolent Coordinating Committee (SNCC). She was a leader in Martin Luther King Jr.'s Southern Christian Leadership Conference (SCLC) during his march from Selma to Montgomery. She is known for her tireless efforts for social justice and her dedication to nonviolent activism.

Gayl Jones
(1949–)

Gayl Jones is an acclaimed novelist known for her evocative storytelling and lyrical prose. Born in 1949 in Lexington, Kentucky, she earned both her master's and doctorate in creative writing from Brown University. Toni Morrison, who was a book editor as well as a literary genius in her own right, published Jones's first novel, *Corregidora*, which catapulted her onto the national literary stage when she was only twenty-five years old. Jones has dedicated her life to writing about the complexities of being Black in America, and her novels grapple with gender, sexuality, violence, poverty, and discrimination. Her books have been nominated for the National Book Award and the Pulitzer Prize for Fiction.

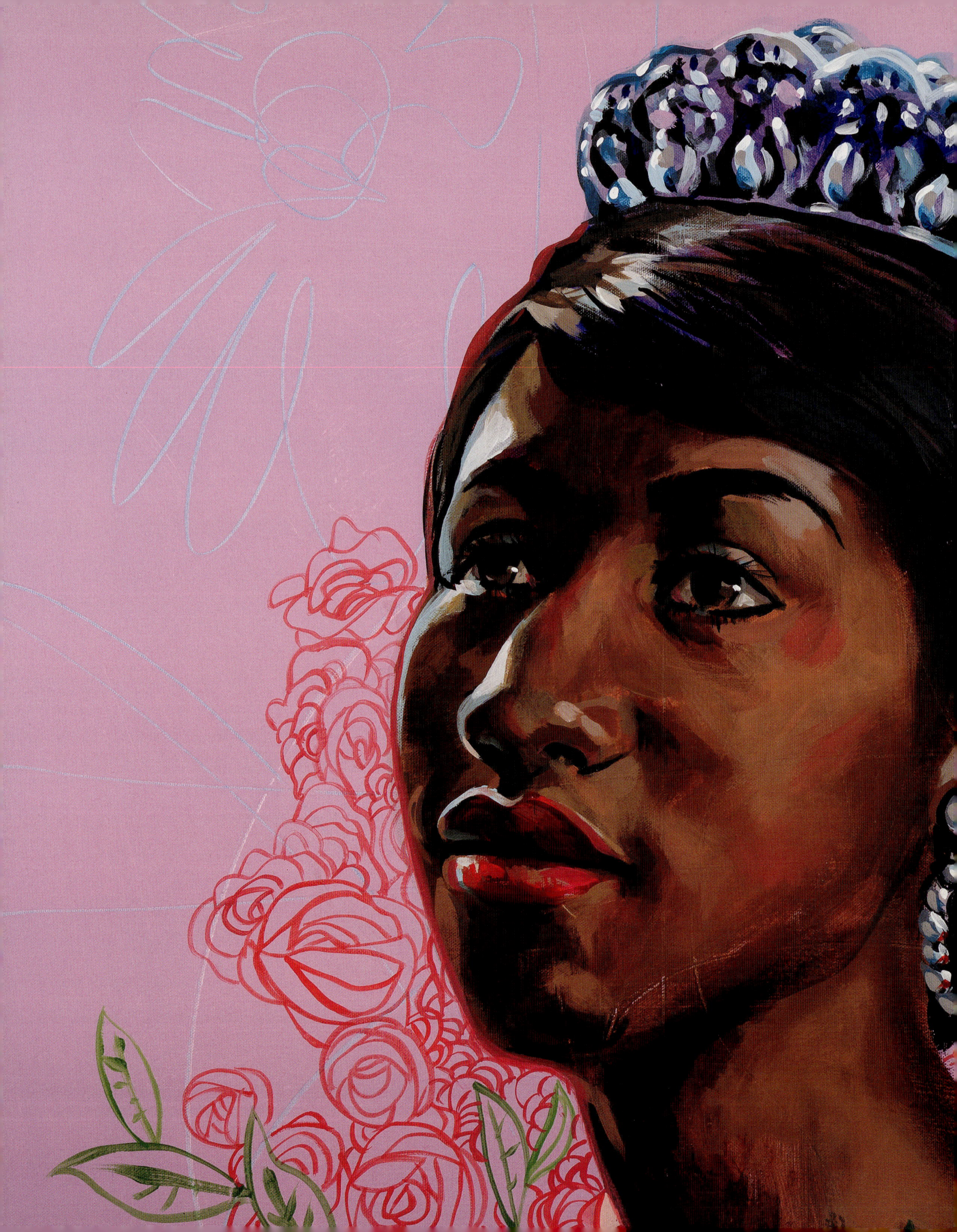

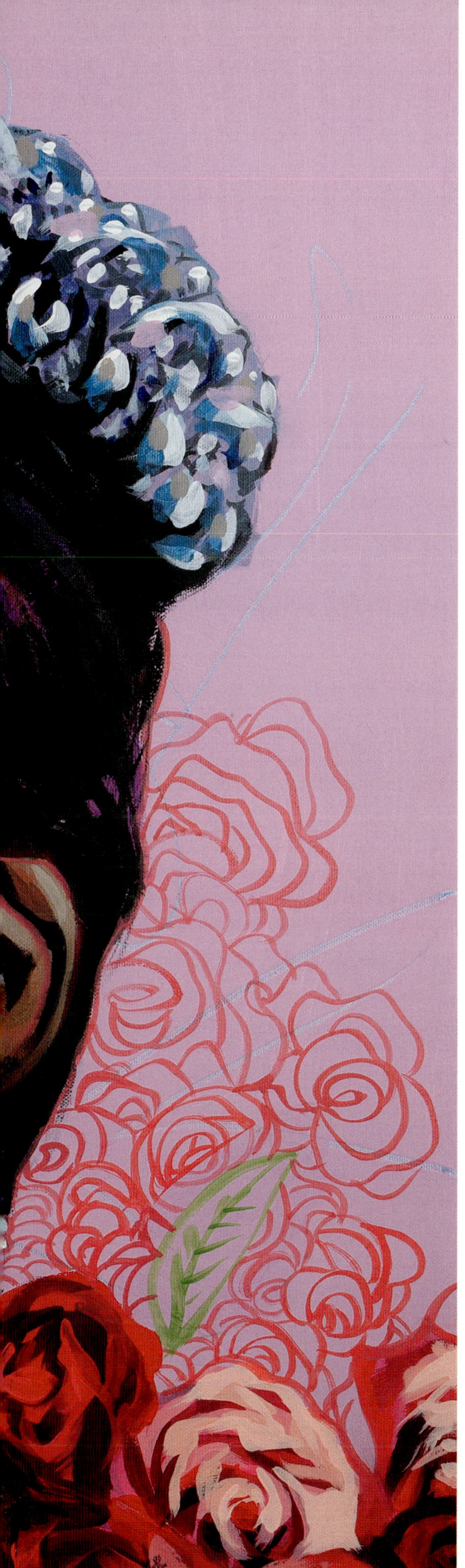

Aretha Franklin
(1942–2018)

Aretha Franklin was a musical powerhouse whose voice captured the hearts of millions around the world. Born in Memphis, Tennessee, in 1942, she grew up in a family of talented musicians and singers who introduced her to gospel music. Franklin demonstrated a natural talent for music from a young age. Her voice was powerful and soulful, and she quickly became one of the most sought-after performers in the music industry. In the 1960s and '70s she had a string of chart-topping hits, including "Respect," "Chain of Fools," and "(You Make Me Feel Like) A Natural Woman." Despite achieving worldwide fame, Franklin never forgot her roots, and her music was always infused with the gospel and soul music that she grew up with. She was an advocate for civil rights throughout her life, and her memorable voice and moving performances inspired people around the world. But Franklin's legacy goes far beyond her incredible talent as a singer and musician. She was a pioneer for women in music, breaking barriers and paving the way for future generations of female artists. She was a trailblazer who refused to be constrained by societal expectations or the limits anyone tried to place on her, and her story will never be forgotten.

LEARNING EXERCISE

By Chase Malone

1. Who Am I?

a. I was born in 1924.

b. I was the first Black woman to serve in Congress.

c. I ran for president as a Democratic party candidate, becoming the first Black woman to do so.

2. Who Am I?

a. I was born in 1940 in Saint Bethlehem, Tennessee.

b. I contracted polio at age five and walked with a leg brace until I was twelve.

c. I won three gold medals in track and field at the 1960 Olympics.

3. Who Am I?

a. I was born in 1930 in Chicago, Illinois.

b. I was the first African American woman to have a play produced on Broadway.

c. Nina Simone wrote a song inspired by my life and work.

4. Who Am I?

a. I was born in 1942 in Mobile, Alabama.

b. I was one of the first African Americans to enroll at the University of Alabama.

c. I worked for the U.S. government, including as Director of Civil Rights and Urban Affairs.

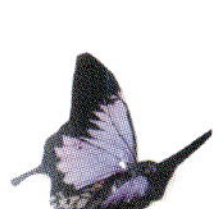

Marryam Moma, *BeDoHave*
(Paper collage)

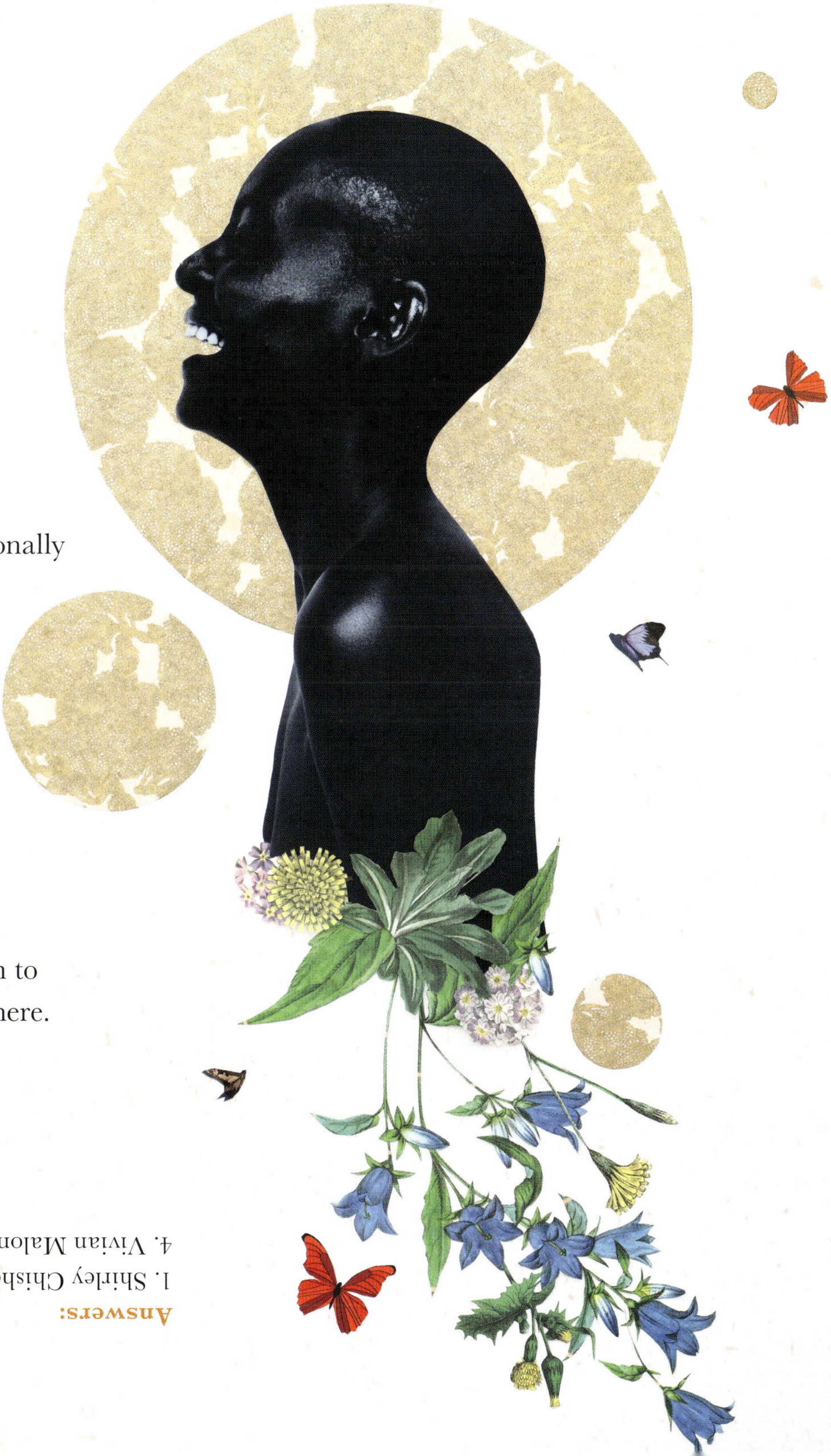

5. Who Am I?

a. I was born in 1935 in Philadelphia, Pennsylvania.

b. I was the third woman to play professionally in the Negro baseball league.

c. I played for the Indianapolis Clowns of the Negro American League.

6. Who Am I?

a. I was born in 1923 in New Orleans, Louisiana.

b. I cofounded the Museum of African American Art in Los Angeles, California.

c. I taught at Scripps College and went on to become the chair of the art department there.

Answers: 1. Shirley Chisholm 2. Wilma Rudolph 3. Lorraine Hansberry 4. Vivian Malone Jones 5. Connie Morgan 6. Samella Lewis

Chapter 7

KIN'FOLK
TALES

ANANSI THE SPIDER: CHARACTER STUDY

Written and illustrated by Demetri Burke

This semicartoonish design is based on the banana spider / golden orb weaver. This spider is found in parts of Africa, including Ghana, as well as in North America, South America, and the Caribbean. Its body incorporates Ghana's kente cloth.

The banana spider / golden orb weaver is known for its web-weaving skills. This can be related to kente cloth, having Anansi weaving kente patterns into his web.

Anansi is a well-traveled man that is eccentric in apparel, jewelry, and hair styling. His appearance morphs with each story and works in combination with his attitude and the landscape he is in. Although his human characteristics are often visible at first, his spider attributes are revealed in subtle details in attire and styling. As the story progresses, you might see an extra hand, eye, or fang reaching out!

Anansi's hair weaves a story in itself. Never the same twice, his updo styles are reminiscent of a spider's body or its web. His hair is diasporic in nature, ranging from Florida wicks, Ghana braids, and Caribbean locs to '90s French rolls and many more styles.

Anansi is an older man with a distinctive gray beard. Although he is young at heart, his age is reflective of being a father himself with multiple children to his name. He is pretty active, with a lanky and statuesque frame.

> **ALTHOUGH HIS HUMAN CHARACTERISTICS ARE OFTEN VISIBLE AT FIRST, HIS SPIDER ATTRIBUTES ARE REVEALED IN SUBTLE DETAILS IN ATTIRE AND STYLING.**

His clothing is reflective of his regalness, adventurousness, and his nature as a traveler. For example, he might wear a jaguar's or a tiger's coat after capturing it, or wear a Rasta shirt to symbolize his stories traveling to Jamaica. They also reference his spiderhood: silk outfits, glittery jewelry to look like the eyes of a spider, furs like that of a tarantula.

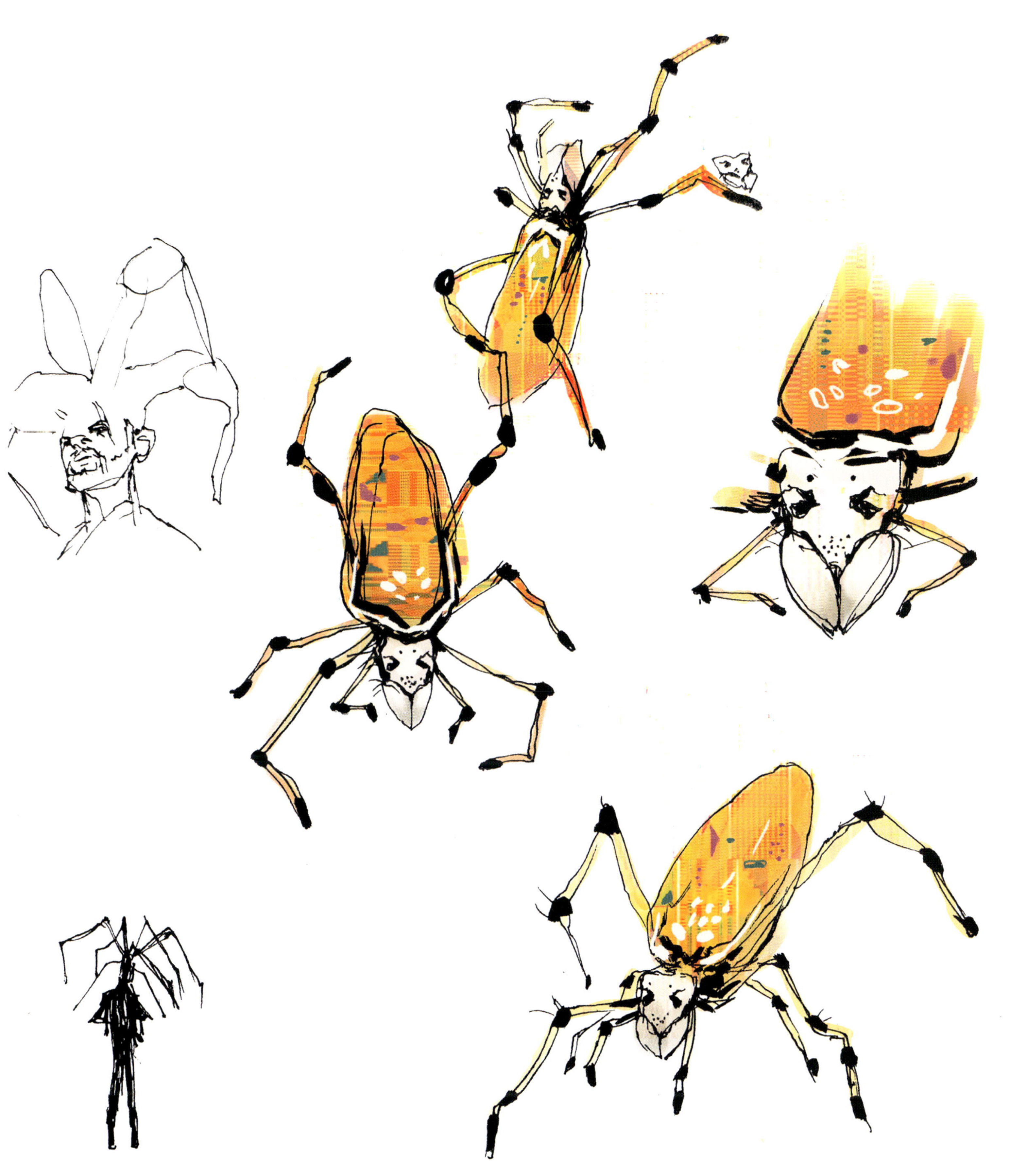

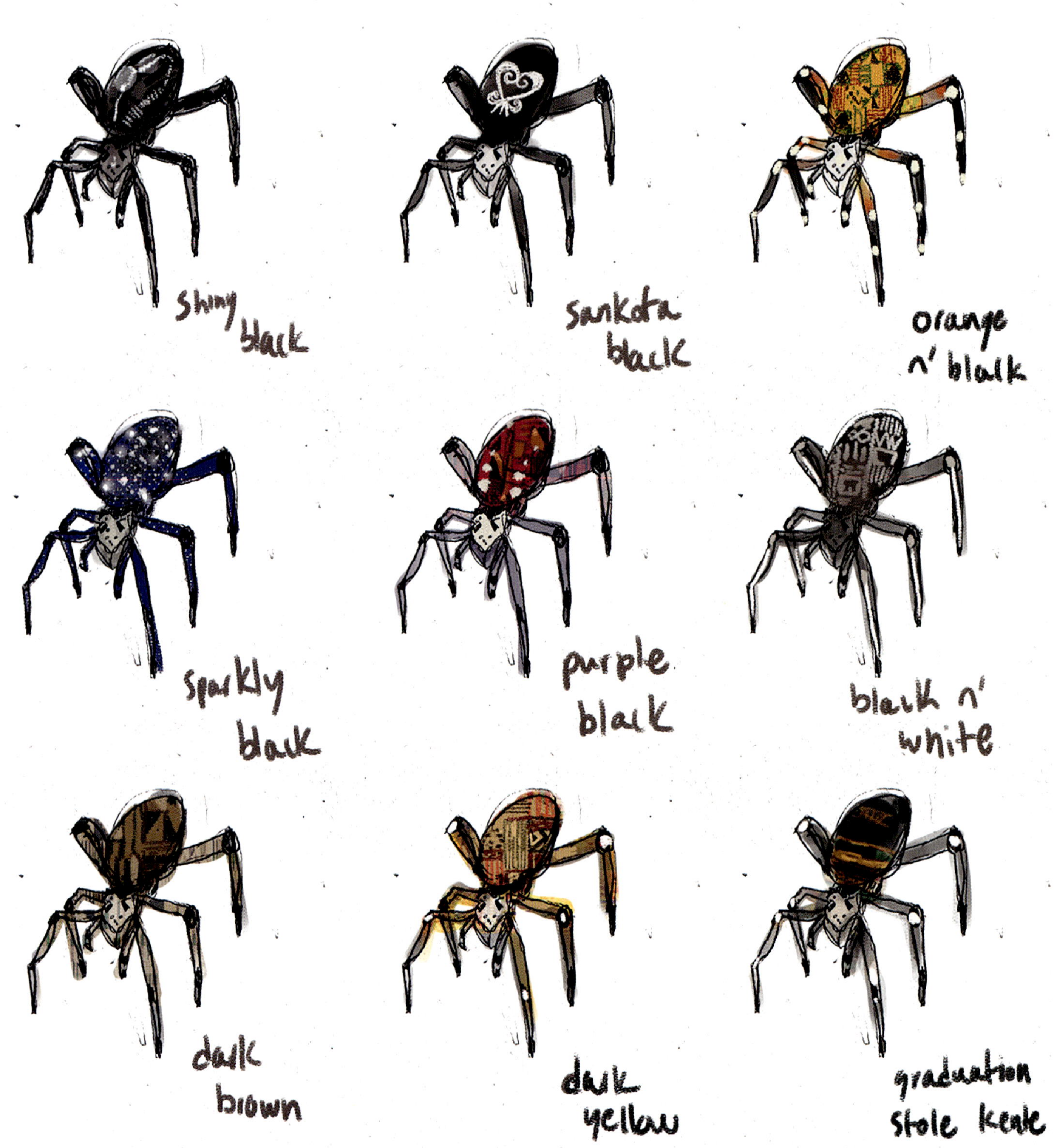

shiny black
sankofa black
orange n' black
sparkly black
purple black
black n' white
dark brown
dark yellow
graduation stole kente

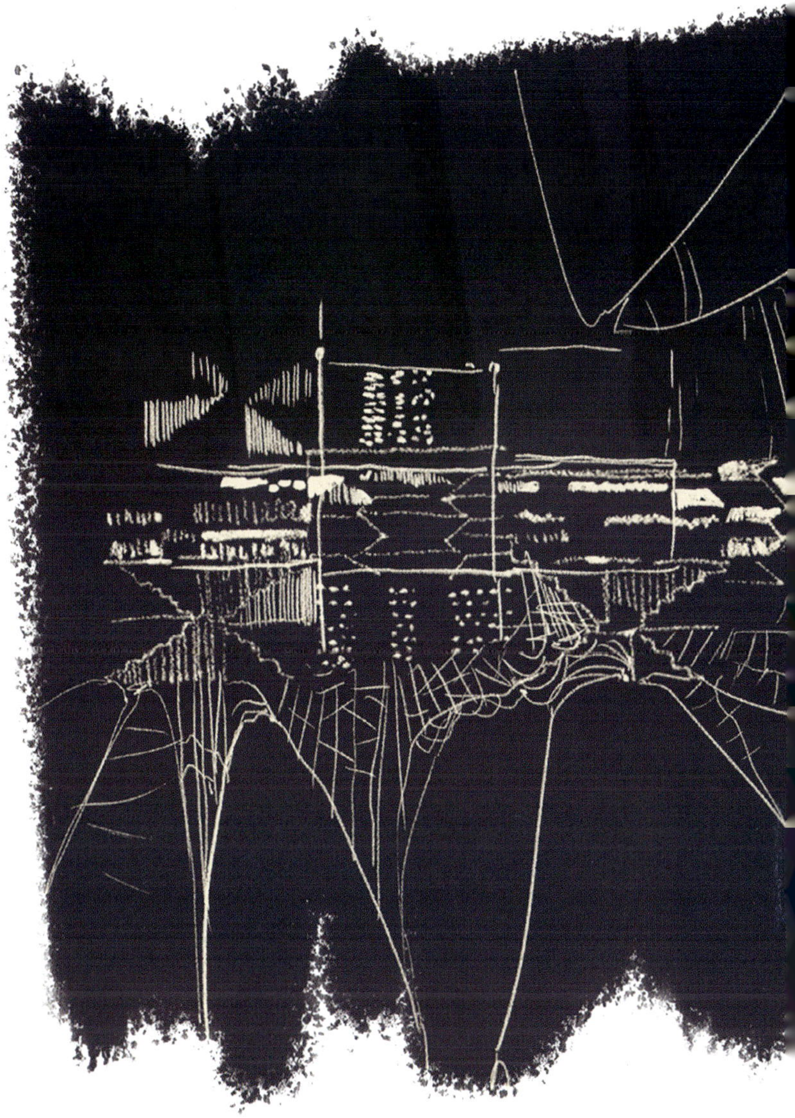

THE BANANA SPIDER / GOLDEN ORB WEAVER

Known for its web-weaving skills. This can be related to kente cloth having Anansi weaving kente patterns into his web.

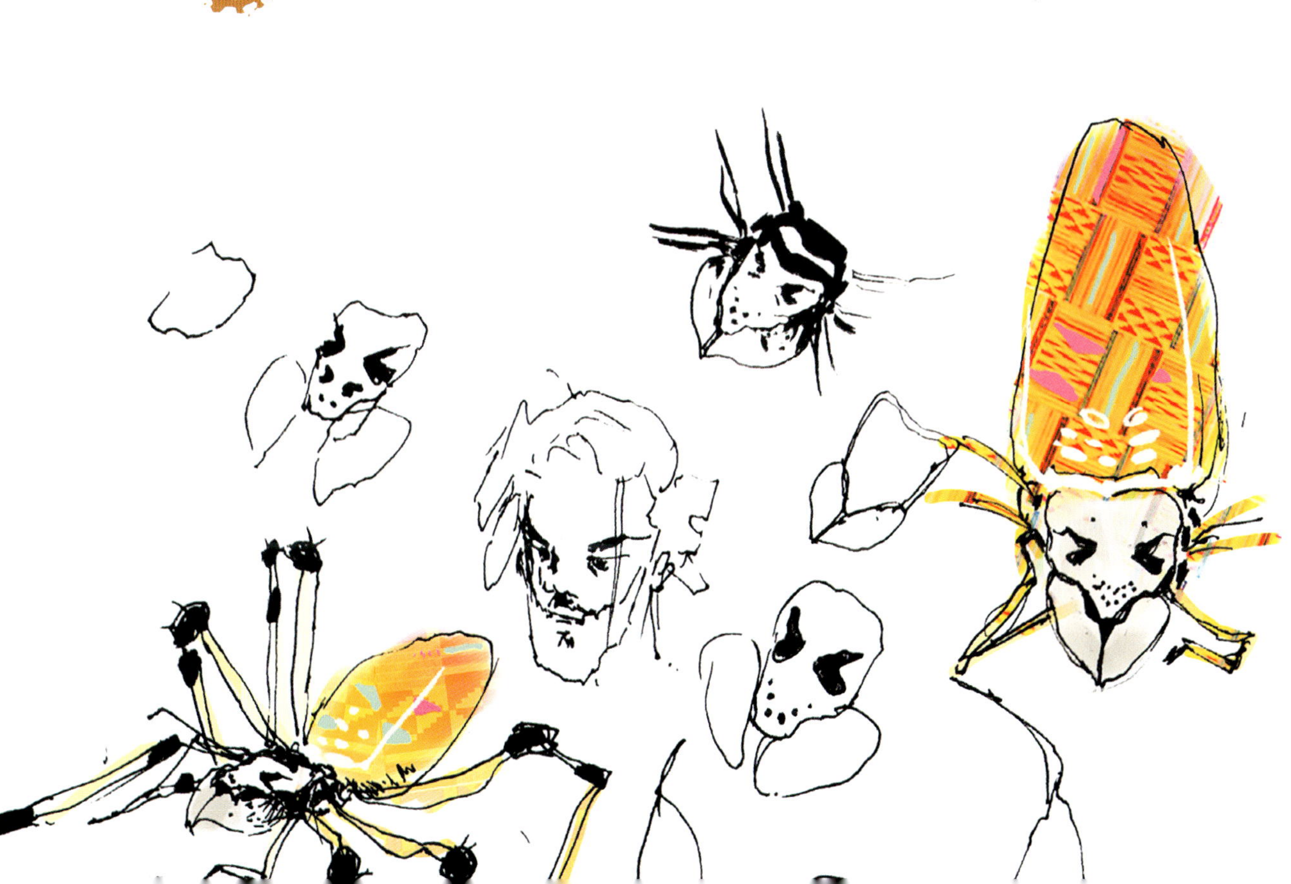

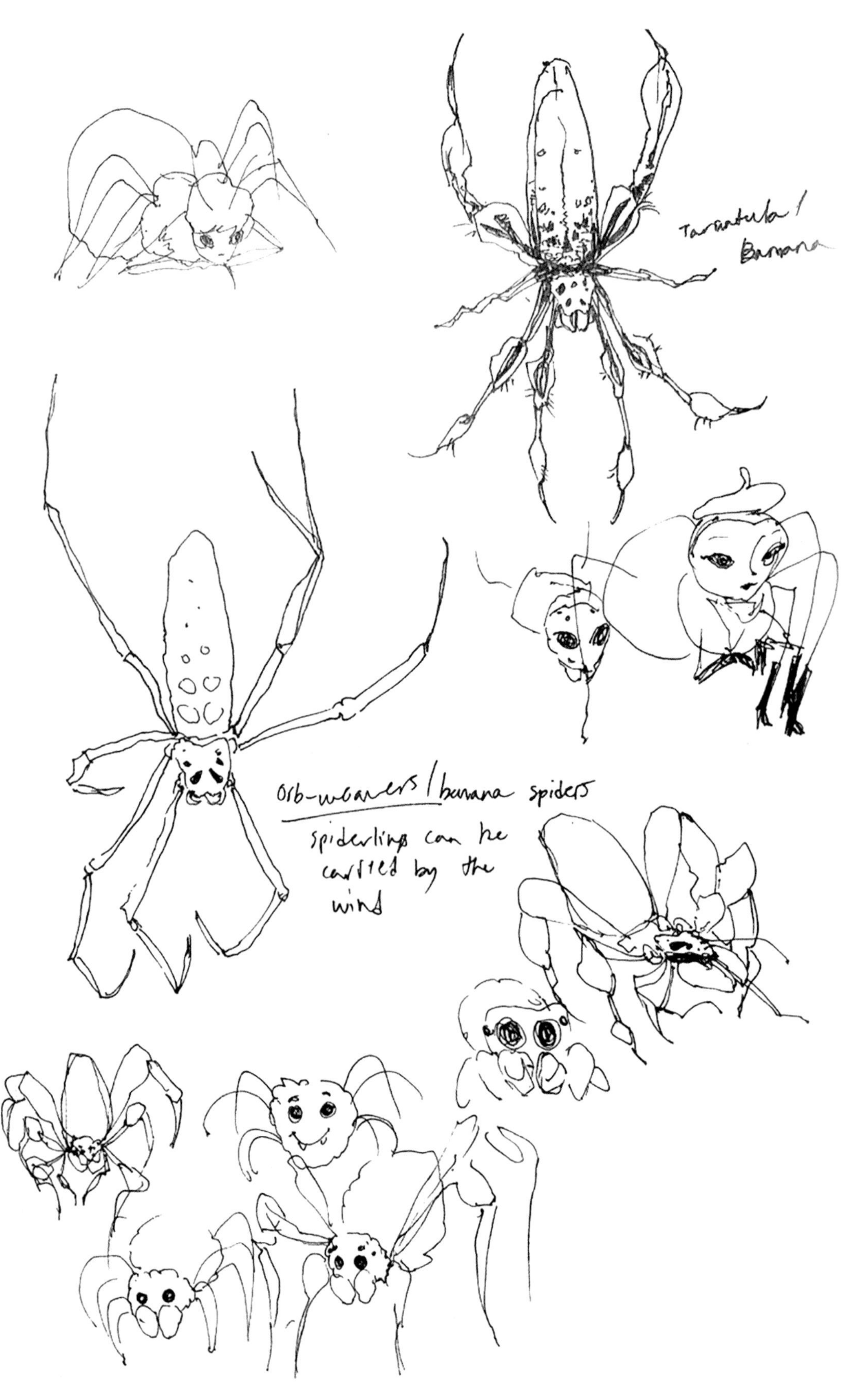

Tarantula/
Banana
orb-weavers/banana spiders
spiderlings can be
carried by the
wind

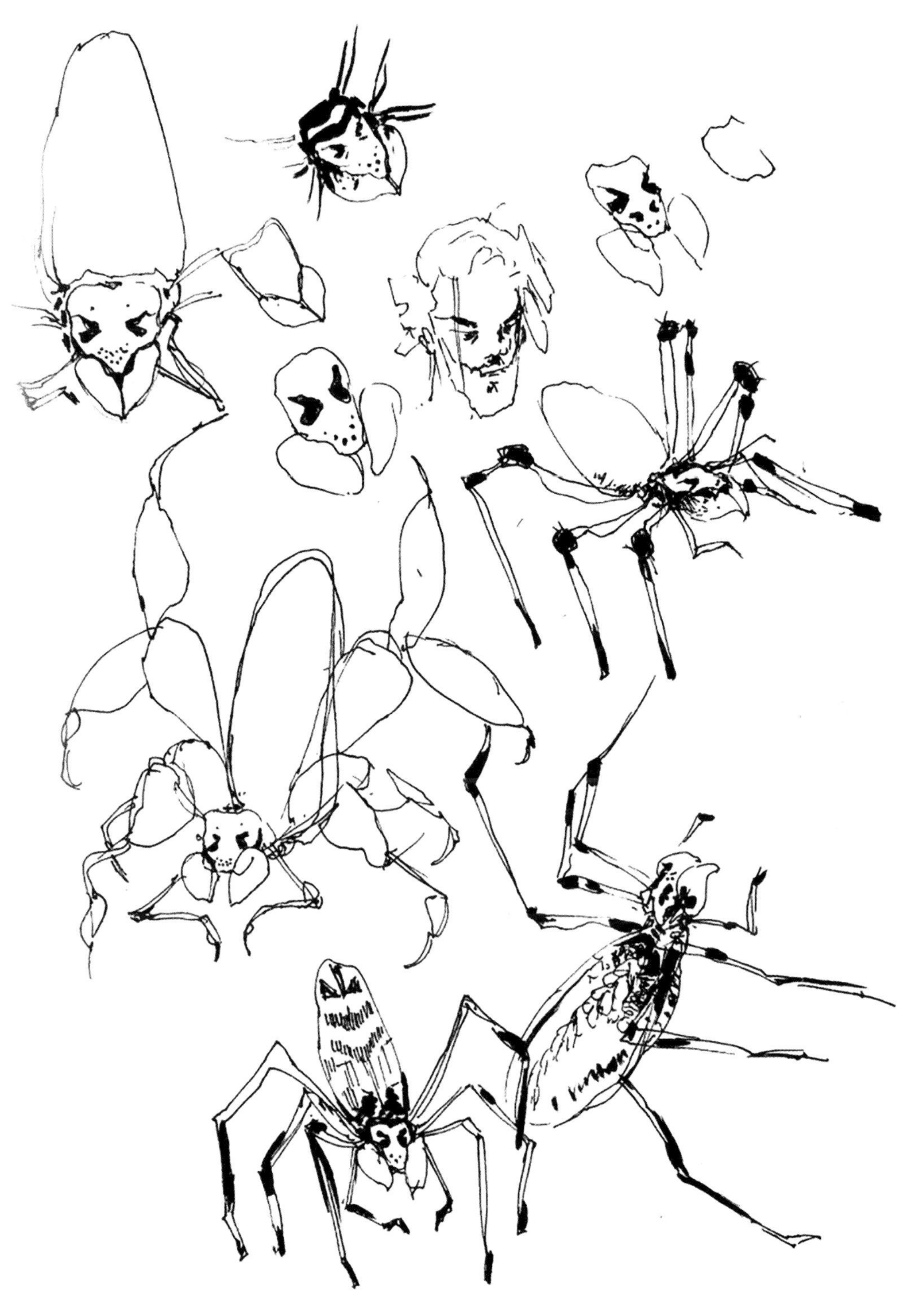

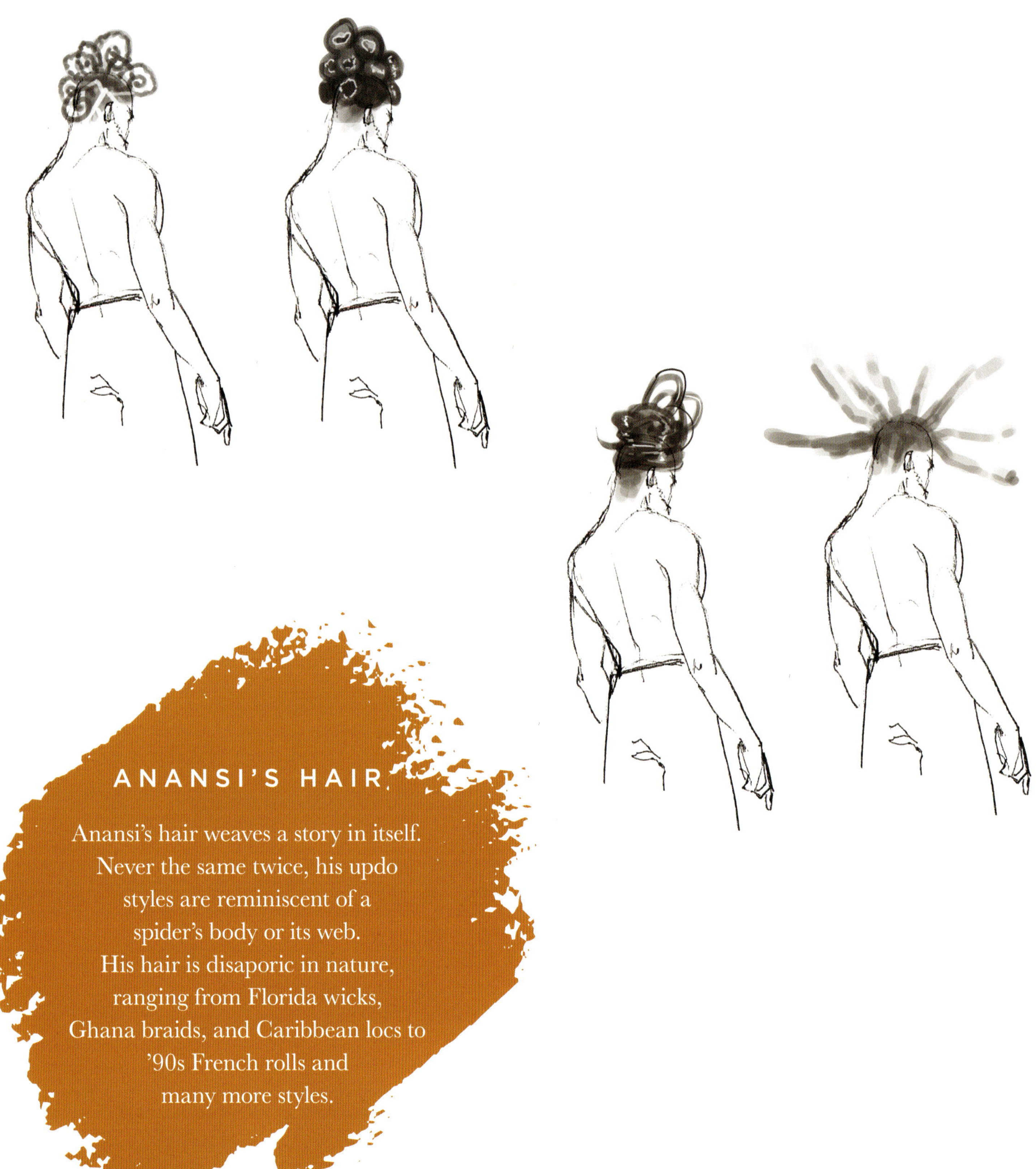

ANANSI'S HAIR

Anansi's hair weaves a story in itself.
Never the same twice, his updo
styles are reminiscent of a
spider's body or its web.
His hair is disaporic in nature,
ranging from Florida wicks,
Ghana braids, and Caribbean locs to
'90s French rolls and
many more styles.

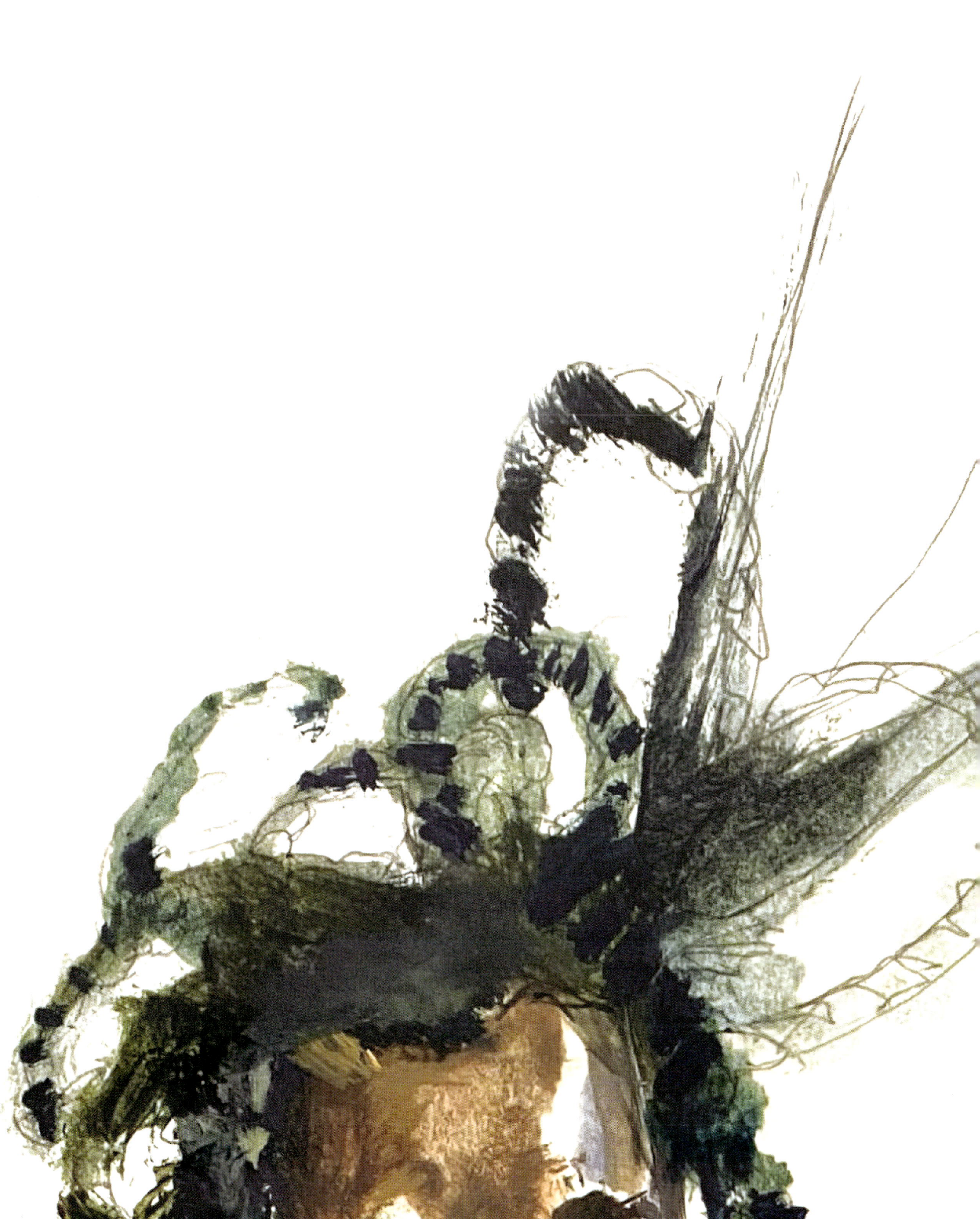

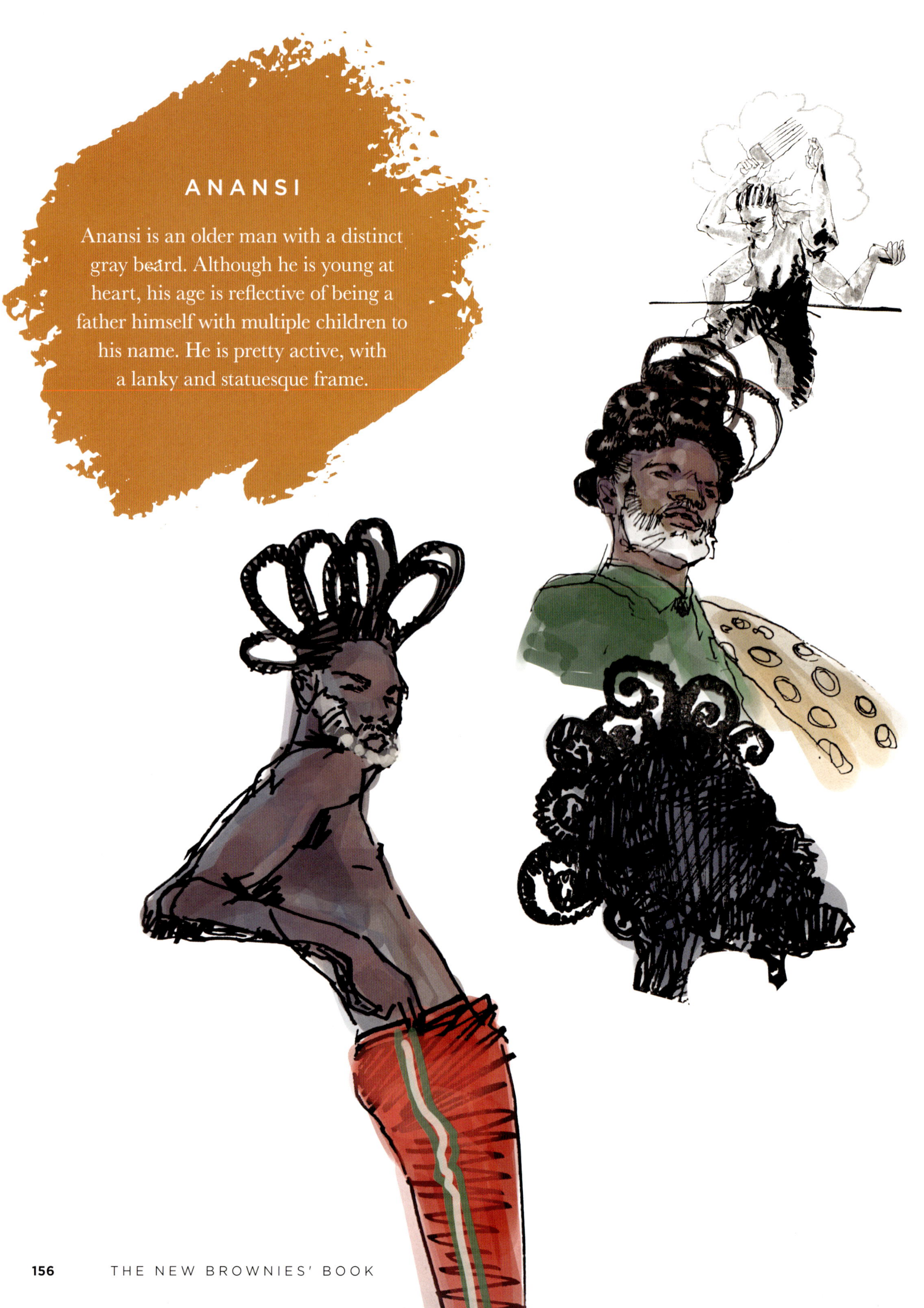

ANANSI

Anansi is an older man with a distinct gray beard. Although he is young at heart, his age is reflective of being a father himself with multiple children to his name. He is pretty active, with a lanky and statuesque frame.

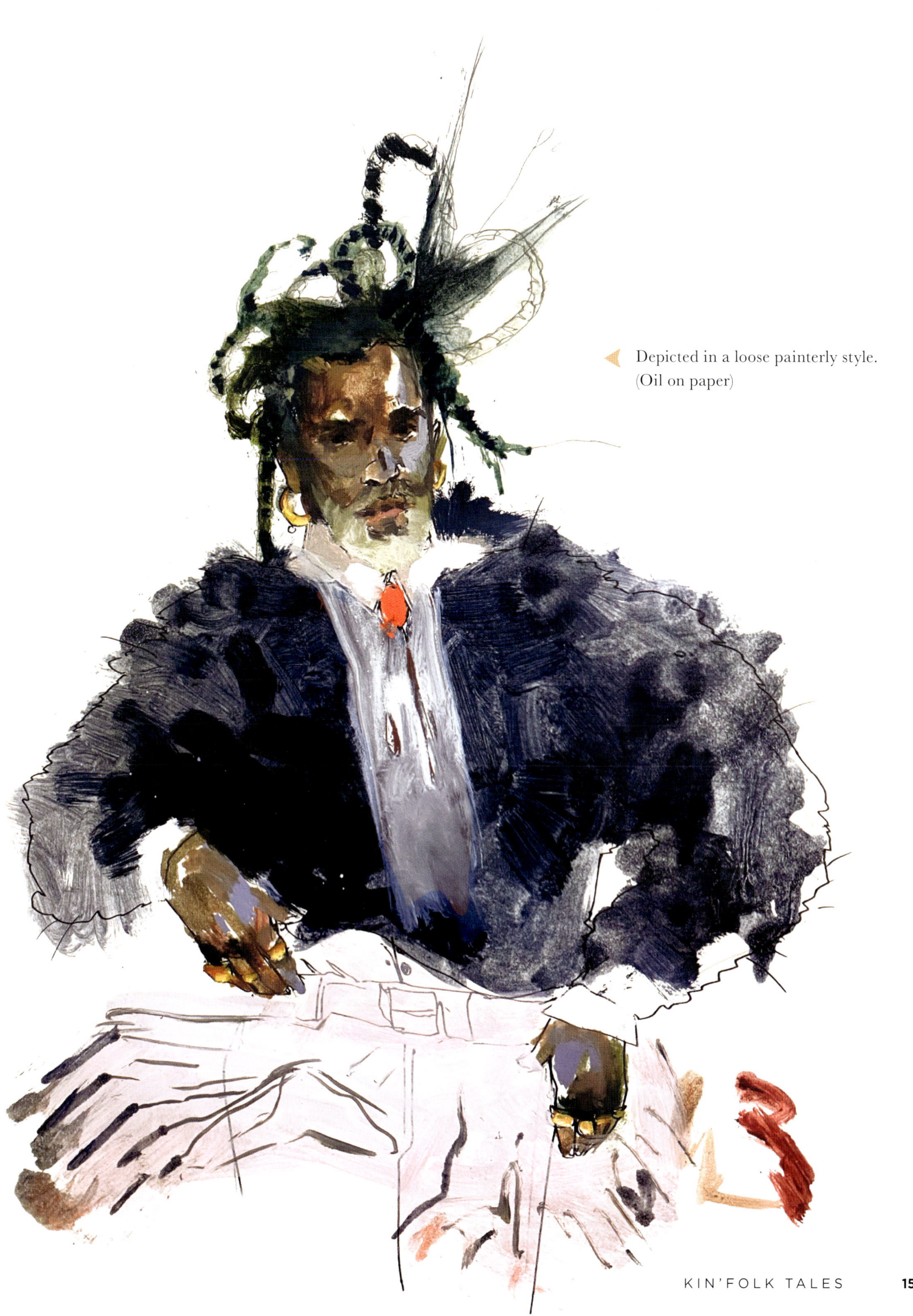

Depicted in a loose painterly style. (Oil on paper)

FOLK SAYINGS

Illustrations by Briana Gordon

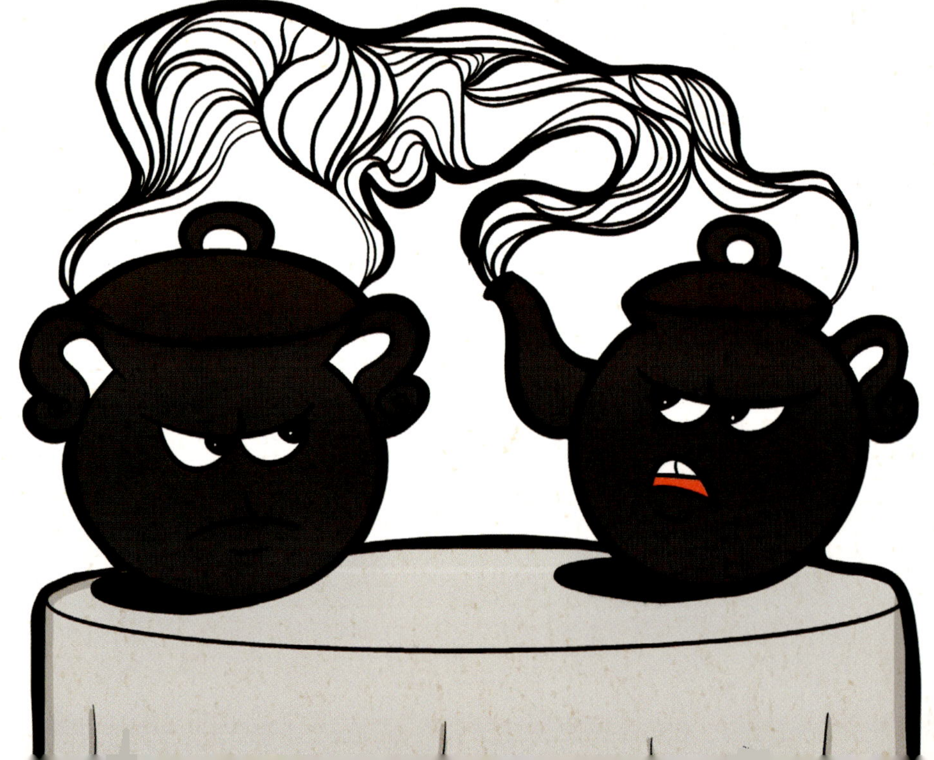

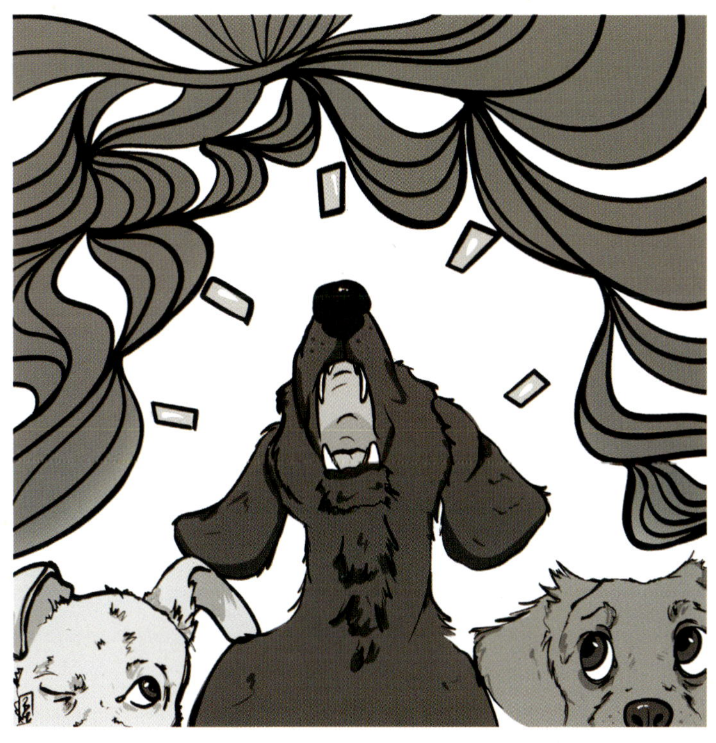

Black don't crack
More than a notion
The squeaky wheel gets the grease
What's done in the dark will come to light
Fix your face
You slow as molasses
If the shoe fits, wear it
The pot can't call the kettle black
If I'm lying I'm flying

Don't bite the hand that feeds ya'
He ain't got the sense the good Lord gave him
Hit dog will holla
Crazy as a road lizard
If you can huh you can hear
Lord, look what the cat dragged in
That is an "A" and "B" situation and I'm gonna
   "C" my way out
All up in the Kool-Aid and don't know the flavor

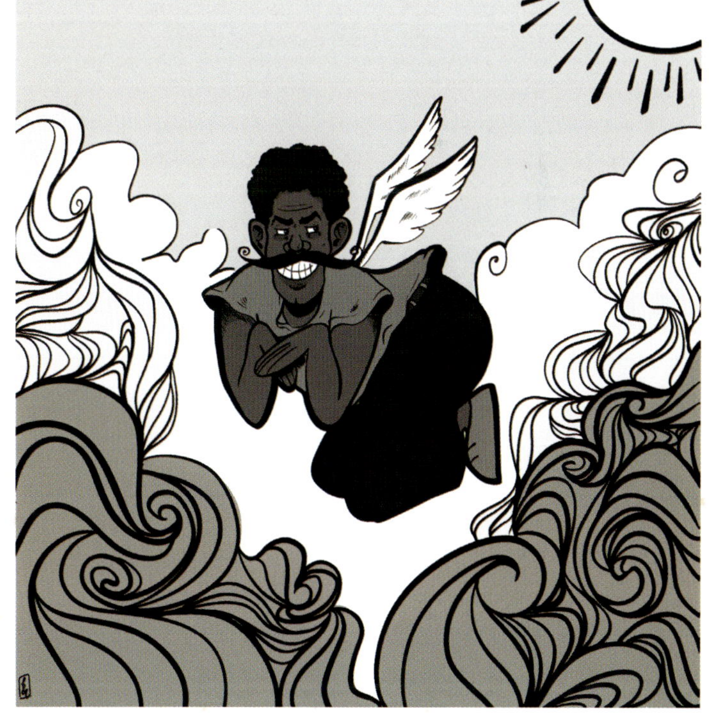

Chapter 8

LIVING
AND DYING

THE TRUTH OF US IS COMPLICATED

By Kai Adia

The simple grace of breath
giving rise to our chest, a mantle
upholding the highest vision of our stories,
the people we meet and the lines
we string together to make the full knot bridge . . .

I think I'm open
to the idea of an unseen hand
playing the keys
Tapping our chests

If it is a creator of love
Watching, guiding, and linking
the soundwaves between us
into heartlines ringing a resounding note
on the bridge.
Just don't forget
This presence moves on our command
Inspired by the sounds we promise
and the motions we make
To live by the mantle

Hold fast and *feel*
the tapping on the chest.

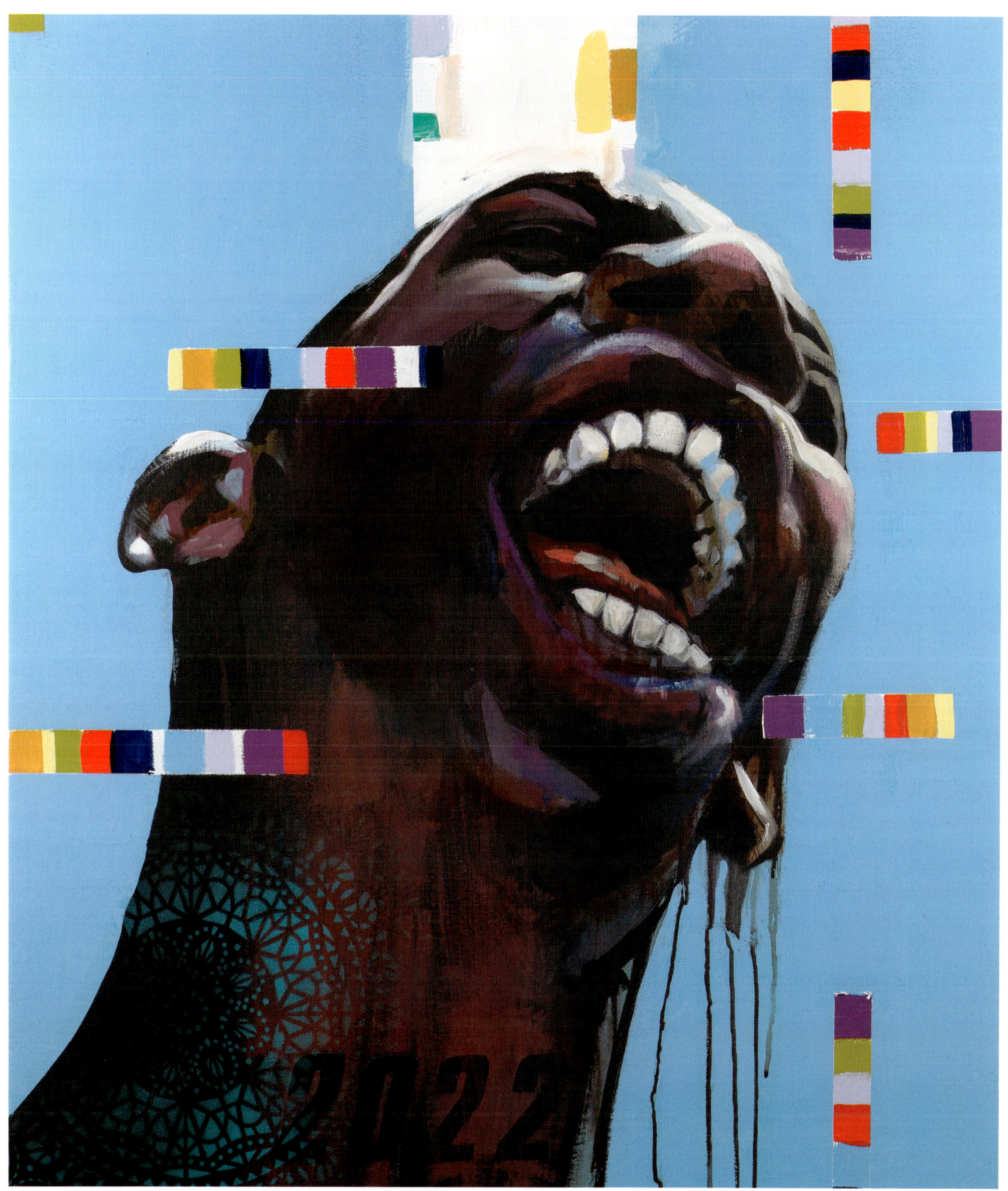

Charly Palmer, *Make Me Wanna Holla*
(Acrylic on canvas)

MY MAMA SICK

By Ida Harris

My mama sick.

She so sick she can't even walk no more.

Something messing with her spine.

She still smoke cigarettes, though.

The long ones, in the soft pack, that go stale quick.

She handles them with her thumb and pointer finger.

Places them between her full lips. She lights a match to the tip then drags menthol through the rolled-up tobacco.

She say she gon' get better.

I believe her.

I daydream about the day she plants her feet firmly onto the ground and stands without my help—without me steadying my young limbs against her grown-up hips for balance, without me guiding her body into the seat of the chair with wheels that spin beneath her weight to make her somewhat mobile.

I imagine her towering over a gaslit stove, slowly scrambling eggs with sprinkles of cheese just for me. I see her hustle and rock and roll her waistline to 1970s disco. I hear her popping her fingers to a fast beat. I go after her when she takes my hand in hers and twirls my skinniness around three times before she introduces me to a playful two-step. She pulls me in close and directs my ankles with her feet. We dance heart to heart to slow jams till the music cease.

I come to at the sound of her voice calling out my name. "Traveeeeeeeeena," she calls.

Mama needs me—needs something—needs me to grab it—now. A tall glass of water, with light ice, a squeeze of lemon, lime, and orange slices.

The tall pill bottle, the flat pill case, the heat pack for her back. I go. I get. I bring.

She fishes out three round pills from the tall bottle and two long pills from the flat one and swallows the water in one gulp. "Mama gon' get better," she says. I believe her.

I believe her when a hospital bed replaces the regular bed in her bedroom.

I believe her every time the visiting nurse stops by to check her pressure, her temperature, her breathing.

I believe her each and every day the aide shows up to help with "activities of daily living": the cooking, the cleaning, the bathing.

I believe her even as our home becomes fractured, broken. Split.

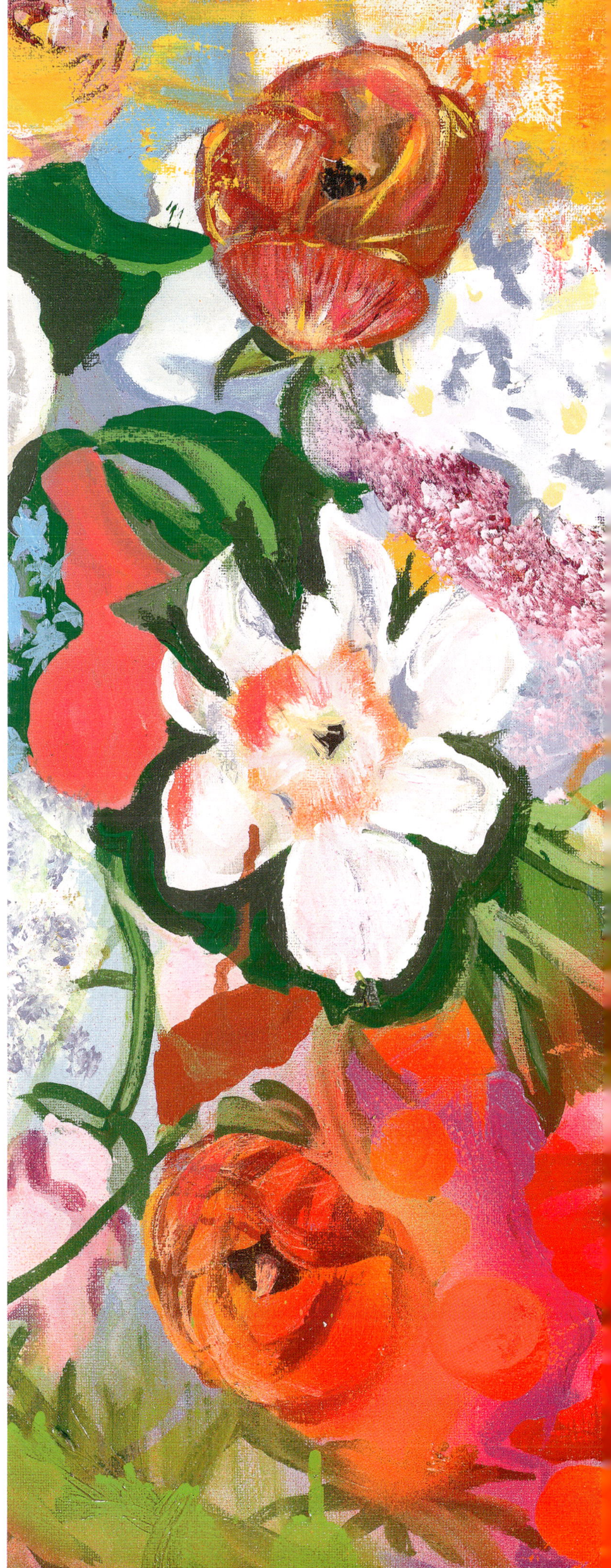

There's a half hour and fourteen miles between us and each hospital visit on Sunday. I counted all thirty minutes on the car ride on the way there.

She smiles wide when I enter the room and wraps her arms around me when I hug her neck. She likes my beaded cornrows. I pat her teeny-weeny Afro. We play Pitty Pat. We eat snacks. We sing songs. Mama likes this song by a lady named Ms. Gloria. She sings it out loud, too: "I Will Survive!"

She say she gon' get better. I believe her.

My mama is sick—so sick she's tired. Not tired of me or playing cards or singing songs but tired as in mostly sleepy. So, on this visit, I climb into her hospital bed and fold myself under the weight of her arm. I throw my legs around hers. I lay cheek to cheek with mama and sing Ms. Gloria's song into her ear till she falls into a deep sleep. I fall behind her—dreaming—of a mama who jumps rope, plays hopscotch, uses a Hula-Hoop, turns cartwheels. I dream of a mama who ain't sick. I wake up. Mama ain't sick no more.

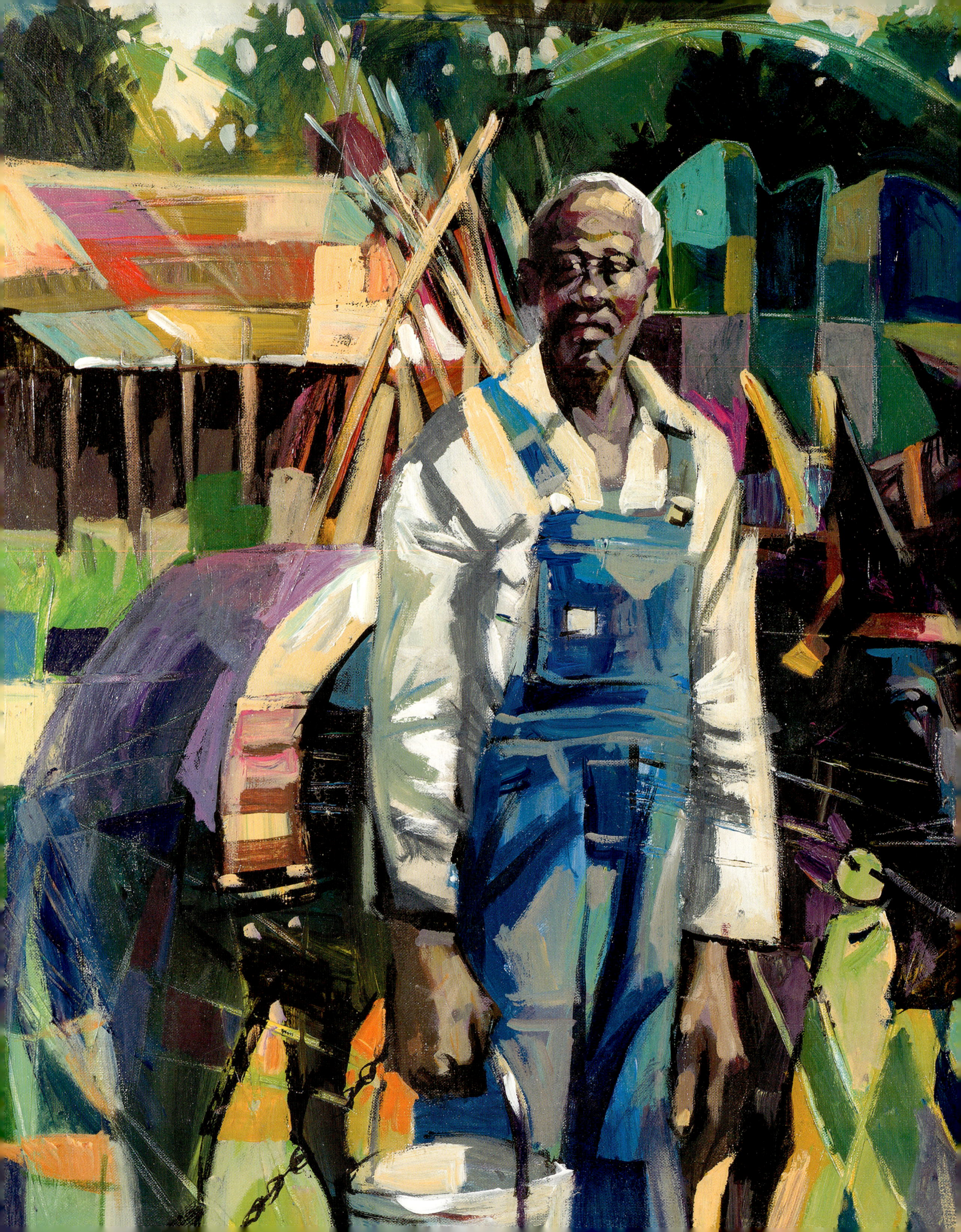

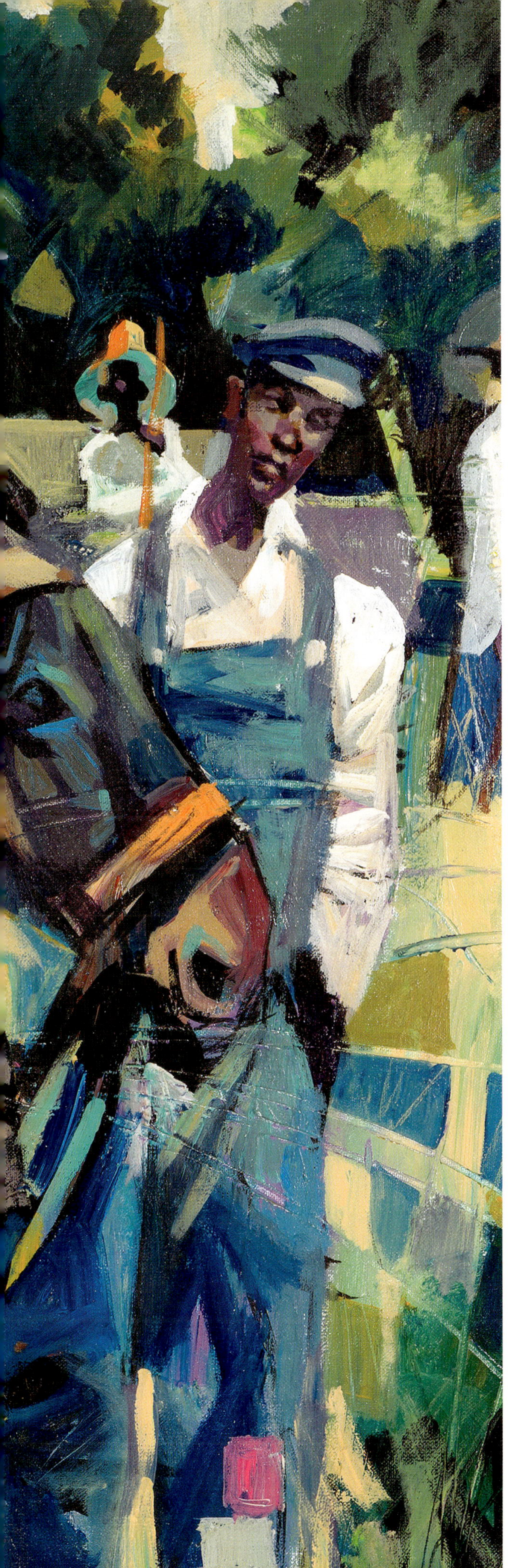

NINE-NIGHTS:
RECLAIMING CARIBBEAN BEREAVEMENT DURING THE PANDEMIC

By Alyasah Ali Sewell

The Ninth Night is being transformed in the face of the coronavirus pandemic.

My understanding of grieving and bereavement comes from my Spanish-Creole-patois-speaking family: My Black mother is from Limón, Costa Rica. The overwhelming majority of her people ended up in the States, staking roots primarily in Brooklyn, New York. We are accustomed to a specific type of Caribbean wake called Nine-Nights, nine dedicated days of grieving centered at the home of the deceased.

I experienced my first wake as a sophomore in high school, when my mother's mother died, and then another one six months later, when her youngest sister died. This is our way of life, our way of coping with grief. It is expected that when the Ninth Night ends, the mourning you can see finds a new home.

Central to the grieving, however, is the togetherness. Starting the day after the burial, family, friends, and neighbors come from near and far to pay their respects to the deceased. There are flowers and cards. Rich, rich black rum cake. Fruit cakes. Coconut cake. Johnny cakes. There are long lines of people waiting to personalize condolences and plate the foods. There are balloons everywhere. We all family now.

We consider wakes not only a mourning period, but also a cause for celebration. The deceased can pass on to join the ancestors, who will protect the living through their journey as well. Our Nine-Nights have come and gone—three times now, three months of pandemic. Still on lock. Still no wakes.

My last remaining maternal aunt finished her journey with glioblastoma. She bookmarked the threats to end my great-aunt's bloodline. Three days after my aunt passed, her youngest son whispered into the night for the last time. Spared by early symptoms, her oldest son would be put on and pulled off ventilators for months. Now, he's long COVID.

The sorrow was so thick. It felt like we were reliving eight nights over and over, and over again. The Ninth Night proving too soon for relief, our conference calls began to serve as wakes. Instead of our bodies heaving with laughter, the fear of grief heaves on our breath. The inability to grieve as a family, together, in shared space, made that Ninth Night of mourning elusive.

Moreover, East Crown Heights, the place where our love was concentrated, still sustains the highest rates of death and the lowest rates of hospitalization in the city. We've seen more body bags than gurneys. Imagine, more heartbreak than hope.

As the hospitals of New York City fell to their burden, public health workers searched for the living from block to block, house to house, street to street. The count of the dead rose so high that the COVID tests ran out. The "officials" said COVID killed anyone found dead those months. They never tested her. Maybe she died of grief.

Locked-out travel in and out of the city meant that we could not host our Nine-Nights. We are a people whose need for it expands as do the angles of the pandemic. Black, Latinx, transnational, immigrant, essential, frontline workers: We are Black diasporic globe-trotters.

We have expanded the generations of our family. Thus, it is only through the trotting that we can mark the hugs we have missed. Only through the trotting can we vacation from the strips of pavement weaving through creeks of landfills and nooks of wastewater treatment plants.

We are meditating through the wind of ambulances. We are wailing our prayers. We are stretching the bridges of life and death. The sirens no longer can tell us when our Nine-Nights begin, much less end.

Instead of letting our heart break in our heart's hand, we call each other on our way to and from essential jobs that we lose if we leave the front line. Our spirits remind us of his voice. Call him now. He was gone when we called him next.

The warm clammy hand of our baby cousin is preferred over the warmth of stethoscopes. Our subdivisions and schools seed distrust in the very system of safety that says it only wants to save our lives. Sometimes the Nine-Nights are the nine friends with whom you learned the djembe. Either way, we are dancing.

We took him home. Even St. Jude couldn't save him. He just wanted to play the Three Ring Circus

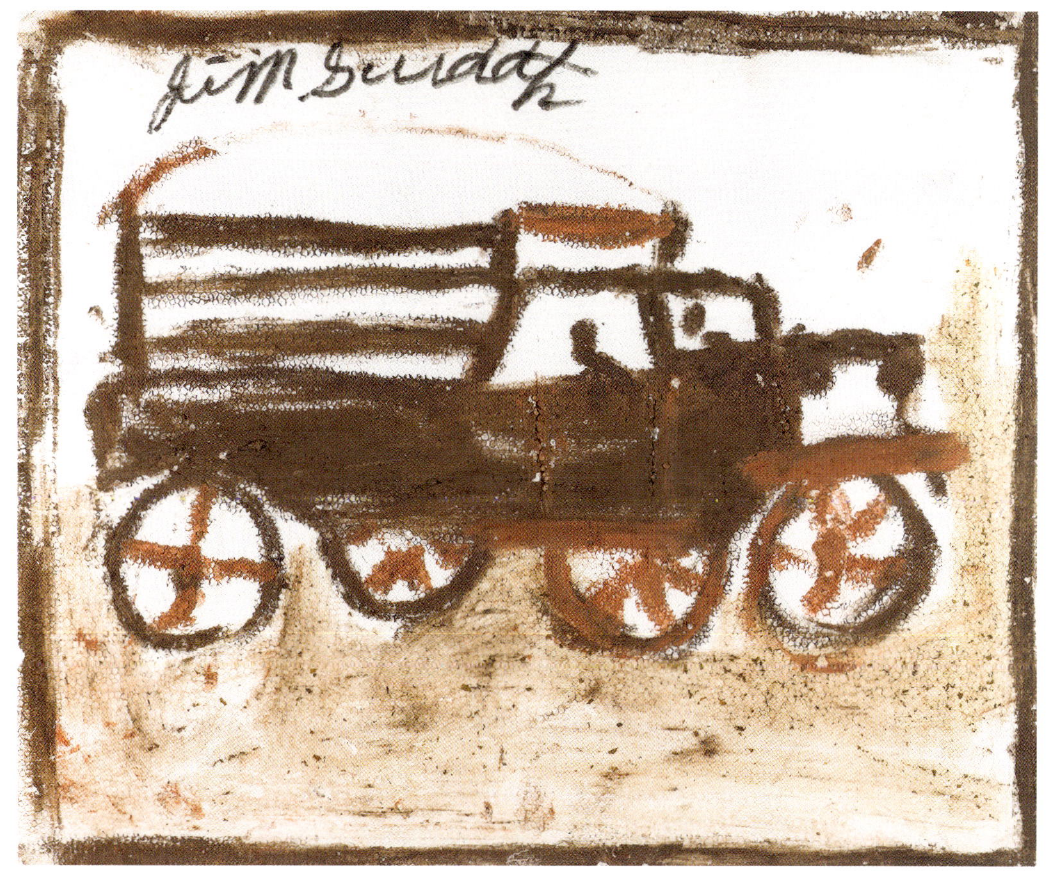

Jimmy Lee Sudduth, *Wagon Truck*
(Hand-mixed paints)

and fight the Teenage Mutant Ninja Turtles. Blinded with sarcomas, he could see the color of all the scenes of *Scooby-Doo*. I know. I made sure he didn't roll off the bed at night. I handed him his pills.

I keep a picture of him in my pocket. When I get scared, I only open my eyes when I hear his name nine times. I cannot remember his Nine-Nights. We were already on our ninth inning of living room baseball by then, heaven. I don't remember physics, but I know what radiation is. His skin browned yellow. He gestures to me to sit at his feet. I breathe his last breath.

We cannot live without that Ninth Night, so we name ourselves after his best friend. Every time we type our names now, we affirm that we are the Ninth Night. We no longer need the candles. We'll keep the sage, though.

When are the tears too much? When are the dry cheeks not enough? How many nights are we allowed to take off before the theaters of grief close to the curtains of release? Burying the dead is no longer just a stage of grief. It is a promise that on the Ninth Night, we will be together, and free.

The COVID pandemic has rendered our bereavement practices impractical. The Nine-Nights of my childhood are gone. We are finding new ways to hug. Technology has unscattered us. Timeline posts. Dance memes. Virtual reunions. We need not experience our Nine-Nights alone. We have set a date for our first night, to visit her grave. Breathe and release, observe our Nine-Nights. See her fat in the next generation's cheeks.

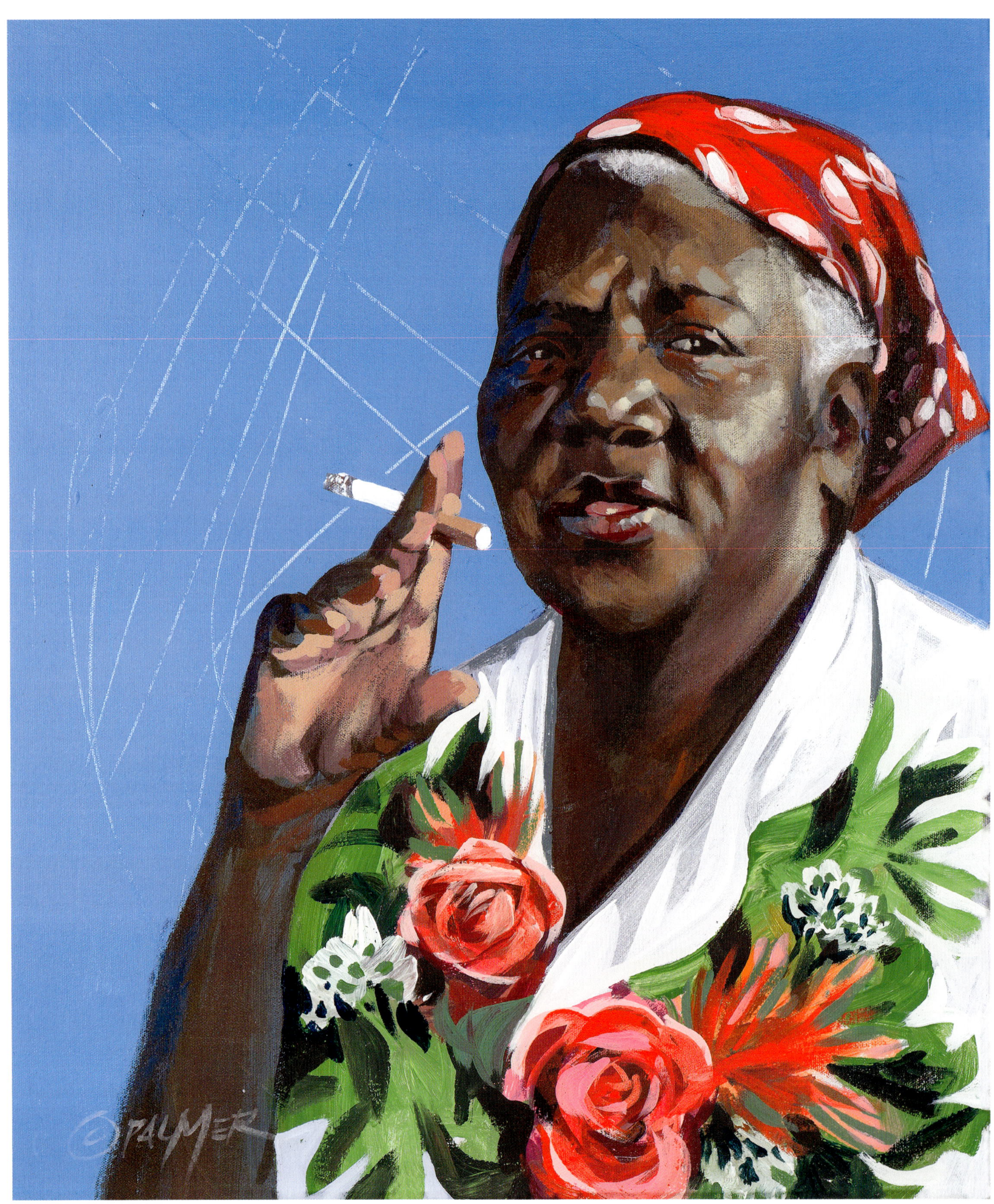

Charly Palmer, *Aunt Mary*
(Acrylic on canvas)

DEATH LEAVES A SCAR, LOVE LEAVES MEMORIES

Wesley Gordon | Age 14

I dedicate this to my grandparents, Lester and Druscilla Faber, for caring for me as a premature baby and for getting me to where I am today.

"Uno!" my aunt screeched, overjoyed. We all cackled as we watched her express her stunning jubilation. It was Thanksgiving, the day to display your love for those essential to your survival. It was an amusing day until it came to a close. As they say, "Nothing lasts forever."

My close family and I were at my grandmother's house for Thanksgiving. My grandfather was also there, but he was comatose in a hospital bed—or at least we thought so.

My grandfather spoiled me as a kid, taking me to McDonald's and Chuck E. Cheese while he sat and enjoyed my company. He took me wherever I needed to be; whether that was school, mixed martial arts, baseball, or back home, he was always there. When I was at his house he would take me to play miniature golf with him and would swim in his pool with me. He would go on rides with me, even though he was tired as well as terrified. I was born three months prematurely, so when I was a baby he would help take care of me. He even retired early when I was born so that he could help me. He came over three days a week even though he lived about an hour away. Overall, he was a big part of my life. He was stubborn, yet he loved me with all his heart. I was at the top of his priorities.

His kindness spread out to others as well. He helped out my mom's friend and allowed her to live at his house long enough that she came to be considered their adopted daughter. He even served the country in the Army for about three years.

One day, however, he became nauseated. He got Alzheimer's disease. His memory became foggier month by month, and he gradually failed to recall what he did that amplified the hearts of others.

As the years passed his illness continued to advance. Fortunately, he generally retained memories about his family—though not all the time. He might call me his granddaughter rather than his grandson. I began to realize that death was catching up to him.

Two weeks prior to Thanksgiving, my mother was driving me to mixed martial arts. I felt strange, mainly because I sensed a depressing aura from her. After class she told me that my grandfather was in the hospital. Apparently, he had fallen down and had become partially paralyzed. ▶

We drove over to the hospital. Once we got there we went up a couple of floors and were asked to stand by in a waiting room. My grandma was there as well. Her eyes were a scarlet red color and never fully opened. There were also about eight others around us. They seemed nervous when they talked to each other, as if the world were about to end. One of them got up anxiously and walked out of the room. She came back with a nurse.

"You cannot see him yet," said the nurse.

The nurse then walked out of the room. The woman's face was filled with ferocity. My mom couldn't help but ask her what happened. An older lady said that one of their family members had gotten into a horrible car crash and was not yet stable. We replied by telling them about our situation. Then the nurse came back and whispered something into each of their ears. Many of them began to cry. The lamentation in the room grew. It made me think about what might happen to my grandfather. The nurse told my mom and I that we could go see my grandfather. We attached visitor stickers to our shirts and walked down the hall to my grandfather's room.

My grandfather and many others that seemed around his age were there. My mom spoke first. "I heard the surgery was a success."

"Yeah, but they did so many terrible things," he replied in a heathery voice.

"H-hi, Grandpa," I said hesitantly.

"Hi, sweetie," he replied.

We both gave him a kiss on the cheek. Right before we were about to leave, a doctor came in with an intimidating needle for my grandpa. My grandfather complained to us that he didn't know what was in the needle and that he didn't want it. The doctor looked at my mom and she said, "Do it!"

I quickly looked away and could tell once they injected the needle, his complaints stopped. We left the hospital, and that was my last visit. After a week he came back home in the hospital bed, close to death.

Silence filled the room as his presence vanished. I haltingly sprang up and then shifted toward the bed, one—"thump!", two—"thump!", three—"thump." I was at the hospital bed studying his body. My heart pumped slowly but with ferocity, like a motorcycle starting to rev up. I scanned his body from his feet up. From the legs, to the stomach, to the neck, to the mouth, and finally the eyes. My heart skipped a beat as I saw them. The glimmer had drained out of his eyes, like a lake becoming waterless.

I stumbled back twice before tumbling onto the couch. My eyes were wide open, just as his were. I looked around as I saw everyone's consternation. I suspected that once someone broke out of their trance, everyone would fall apart.

First came my grandmother, gushing out tears like a broken fire hydrant. Instantly my mom and aunt started to hassle about whom to call. Soon after, my aunt swiftly left the room, and my mom told me to go with her.

I got up off the couch and limped with a glitch in my step toward my aunt. She was lying down on her stomach with her head directly on the comforter. I rubbed her back trying to help her relax. Then she sobbed, saying, "Not my daddy!" and repeating it. It echoed unceasingly as she reflected back on her memories.

After a while my mom entered the room and told me that I could go to my room. My mind felt like a heavy textbook on a subject I loathe. I lay down in bed, desperately scrolling through my phone to find something to make myself feel better.

But then, my dad tapped on the door asking, "Wesley, can I come in?"

I said, "Yes," in a long, croaky voice.

"Are you okay?" he asked.

I responded "No." I continued, "I miss him so much, and now he is gone!" taking an unwilling breath in between each syllable.

Then he told me, "Death leaves a scar, love leaves memories."

Chapter 9

OLD WOMAN

BY ANOTHER NAME

By Charly Palmer

When I took the call, the voice I met was gentle, cracked, aged, and questioning: "Can I speak to Charles Palmer?"

I dislike the name Charles.

Besides, my name is Charly with an *ly*, but I was raised not to correct elders. My wife was raised similarly. She has great-aunts who have called her Kerena her whole life—yet her name is Karida.

She humbly accepts it.

I had no idea who the elder was on the other end of this call, but I simply acknowledged myself as Charles. It was the right thing to do.

"Yes, ma'am, this is Charles."

"Hi Charles, this is Ntozake Shange."

There are rare moments in my life when I am a fan. This was one of those moments. I didn't scream, fumble my words, or freeze. I'm way too cool for that, but the smile on my face was confirmation that I, newly christened Charles Palmer by Ntozake Shange, was a huge fan.

"I believe that Halima told you that I would be calling."

"Yes, ma'am, I mean madam, I mean . . . ," I fumbled my words.

This was Sister Shange calling me. You have to understand—even if you don't. Shange is one of the most important writers of the Black Arts Movement, and here she was calling me—Charles.

"You have a pleasant voice, young man," she said. "Halima told me to be expecting your call."

"Thank you!" I said, adding some bass to my voice.

"I've been enjoying your website. I love your art."

"Thank you, ma'am."

"I've recently completed a poem and I was hoping that you would put images to my words."

She struggled to breathe between her words.

"I'll have my assistant email you the poem and give you a few days to digest the words, and I'll give you a call back."

A couple days later, when she called, I immediately recognized the voice and acknowledged the name she bestowed upon me.

"Is this Charles?" Ntozake asked. "Yes, how are you doing, Ms. Shange?" "Young man, my friends call me Zake."

I didn't know if she was inviting me to be a friend, so I waited for a clearer invitation.

That clarity never came.

"Have you had time to read the poem?" she asked.

"Yes, ma'am, I mean Ms. Shange, I mean Zake," I say, still fumbling. She chuckled.

"What do you think?"

"I loved it!" I told Zake. "I've already started sketching some ideas."

Working with Zake wasn't a job for me. It was a gift I humbly received. One of the reasons working with Zake never felt like work is that we never once discussed price. And if you know anything about Charly Palmer, then you know I bring up budget details within the first five minutes of a business call.

I looked forward to each and every conversation, which I refused to call meetings. Regarding our calls as meetings would diminish how much I truly cherished these calls. They became a ritual that lasted three months. As we were wrapping up this project, we made plans to meet in person to start working on her next book.

"Charles, I would love to meet you," Zake said one day.

I smiled. The thought had crossed my mind more than once—more than twice. "I would happily make those arrangements," I said.

I had another project to complete and hoped to see her the following month. We continued to talk every few days—and then we didn't. Days passed. I called again—no answer. I reached out to our mutual friend, Halima—no answer. I waited patiently, though, feeling a bit rejected by the interruption of our once routine phone calls.

As I attended an art show at a local gallery, a friend walked up to me and asked, "Weren't you working on a project with Ntozake Shange?"

"Yes," I replied.

"Have you heard the news?" my friend continued. "She passed away this morning."

My heart sank as I replayed our last words in my mind several times.

"I'm looking forward to meeting you," I said. Replying in her frail voice, "That would be nice, Charles."

I wouldn't mind being called Charles once again.

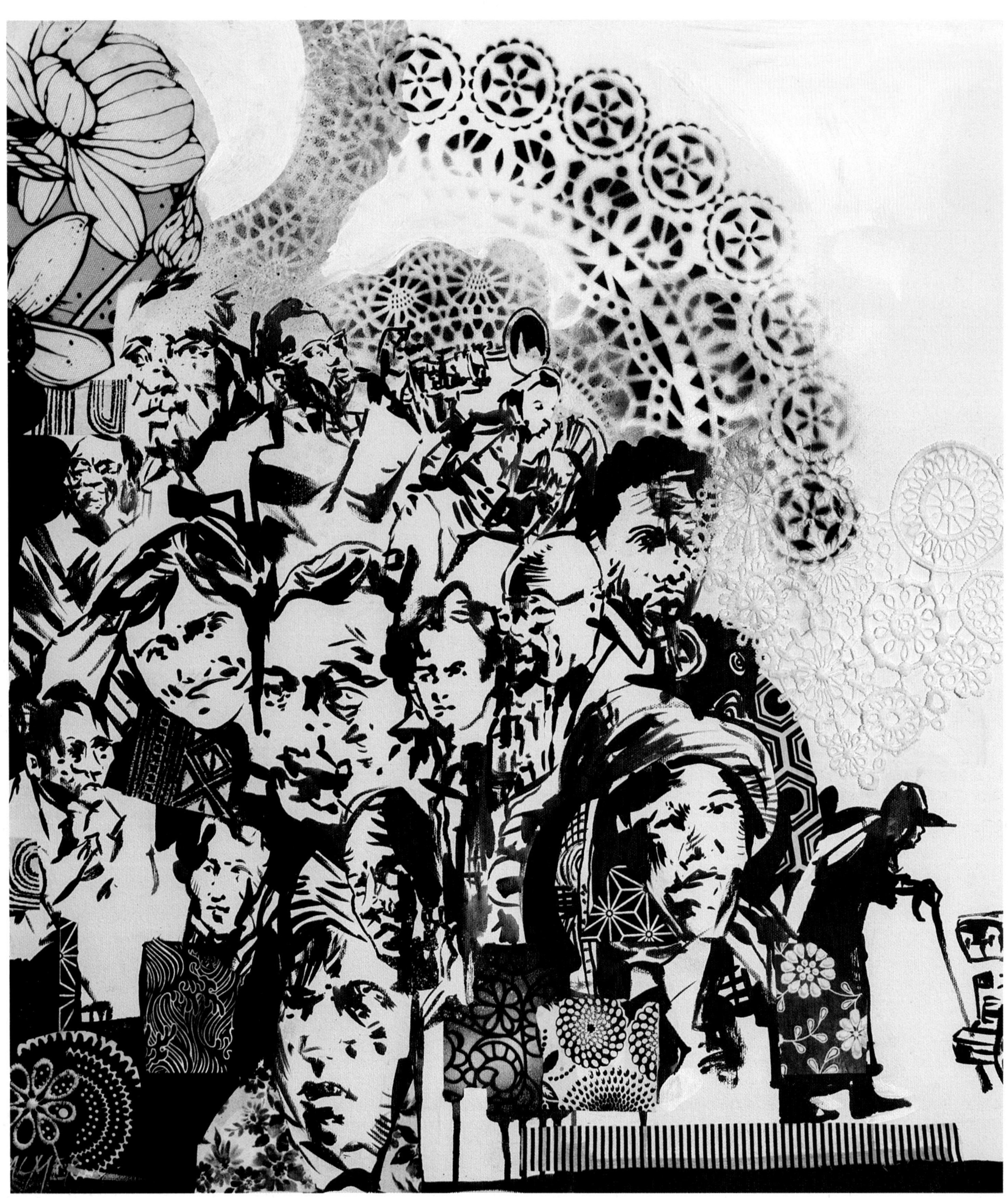

Charly Palmer, *I Am an Old Woman*
(Black gesso on canvas)

EXCERPT FROM
I AM AN OLD WOMAN

By Ntozake Shange

i bet the haitian villagers of jacques roumain
could use a machete to swipe the black face off him

we mustn't discuss race there are some white
people here
besides it disturbs the african landlords
as does the brooding of sterling brown

the violent impudence of a young leroi jones
even when he walked and raised hell in an
  alphabet city

we could tell he was of jersey
but I never claimed that
now oliver lake and reggie workman live there
had a spot dedicated to new black music

written alive after the spring of 1740
are calling for the lost generation
to find paul laurence dunbar and bessie smith
before al johnson realizes he had stumbled
  upon the
real black gold

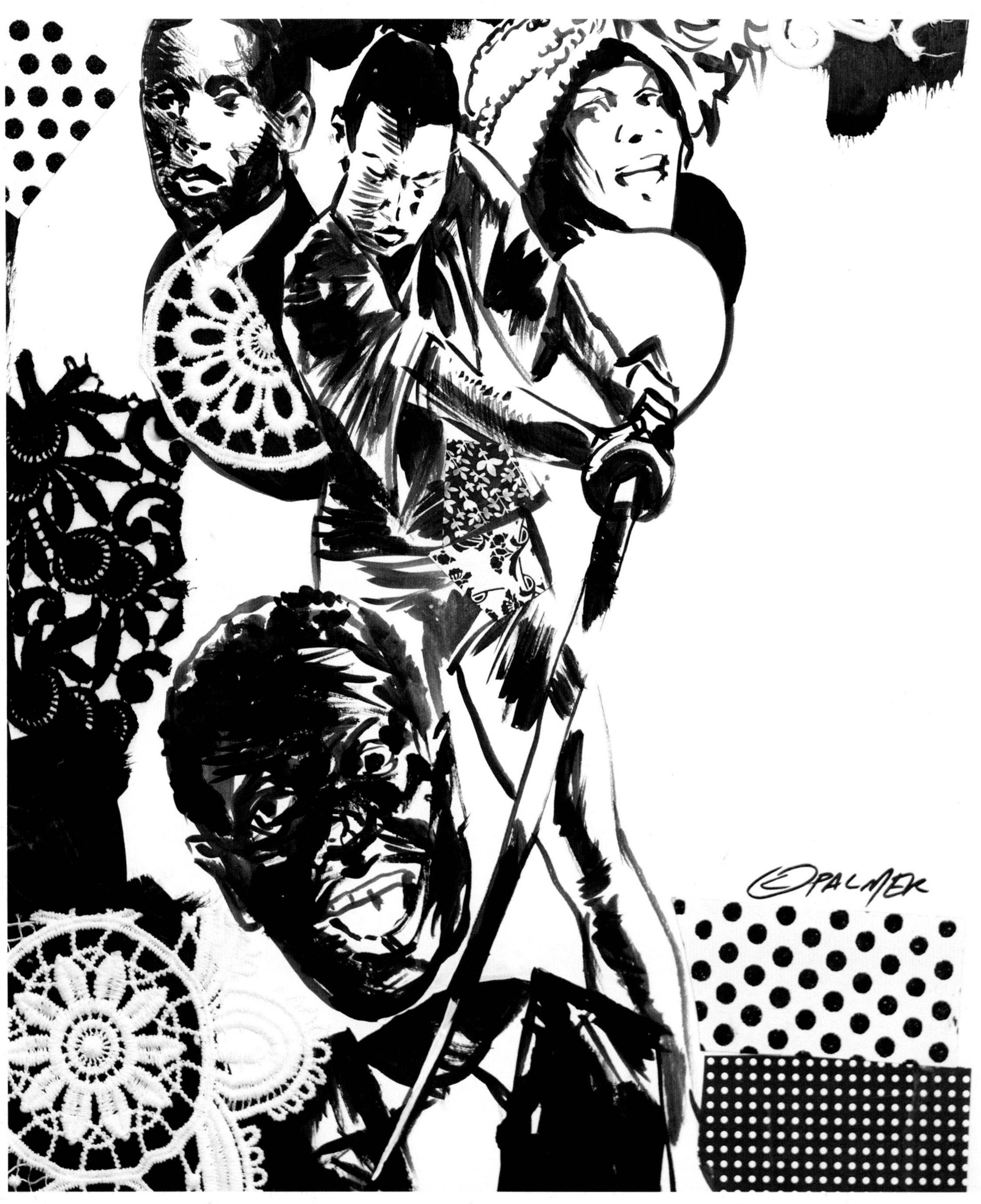

Charly Palmer, *Al Jolson*
(Black gesso on canvas)

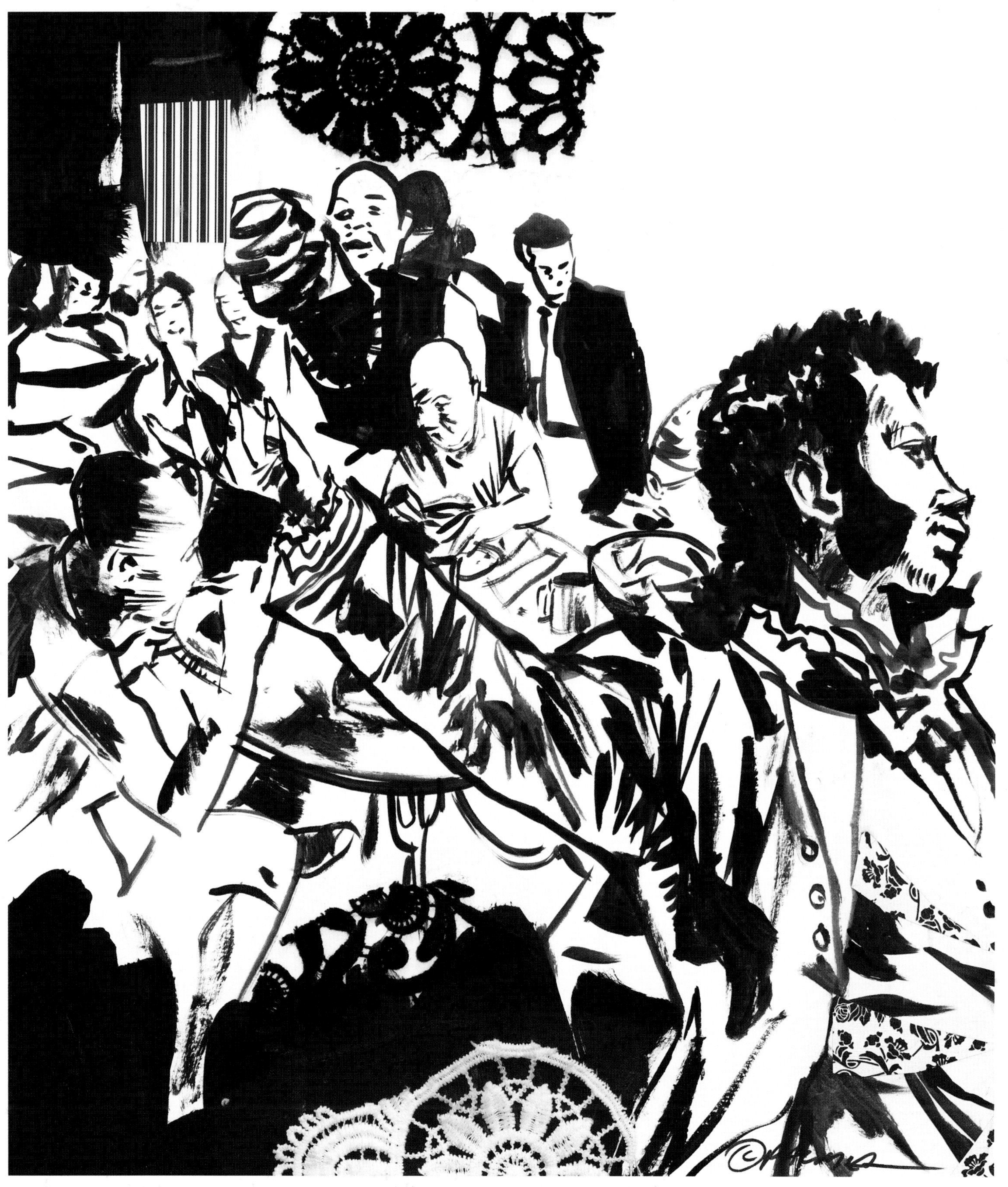

Charly Palmer, *Companionship*
(Black gesso on canvas)

COMING AND GOING

F R O M

By Karida L. Brown

i am from
the departures and arrivals of my ancestors
surf, and turf
coal, mountains, appalachia
gone home

a peripatetic improvisation
a lil' bit of Yoruba, Zulu, San, Xhosa, Ndebele,
  Sotho
south, country, long island, and always the A
it is not a geography

i was here
before form
we brought color to earth
so far back from the universe
came here this time so you could see and believe
outside the lines

i come, straight outta . . .
Richard's heart and Nita's prayers
Charlene and Mary's wisdom,
from Shirley's mighty laugh
and Larry's kind eyes.

i hail from the legend of Leona's cusses,
and Major's quiet imagination
from the smell of Mamie's kitchen
the fertile soil of Thornton's garden

i done came from,
common sense that ain't so common
cooked food, i see you, respect
the only real place

Love.

i am a direct descendant of
Black music, food, and dance
Blackety-Black sayings and jokes
a big 'ole Black family
and the Black Radical Tradition

Diane Nash, Joyce Ladner, and June Jordan
W. E. B. Du Bois, Stuart Hall, Carter G. Woodson
learn them
i come from a people who make a way out of no way
who make ways for others
when you feel me coming
make way.

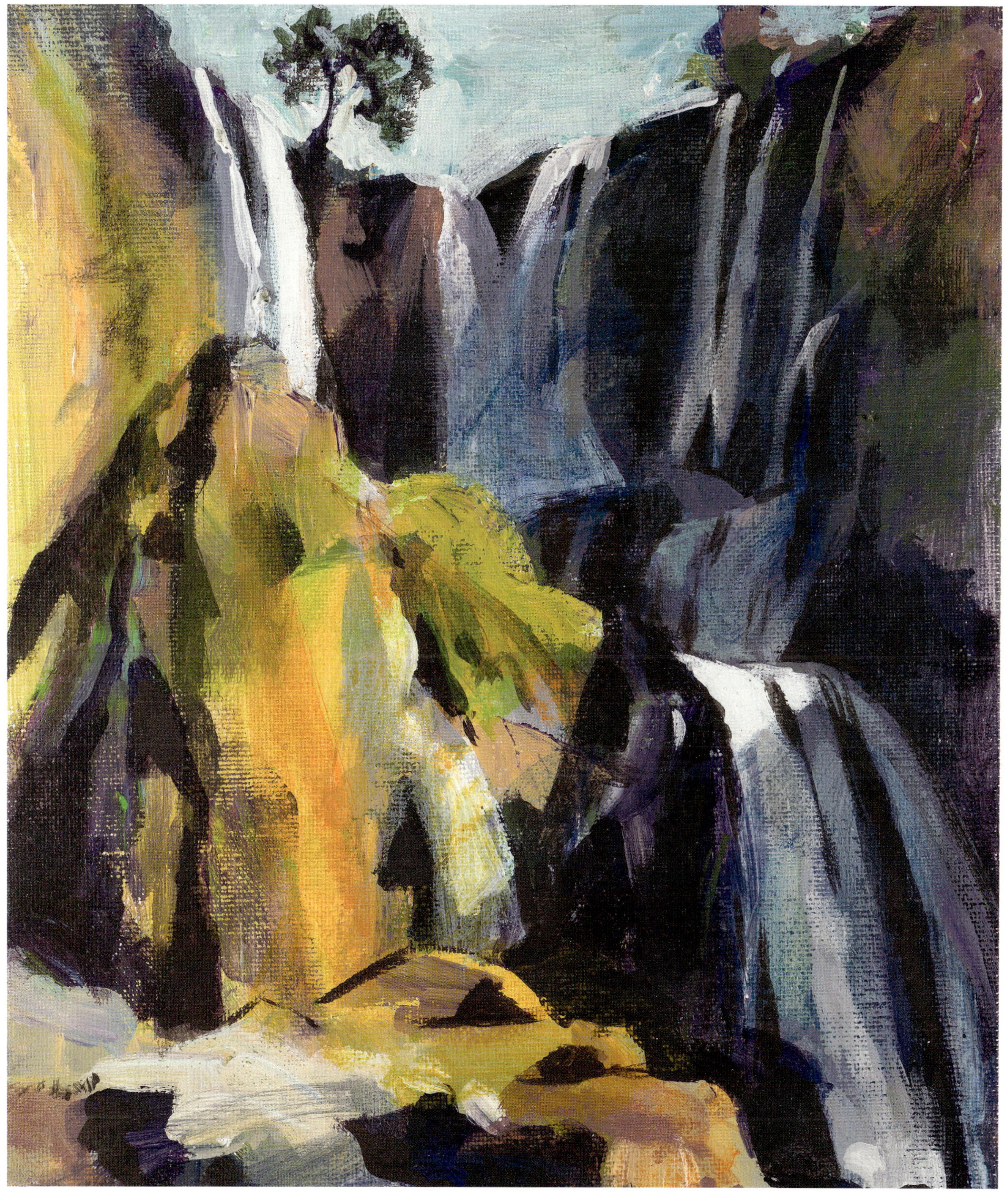

Charly Palmer, *Chasing Waterfalls*
(Acrylic on canvas)

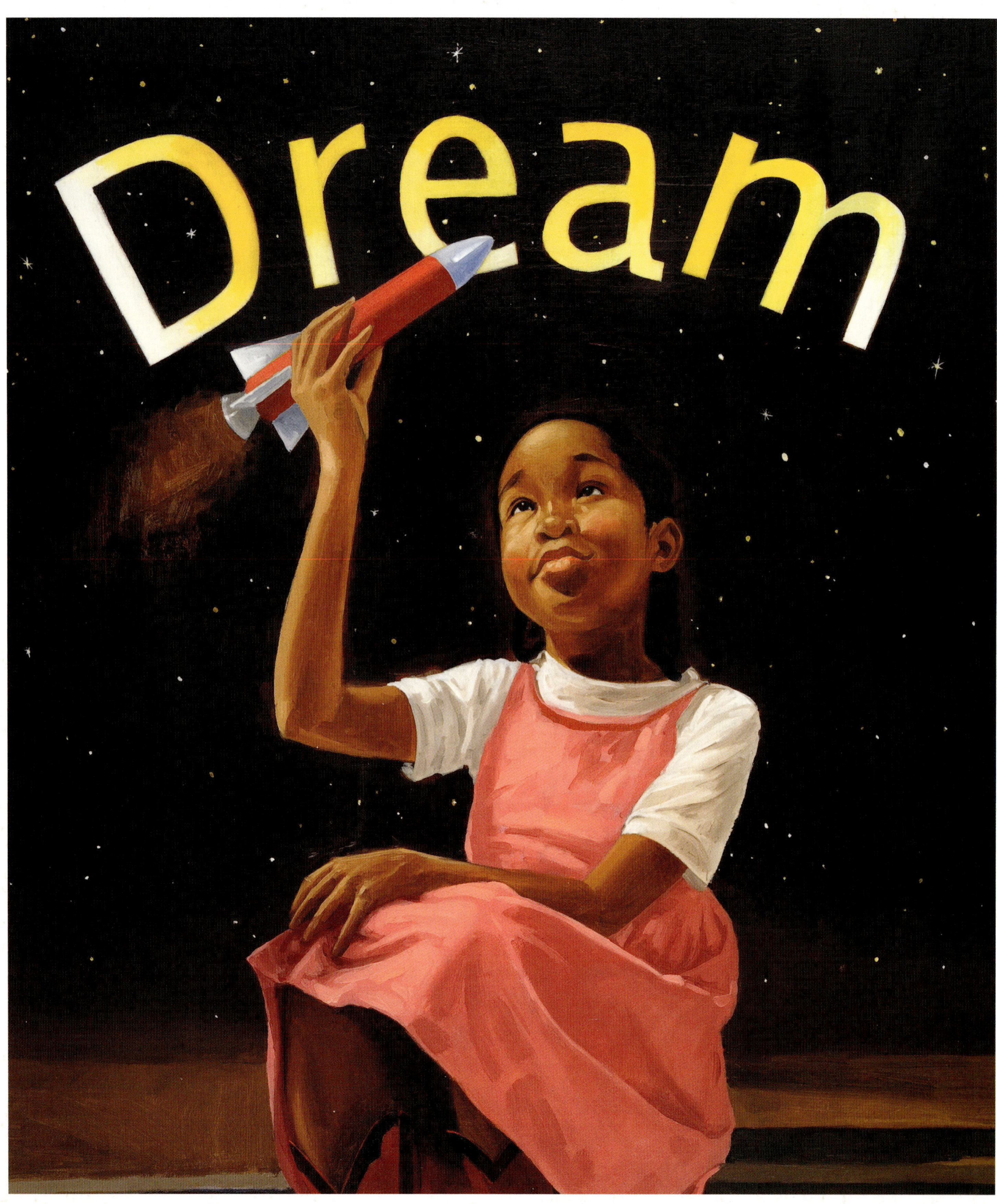

James Ransome, *Dream*
(Acrylic and oil)

A LEAP OF FAITH

By Alicia Edwards

My mother immigrated to the United States from Jamaica in the late 1970s. In Jamaica, America was always seen as the land of opportunity, and if you were ambitious, that was where you belonged. People who immigrated to America, no matter how skilled or unskilled they were, somehow managed to send money back home to their families. This gave everyone there the impression that a life in America was an abundant one; if you wanted to have more, you had to go there.

My parents met in New York one day just walking in the park. They quickly fell in love and started a family, including me, the only girl, and my two brothers. I always felt like we had something special being the children of immigrants. We had a strong sense of coming from somewhere and being able to go back there, eating ackee and saltfish for breakfast and speaking Patwa. It was like our own thing, and we had a space that was for us and others like us.

When I was a child I wanted to be a teacher because that was the only type of professional I saw. As I got older and found a love for reading, I decided that I wanted to be a writer. My parents encouraged me to keep a diary and to write poetry, but it seemed that they always saw it as a passion project or a hobby, not something I could do for a living. They always encouraged me to choose a profession that required a license. They wanted me to choose a career that limited who could do your job because, in their minds, that would ensure a demand for my skills. My parents defined success as being able to keep a job, make a good living, and buy a house. There wasn't really any room in their definition for being happy every day when you go to your job. In fact, that never even came up. ▶

We did not grow up having wealth. We didn't even know anyone who had money. It felt like that was something reserved for white people. The closest we came to people with money was the white family that my best friend's mother worked for in Brooklyn Heights. They owned a beautiful brownstone as well as a vacation home in East Hampton, New York. As we got older, we would accompany them to their vacation home in the summers. Although we stuck out like a sore thumb because we were the only Black people in sight, we got to know a lot of other white families who were interesting in so many ways. They were not just doctors and lawyers, which seemed to be our family's only version of what could make someone rich.

For example, there was a man who made wood furniture and started a company doing so. And a professor who did research in Tanzania for six months out of the year. And a newscaster. And a fine artist. And a realtor who made over $300,000 just by renting homes in East Hampton in the summer. There was also a writer who released a book every two years and still managed to live very comfortably! Why were our parents setting us up for a life of work that would surely require long hours as the only option to live comfortably when there was so much more out there for us? I felt like the white people we encountered knew a secret we didn't: that building wealth did not require you to choose a profession you did not enjoy. It was quite the opposite.

I still listened to my parents and aspired to get that coveted professional license. I originally enrolled in college at Temple University as a pharmacy major, but I eventually switched to business because I had more interest there. Earning my bachelor of business administration in accounting provided me with the opportunity to do something I was interested in and still get the professional designation my parents wanted me to have. I became an accountant and eventually earned my license as a CPA (certified public accountant). I landed a job at a prestigious accounting firm and bought a house, only to later realize that none of this made me happy. I was miserable going to the office every day.

I've always loved finance, as saving and investing money came naturally to me. I knew I wanted to start my own practice where I could help others make better financial decisions and ultimately build wealth on their own. However, I was overcome with fear. I did not want to be a disappointment. I didn't know how to go about getting clients, and I was scared, so I stayed in corporate America for more than fifteen years. Looking back, I did learn a lot about how to manage a team and become efficient in my work. But it was not until I took a leap of faith and started my own CPA practice that I realized why I loved finance in the first place. I love helping others build wealth and get the financial freedom they need to truly live the life they want.

I targeted mainly Black clients because I felt like they needed my help the most. I also wanted to help members of my own community. I absolutely love guiding my clients to not only develop thriving businesses, but also to build wealth for themselves and their families using the many avenues business owners have available to them to do just that. Owning your own business is the best-kept secret to building wealth because it allows you to keep so much more of what you earn. I still have my dreams of becoming a writer, and I started working on a book discussing personal finance and career enjoyment. Things have really come full circle for me.

What I have learned in my life and career is that overlooking your happiness solely for financial stability is a waste of time. This is because you can only pretend for so long before it starts to eat at your soul. There is no passion to be found in life if you aren't willing to take risks. My mother took a leap of faith immigrating to the United States without any money or any support, believing that she would find a job and a community and make a life for herself. One generation later, I took a leap of faith by starting my business, which now provides me with the flexibility to be there for my children and to bring home more money than I did when I was working in corporate America. We should not just look to make a living; we should look to make a change. Don't look for a career to fall back on; look for a career that you love and are passionate about.

I often take calls from clients and unintentionally stay on the phone for hours without getting paid because I am excited to talk to them. Providing them with the valuable information they need to thrive financially brings me a sense of fulfillment and joy. I am sure you hear this often, but please take it to heart: If you love your work, the money will come.

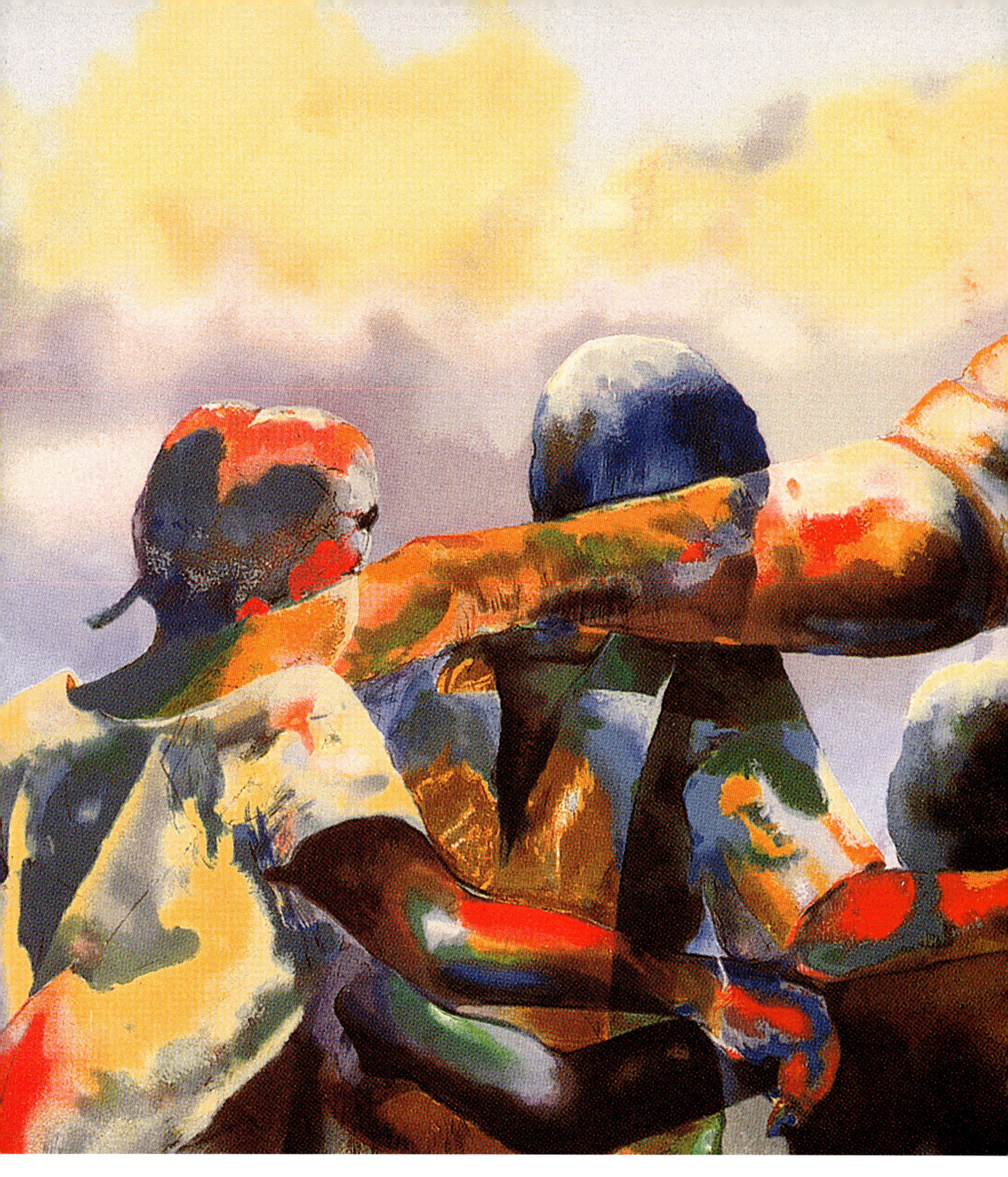

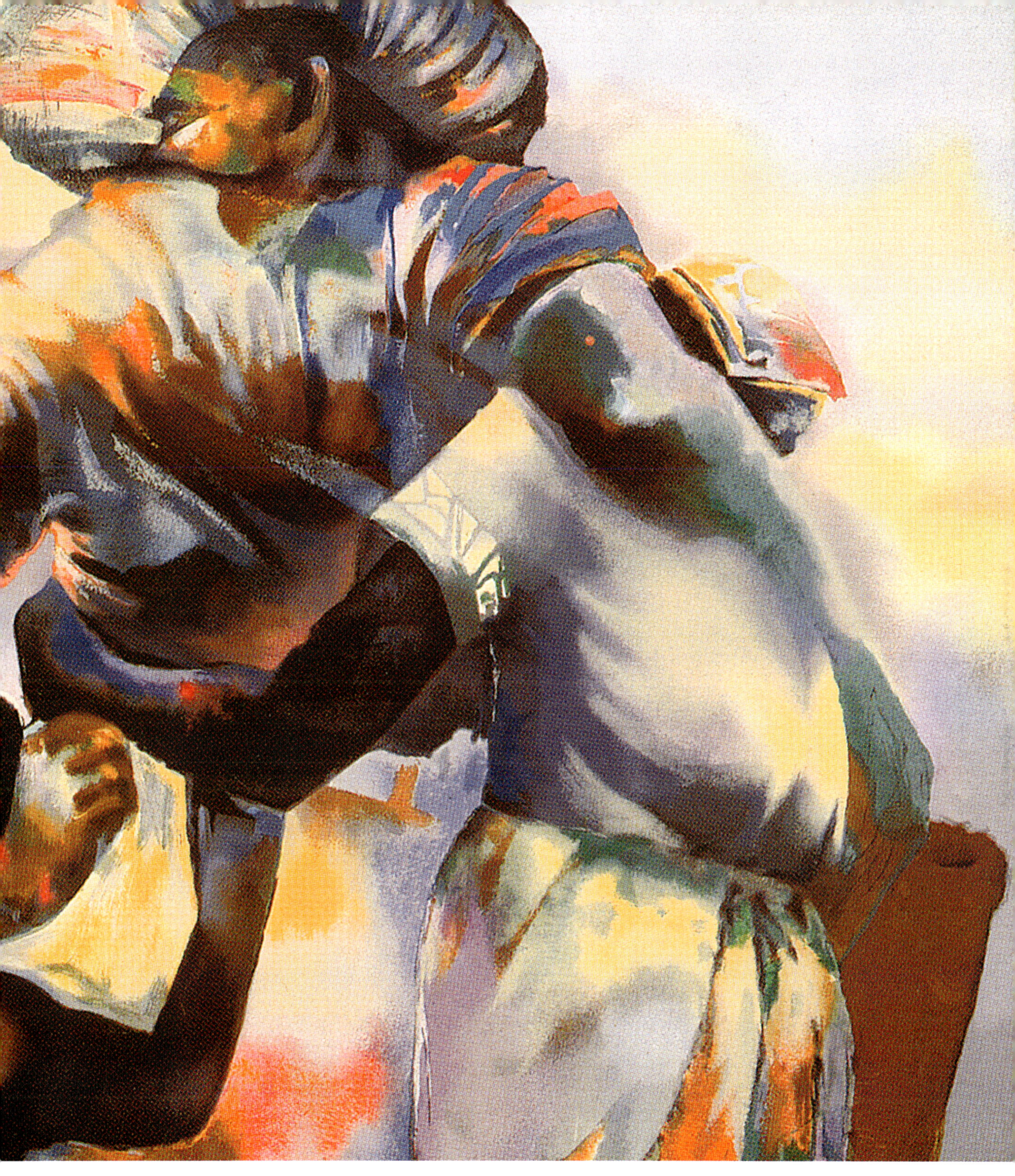

Paul Goodnight, *In Arm's Reach*
(Acrylic, oil, pencil, and charcoal)

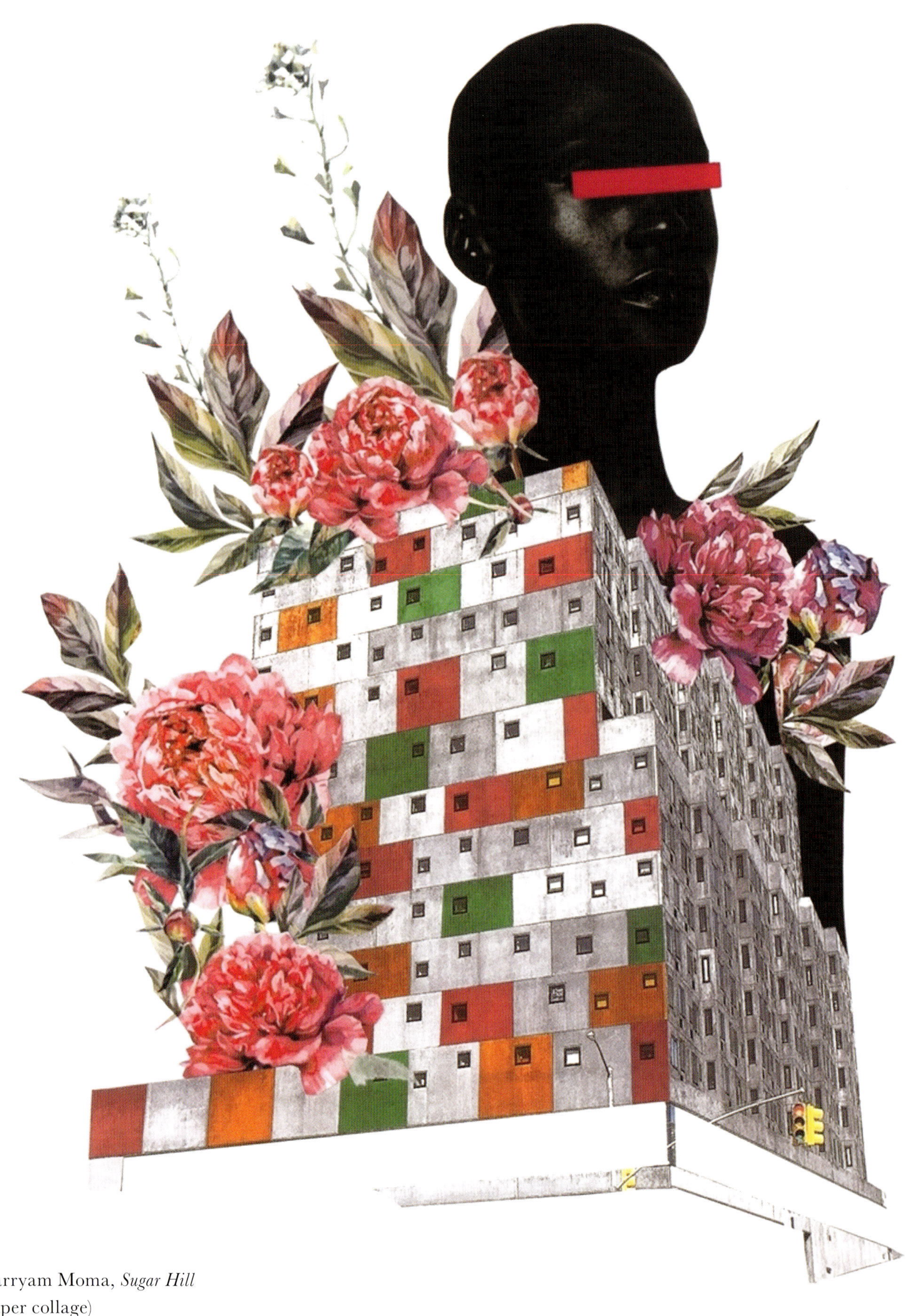

Marryam Moma, *Sugar Hill*
(Paper collage)

PROGRESS

Mekhi Yant | Fisk University, Class of 2023

What would you say is the most important part of life? Hopefully you would say progress. Progress is a very necessary part of life. You can give progress the credit for evolution, contributions, and resolution. Without progress, African Americans would not have voting rights, citizenship, or even be free from bondage. Without progress, schools, restaurants, and even public restrooms would still be segregated. Without progress, cities, communities, and the entire country wouldn't have half the advancements they have today. If it were not for progress, dreams would never become reality. This is not to mention how important progress is for an individual. Obviously, if it were not for progress, youth would not mature into adults.

Benjamin Franklin once said, "Without continual growth and progress, such words as *improvement*, *achievement*, and *success* have no meaning." That's the true way to judge someone's character, through their progress and growth. If one can grow in the face of obstacles and challenges, then one can surely improve, achieve, and succeed. Of course, it isn't going to be easy, but nothing great is.

The key to progress is persistence. President Barack Obama once said, "If you're walking down the right path and you're willing to keep walking, eventually you'll make progress." See, the key word is *eventually*. Progress will come, but you have to keep moving forward. Little by little, step-by-step. No one has ever made major progress in just one step.

"Persistence is key." Despite how cliché it may sound, it is true. Kobe Bryant didn't break a record with his first jump shot. Michael Jackson didn't make a hit with his first note. Viola Davis didn't win an Academy Award at her first audition.

> **WHILE PROGRESS OFTEN RESULTS IN SUCCESS AND MANY ACCOLADES, THEY ARE NOT THE GREATEST UPSIDE OF PROGRESS.**

Yet each persisted at their own craft and progress surely followed.

While progress often results in success and many accolades, they are not the greatest upside of progress. You see, the greatest upside to making progress is knowing that you've earned it and deserve it. This is a feeling nobody can take from you. Self-validation, self-preservation, self-accomplishment! ▶

So, for those who are experiencing what seems to be a continuous string of failures, there is only one way to change that. Persevere. For those who have yet to reach their goals, there is only one way to reach them. Persevere. For those who are having a continuous string of successes, there is only one way to continue such success. Persevere. If you are not yet where you want to be in your endeavors, that means one of the two things: Either you have not yet done enough. Keep going! Or it is simply not your time yet. Keep going!

See, those who have reached a magnitude of success in their field realized that progress takes perseverance and just chose never to give up. Nevertheless, perseverance requires much sacrifice, just as all progress does. For instance, our ancestors were forced to sacrifice their rights, their pride, and their well-being for our community to make progress. Progress requires a sacrifice of free time and in some cases even relationships. Anything worth having is worth sacrificing for, whether it is a dream, a cause, or your own personal welfare. If you personally feel that you should be making progress at something, then you would be doing yourself a disservice by not sacrificing for it.

But perseverance and sacrifice does not just come from the woodwork; it comes from a mindset of relentless determination. See, determination pushes an individual past their own limits, if they had any to begin with. One who is determined is one who is not satisfied until the job is done. It doesn't matter how persistent they have to be or how much they have to sacrifice. It doesn't matter how hard they have to work or how many times they have failed. The late, great Kobe Bryant once said, "Once you know what failure feels like, determination chases success." That's truly what progress is: perseverance, sacrifice, and determination. These are the guidelines for improvement and growth, the stepping stone to success.

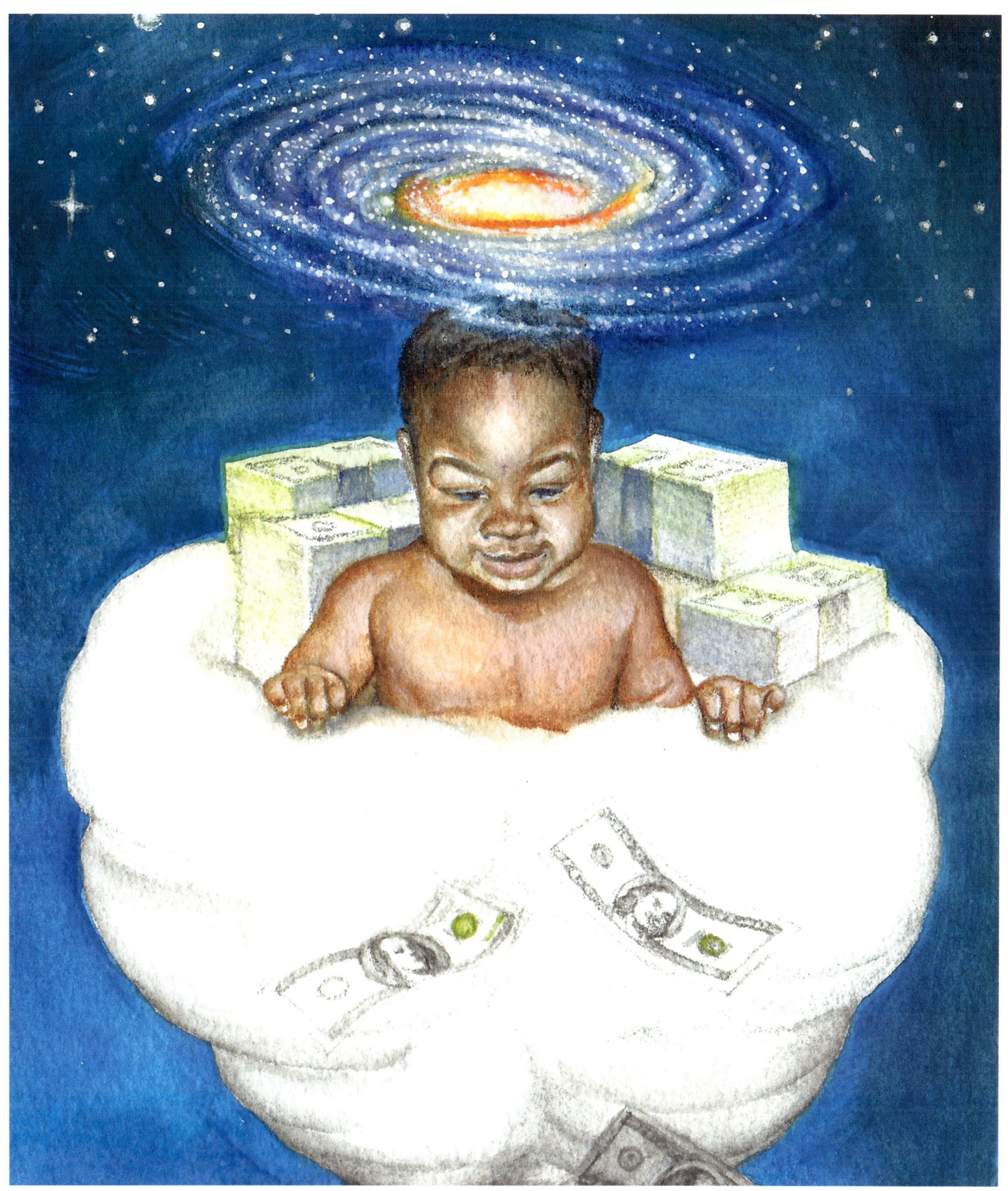

Fabian Williams, *Blessings from Baby New Year*
(Watercolor)

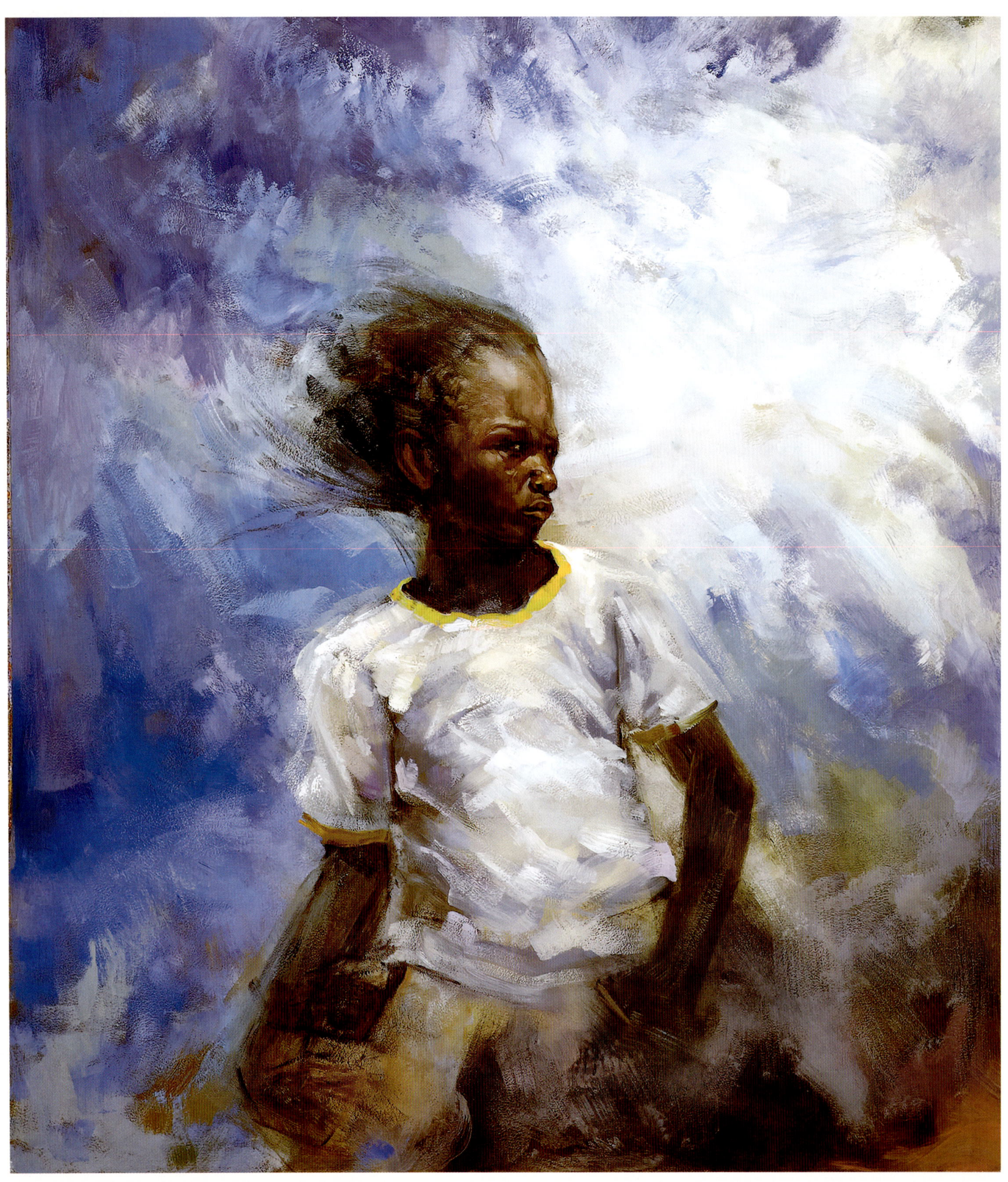

Tyrone Geter, *Curve*
(Acrylic on canvas)

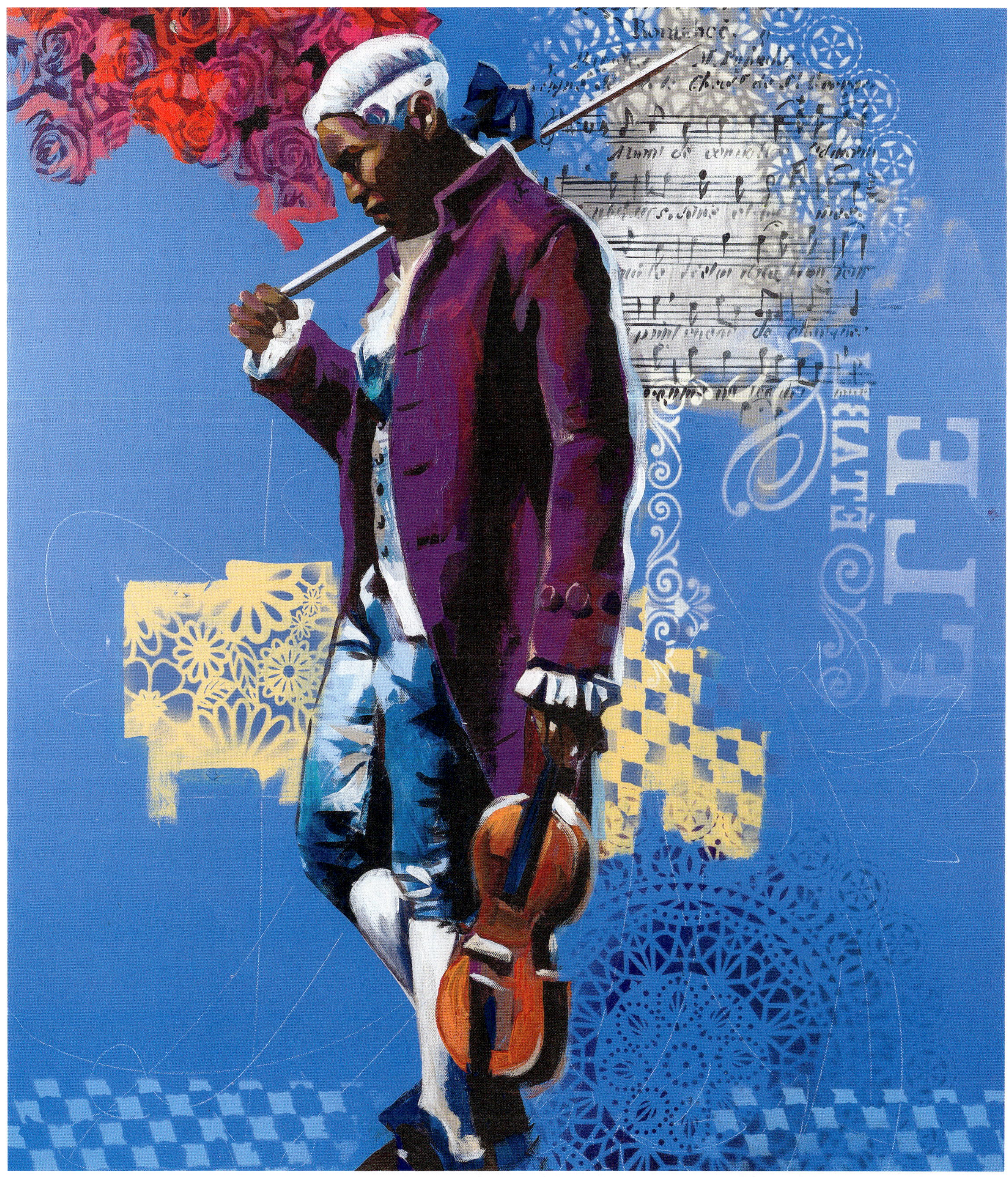

Charly Palmer, *Chevalier*
(Acrylic on canvas)

CONTRIBUTOR BIOS

Kai Adia is the cofounder of Bee Infinite Publishing and a Los Angeles–based writer of poetry and short stories that focus on science fiction, fantasy, and environmental concerns. In 2020 she published and illustrated her debut poetry collection, *The Depths of Anima*, and in 2022 Adia read from her collection on the poetry stage at the Los Angeles Times Festival of Books. To learn more about her current projects, visit www.beeinfinite.org and www.kaiadia.com.

Lavett Ballard is a mixed-media visual artist based in New Jersey. She holds an MFA in studio art from the University of the Arts in Philadelphia. Ballard's art was commissioned as a cover for *Time* magazine's special Women of the Year double edition in March 2023. Ballard's art is a reimagined visual narrative that reflects social issues affecting primarily Black women within a historical context.

Jamaal Barber was born in Virginia and raised in North Carolina. In 2013, after seeing a screen-printing demo at a local art store, Barber started experimenting with printmaking and made it his primary focus. His woodcuts and mixed-media prints can be seen on display at ZuCot Gallery in Atlanta. His work has also been included in the Decatur Arts Festival, Atlanta Print Biennial, and other shows in the Atlanta area. Barber has done work for Twitter, the *New York Times*, Penguin Random House, Black Art in America, and Emory University. Barber now resides in Atlanta with his wife and two children.

Asante Guzik Bates is a sophomore at Fisk University, class of 2025. She served on the *New Brownies' Book* student editorial board through the John Lewis Center for Social Justice at Fisk.

Bertice Berry, PhD, is an award-winning sociologist, author, and lecturer. Her new novel, *BlackWorld*, features the cover art of Charly Palmer.

Lillian Blades was born in Nassau, Bahamas, and currently resides in Atlanta. Blades's works are predominantly mixed-media assemblages made with an assortment of materials, both found and constructed by her in her studio. Her childhood home of Bahamas, ancestral background of West Africa, and her late mother, who was a seamstress, influence her art. These influences appear through use of her color palette and objects that evoke memory and history.

Demetri Burke is a young artist residing in Atlanta. He holds a BFA in studio art from Georgia State University, and his work has been shown nationally in galleries, museums, publications, and online exhibitions. He uses mixed media, including charcoal, oil paint, and found images, to express narratives of identity and culture on canvas. Abstraction, montage, and realistic rendering are key parts in his creation process. In 2022 he had his debut solo exhibition, *And Then We Heard the Thunder.* ▶

Shannon Byrd, a native Atlantan, has lived her entire life immersed in the arts. The daughter of performing artists, she is also a comedian and actor as well as leader and cofounder of an African dance collective. She is so happy to finally work creatively alongside her husband, KEEF Cross, in this amazing project.

Kevin Cole is an artist whose work is based on the relationship between sight, sound, and color. Cole's work deals with music from the African American community, such as jazz, rap, hip-hop, gospel, and blues, and thus is rooted in a place of targeted tragedy. Its curvilinear twists, knots, and loops are fed by the energy found in the souls of all those who toil and triumph every day against the odds and against the unheralded tragedies of life.

Alfred Conteh is a leader in the vanguard of American portraiture. He uses his studio practice to explore his identity and personal history from several different perspectives. He was born in Fort Valley, Georgia, and is now based in Atlanta; his mother is African American and his father is from Sierra Leone, West Africa. Conteh's work concerns the ways African Americans have dealt with disparities affecting their communities for generations, especially in the southern United States.

KEEF Cross is a retired tattoo artist who works as a freelance artist and graphic novelist based out of Atlanta. Having made a name for himself with the graphic novel *DayBlack*, KEEF was excited for the opportunity to work with his wife to make something their kids could also enjoy while tackling social issues within the Black community.

Amber Curtis graduated from Fisk University as a part of the class of 2022. She served on the *New Brownies' Book* student editorial board through the John Lewis Center for Social Justice at Fisk.

Joy Angela DeGruy, PhD, holds a BS in communication, master's degrees in both social work and clinical psychology, and a PhD in social work research. Dr. DeGruy's research focuses on the intersection of racism, trauma, violence, and American chattel slavery with a focus on reparations and healing.

James Denmark was born in Winter Haven, Florida, in 1936. He earned his MFA at Pratt Institute of Fine Arts in New York. During this period Denmark was heavily influenced by the abstract expressionists Jackson Pollock, Clyfford Still, and Willem de Kooning. The African American masters Norman Lewis, Romare Bearden, Jacob Lawrence, and Ernest Crichlow instilled in him an appreciation of African American artistic heritage. Denmark's collages, watercolors, woodcuts, and reproductions are sought by galleries and collectors worldwide. He lives and works in Brooklyn, New York.

Waverly Duck, PhD, is a native of Detroit and the North Hall Chair Endowed Professor of Sociology at the University of California, Santa Barbara.

Alice Faye Duncan is the author of *Memphis, Martin, and the Mountaintop*, which received a 2019 Coretta Scott King Illustrator Honor. Her most recent books for children include *Yellow Dog Blues*, *This Train Is Bound for Glory*, and *Coretta's Journey*.

Alicia Edwards is a CPA, real estate investor, and occasional writer. She is currently working on her first novel, which is loosely based on her coming-of-age story.

Lynthia Edwards is a fine artist whose work illuminates the world of the southern Black girl experience. Born and raised in Alexander City, a small Alabama town, she sees herself in her subjects. Inspired by historical research and shaped by personal experience, her work reveals the colors, complexity, physical beauty, and internal elegance of her subjects. She captures viewers with color and engaging imagery—telling the stories of her subjects without shrinking from the ugly truths they sometimes reveal.

Tyrone Geter has built an international reputation as an artist, painter, sculptor, illustrator, and teacher. A recently retired associate professor of art at Benedict College in Columbia, South Carolina, Geter grew up in Anniston, Alabama, during a time defined by strict segregation laws and social injustice. The immediacy of racial violence in Anniston during the civil rights era and an inherited legacy of spiritual strength inform and shape Geter's work. He received his MFA from Ohio University in 1978 with an emphasis on painting and drawing. His figures embody history while simultaneously speaking of a spiritual world overflowing with compassion and empathy.

Paul Goodnight is a fine artist whose work seeks to blend the line between abstraction and representation, with a focus on human form. Born in Chicago in 1946 and raised in Roxbury, Massachusetts, and New London, Connecticut, Goodnight received his BFA and an honorary MFA from the Massachusetts College of Art. His learning continued under the tutelage of Paul Rahilly, John Biggers, and Chuck Stigliano. Goodnight's work has been featured in films such as *Ghost, The Preacher's Wife*, and *Gone Baby Gone*, among others, and on many television programs, including *Seinfeld* and *The Fresh Prince of Bel Air*.

Briana Gordon is an Atlanta-based artist whose work centers on themes of peace, growth, self-love, and self-reflection. She makes both digital artwork and traditional paintings in a variety of media, including acrylic, oil, watercolor, and gouache. Gordon's work has been shown in several galleries in Atlanta, including Peters Street Station, Future Gallery, and Cat Eye Creative.

Wesley Gordon is a sophomore high school student with a passion for mathematics, track, and mixed martial arts. Although English wasn't originally his forte, his parents' continual encouragement eventually led to a love of language arts. Gordon lives in Los Angeles with his parents, and in his free time he likes to hang with his friends and watch anime.

Ida Harris is an essayist and journalist writing at the intersection of Blackness and womanhood. Harris is a published author whose work is included in the anthology *Bigger Than Bravery: Black Resilience and Reclamation in a Time of Pandemic*. Her work is featured in the *Boston Review, Teen Vogue, ELLE, Essence, Yes! Magazine, USA Today*, and more. As a New York native she represents South Jamaica,

Queens, and considers the Deep South home. She currently heads *MadameNoire* as managing editor.

April Harrison is a self-taught award-winning artist and illustrator who has been professionally involved in art for more than twenty years. She creates rich mixed-media paintings that reveal her unshakable belief in the strength of faith, family, and friendship. Her adept use of color and collaging with specialty paper and magazine prints, as well as her audacious repurposing of found objects in her work, adds a physical reality and a quiltlike quality that roots it within an African American artistic tradition.

Latoya Hobbs is an artist, wife, and mother of two from Little Rock, Arkansas, currently living in Baltimore. She received her BA in painting from the University of Arkansas at Little Rock and MFA in printmaking from Purdue University. Hobbs's work portrays figurative imagery that addresses beauty, cultural identity, and womanhood as they relate to women of the African diaspora.

Marcus Anthony Hunter, PhD, is the Scott Waugh Endowed Chair in the Division of the Social Sciences and a professor of sociology and African American studies at UCLA. He is the coiner of #BlackLivesMatter and author of four books, including *Radical Reparations* (HarperCollins/ Amistad 2023).

Zoe Jones says, "My name is Zoe, and I am five years old. I love my family and playing. I can kick monsters' butts and they go away."

Magana J. Kabugi, PhD, is an assistant professor of English and the director of the University Writing Center at Fisk University. His research focuses on twentieth- and twenty-first-century African American literature and the intellectual history of higher education (with an emphasis on Historically Black Colleges and Universities). His work has been featured in national publications, including *HBCU Digest* and *Diverse Issues in Higher Education.*

Leonard Maiden is an artist who mines the aesthetic potential of African American imagery through experience and the whimsy of imagination. Maiden states, "I feel a visual affinity for dark skin shining in the southern summer sun against the background of countrysides, small-town shops, and cotton fields of the South and the way it's expressed through the activity of painting." The core content of his work is inspired by his parents, who grew up on farms in Louisiana and Mississippi, and his grandfather, who raised cotton in Mississippi. His paintings portray symbols of independence, family ties, and strength.

Chase Malone is an art history major at Spelman College. She enjoys the study of African American art and literature.

Jasmine Mitchell is a senior at Fisk University, class of 2023. She served on the *New Brownies' Book* student editorial board through the John Lewis Center for Social Justice at Fisk.

Marryam Moma is a Tanzanian-Nigerian visual artist who holds a bachelor's degree in architecture from the Tyler School of Art, Temple University, in Philadelphia. Moma melds repurposed hand-cut pieces, paper, and media into fresh, layered imagery with new associations. Her art practice aims to empower and uplift the Black body, especially the Black female body. It unveils magic within this race, breaking collective contemporary stereotypes and changing perceptions of Black women, allowing society to rediscover them as powerful, complex, beautiful, revered, and valuable.

Tracy Murrell is drawn to images of the female form; silhouettes of women are of particular interest to her. Murrell sees the poise and energy women inhabit in the world, which is so often commodified in popular media. In response to this, she offers countersymbols of women as figures personifying grace and strength. In her work she uses silhouettes to recontextualize images from popular culture to use as entry points for deeper conversations on gender, race, and the perceptions of beauty.

Courtney J. Patterson-Faye, PhD, is an assistant professor of sociology at Wesleyan University. Her work, steeped in both African American studies and sociology, utilizes Black feminist thought, fat studies, fashion, sexuality, and cultural sociology to shift how the world regards the bodies and minds of Black women. She has published in *The New Black Sociologists*, *Sexualities*, *Contemporary Black Female Sexualities*, and the *Du Bois Review*.

Derek Phillips is a mixed-media artist and printmaker who lives and works in Lawrenceville, Georgia, right outside his hometown of Atlanta. His art pays homage to the African American experience, which he calls the tragedies and triumphs of what it is to be Black in America. His primary goal when creating is to inspire, enlighten, encourage, and educate through his work.

Laurence Ralph, PhD, is a professor of anthropology at Princeton University and the director of the Center on Transnational Policing. Ralph's latest book, *Torture Letters: Reckoning with Police Violence* (University of Chicago Press, 2020), explores a decades-long scandal in which 125 people were tortured while in police custody.

James Ransome is an illustrator born in Rich Square, North Carolina. The Children's Book Council named him as one of seventy-five authors and illustrators everyone should know. Currently a member of the Society of Illustrators, Ransome has received both the Coretta Scott King Award for Illustration and the IBBY Honor Award for his book *The Creation*. He has also received a Coretta Scott King Honor Award for Illustration for *Uncle Jed's Barbershop,* which was selected as an ALA ▶

Notable Book and a feature on *Reading Rainbow*. Ransome lives in Rhinebeck, New York, with his wife, Lesa Cline-Ransome, a writer of children's books, their four children, and one Saint Bernard.

Tokie Rome-Taylor is a photographer interested in ethnography, identity, and representation. Her multimedia practice is grounded in the understanding that self-perception and sense of belonging in a society begins in childhood. She uses children as subjects to speak of a sense of belonging. These images of Black and brown children reexamine history and tradition through photographic portraits that counter inaccurate stereotypical, subjugated, and inferior depictions of people of color.

Alyasah "Ali" Sewell, PhD, is an associate professor of sociology at Emory University. They are trained as a medical sociologist, a social psychologist, and a social science research methodologist. Born in Atlanta to African and Latinx Caribbean immigrants, Ali found their voice on the spoken word stage as a young adult. They were politicized by 9/11, which occurred two weeks after they started college. A researcher at heart, they embraced sociology to sustain their childhood vision of being an artist, writer, and activist. Their mantra is "Good times! It's all love; working on it being all justice."

Ntozake Shange was a poet, performance artist, playwright, and novelist. Born Paulette Williams on October 18, 1948, in Trenton, New Jersey, Shange earned a bachelor's degree in American studies from Barnard College in 1970 and then left New York to pursue graduate studies at the University of Southern California. It was during this time that she took the names *Ntozake* ("she who comes into her own things") and *Shange* ("she who walks like a lion") from the Zulu dialect Xhosa. Shange is perhaps most famous for her play *For Colored Girls Who Have Considered Suicide/When the Rainbow Is Enuf* (1975).

Danny Simmons is an American abstract painter from Queens, New York, who once coined his painting style as "neo-African abstract expressionism." His talent and passion for the arts reaches beyond the canvas; he is a published author, poet, painter, and art philanthropist.

Jimmy Lee Sudduth was born in 1910 in Caines Ridge, Alabama. He began making art as a young boy and went on to become a celebrated artist. Throughout his career he preferred to paint using natural materials as his pigments and his own hands as his brushes. He died in 2007 at the ripe old age of 97.

Daikerra Sweat is a senior at Fisk University, class of 2023. She served on the *New Brownies' Book* student editorial board through the John Lewis Center for Social Justice at Fisk.

Halima Taha is an art advocate and professional offering curatorial, appraisal, planning, writing, and management services. She is the author of *Collecting African American Art: Works on Paper and Canvas*, the first book to validate Black artworks as viable market assets and commodities. Taha is a professional speaker and arts writer for *Artnet*, *Black Art in America*, *Pigment*, *Tribes*, and *Sugarcane* magazine.

Frank X Walker, PhD, is the first African American writer to be named the poet laureate of Kentucky. A multidisciplinary artist, writer, and educator, Walker has published eleven collections of poetry and a children's book, *A Is for Affrilachia*. He is a professor of English and African American and Africana studies and the director of the MFA in creative writing program at the University of Kentucky. A Cave Canem fellow, he has also been honored with a Lannan Literary Fellowship for Poetry.

Fabian Williams, a.k.a Occasional Superstar, is an artist born and raised in Fayetteville, North Carolina. He now lives in Atlanta. Williams received a BFA from East Carolina University in illustration. After working for thirteen years in the advertising industry with clients including Nike, Warner Brothers, and HBO, he moved to a purely expressive practice outside the commercial space to express more political and socially relevant contemporary themes.

Mekhi Yant is a senior at Fisk University, class of 2023. He served on the *New Brownies' Book* student editorial board through the John Lewis Center for Social Justice at Fisk.

Damon Young is a contributing columnist to the *Washington Post Magazine* and writes about the angst, anxieties, and absurdities of American life—specifically culture, class, money, and race. He is the author of *What Doesn't Kill You Makes You Blacker: A Memoir in Essays*, which won the 2020 Thurber Prize for American Humor. He is also the cofounder of the culture blog VerySmartBrothas and was a contributing opinion writer for the *New York Times* and a columnist for *GQ*.

ACKNOWLEDGMENTS

To our beloved readers and supporters,

As we reflect on the journey of producing *The New Brownies' Book*, we are filled with gratitude for every person who has crossed our path along the way. It's with humble hearts that we graciously thank each and every one of you that have supported us through this endeavor.

Firstly, we would like to express our love and gratitude to our amazing family, who have been with us every step of the way. Your unconditional love and support have been the driving force behind our creativity and perseverance. Thank you for your encouragement, your patience, and your unwavering belief in us. We could not have done it without you.

To our editor extraordinaire, Natalie Butterfield, and our publisher, Chronicle Books: Thank you for believing in our vision for this book and for helping us to bring it to life. Your insights, expertise, and guidance have been invaluable. Thank you for sharing our passion for storytelling and for working tirelessly to create a beautiful piece of literature that we can be proud of.

To the sixty artists and writers who so generously contributed original works to make this book a master-piece: Thank you from the bottom of our hearts.

To all the educators and librarians who have embraced our book: Thank you for introducing it to your students and patrons. Your dedication to promoting literacy and fostering a love of reading in young people is truly admirable, and we are grateful for the opportunity to be a part of that mission.

And to our readers, both young and old, who have picked up our book and allowed it to touch your hearts, we are forever grateful. Your support means everything to us, and we are humbled by the thought that the words and illustrations presented in this collective love letter have brought joy and wonder to your lives.

At the heart of everything we do is Black love. We believe in the power of books to inspire, to educate, and to bring people together. We hope that our book has done just that, whether it's through a shared moment of wonder between a parent and child, a classroom discussion about the themes and messages in the story, or a personal reflection on the experiences and emotions that the book has brought to the surface.

In writing this book, we have experienced moments of great joy, frustration, fear, and accomplishment. We have learned so much about ourselves and about the creative process, and we are grateful for every moment of it. We look forward to continuing this journey, and we hope that our future endeavors will continue to inspire and delight our readers.

Once again, to all our supporters, we thank you from the bottom of our hearts. May our book reflect the love, hope, and imagination that we all carry with us, and may it bring joy to your lives for years to come.

With love and gratitude,
Karida and Charly

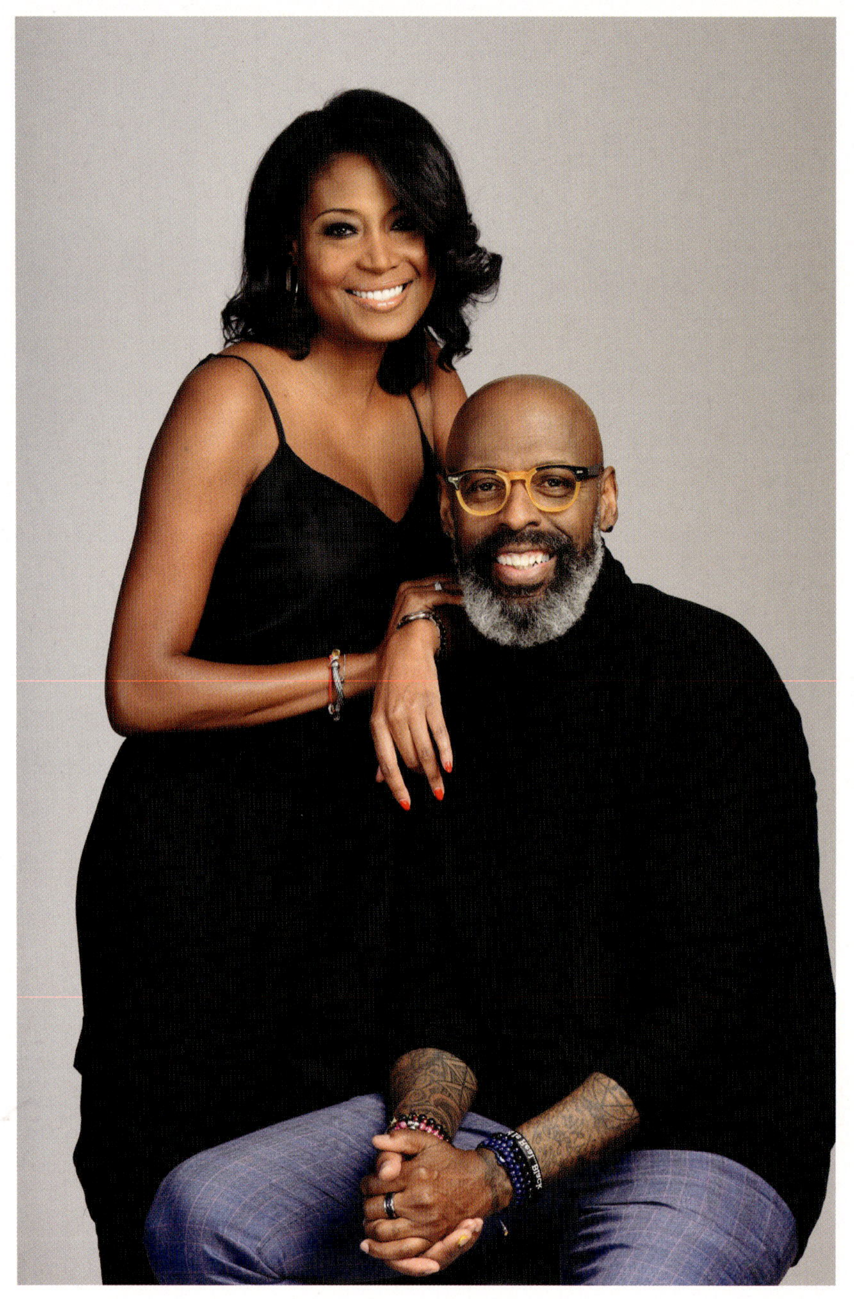

Dr. Karida L. Brown is a sociologist, educator, and writer whose research focuses on the relationship between race, social transformations, and communal memory. She is a professor of sociology at Emory University, the inaugural Diane Nash Descendants of the Emancipation Chair at Fisk University's John Lewis Center for Social Justice, and the director of Racial Equity & Action for the Los Angeles Lakers.

Charly Palmer is an award-winning fine artist, graphic designer, and illustrator. His artwork bears witness to African ancestry and contemporary experiences, from his paintings to his illustrated children's books, including *The Teachers March! How Selma's Teachers Changed History*. He teaches at Spelman College and lives in Atlanta with his wife, Dr. Karida L. Brown, and their two pugs, Pugsly and Blu.